WHEN THE SPIRITS
DANCE MAMBO

ALSO BY MARTA MORENO VEGA

The Altar of My Soul

MARTA MORENO VEGA

WHEN THE SPIRITS DANCE MAMBO

GROWING UP NUYORICAN IN EL BARRIO

THREE RIVERS PRESS
NEW YORK

B
VegA,M

Published by Three Rivers Press, New York, New York.
Member of the Crown Publishing Group, a division of Random House, Inc.

www.crownpublishing.com

THREE RIVERS PRESS is a registered trademark and the Three Rivers Press colophon is a trademark of Random House, Inc.

Printed in the United States of America

DESIGN BY ELINA D. NUDELMAN

Library of Congress Cataloging-in-Publication Data
When the spirits dance mambo : a memoir / by Marta Morengo Vega.—1st ed.
    1. Vega, Marta Moreno. 2. Puerto Rican women—New York (State)—
New York—Biography. 3. Puerto Ricans—New York (State)—New York—
Biography. 4. Puerto Ricans—New York (State)—New York—Social life
and customs. 5. Puerto Ricans—New York (State)—New York—Social
conditions. 6. Ethnic neighborhoods—New York (State)—New York. 7.
Harlem (New York, N.Y.)—Biography. 8. New York (N.Y.)—Biography. 9.
Harlem (New York, N.Y.)—Social conditions. 10. New York (N.Y.)—Social
conditions. I. Title.
F128.9.P85V438   2004
974.7'004687295'0922—dc22   2003027912

ISBN 1-4000-4924-5

10 9 8 7 6 5 4 3 2 1

First Edition

THIS BOOK IS A TRIBUTE TO ALL THE

ABUELAS/OS, PARENTS, AND EXTENDED FAMILY

BORN IN PUERTO RICO WHO CREATED "EL BARRIO"

SO THAT THOSE OF US BORN AWAY

FROM THEIR BELOVED ISLAND WOULD ALWAYS HAVE

A RACIAL AND CULTURAL UNDERSTANDING

OF OUR PLACE IN THE WORLD

WHEN THE SPIRITS DANCE MAMBO

ONE

In Abuela's World

Yo traigo mis flores acabaditas de cortar de varios colores mis flores para tu altar: príncipes de pura sangre para Changó . . .

I bring my fresh-cut flowers of many colors for your altar: deep, blood red roses for Changó . . .

— CELINA Y REUTILIO, "A SANTA BÁRBARA"

As the music plays, breathe in slowly. Feel the air flow through your body. Close your eyes and hold your breath. When the air feels like it's going to explode inside your chest, hold it longer. Now let it out. Listen. Listen to your heart and to the *ta-ta-ta, ta-ta* of the *clave*. Let the clapping rhythm of those two mahogany sticks travel through your body, throbbing in every part of you. Know that if you do not move to the beat, you will burst. That's mambo.

I grew up surrounded by the pulsating rhythms of Tito Puente and Machito and the teasing, sensual songs of Graciela. The deep, robust voice of Celia Cruz brought Africa to our home. In our cramped living room on 102nd Street, my brother taught me to mambo. There, too, my father took my mother in his dark, powerful arms and they swayed to the tune of a *jíbaro* ballad. In the bed we shared, my older sister cried herself to sleep while the radio crooned a brokenhearted lament. And my grandmother, cleaning her altar to the spirits of our ancestors, played songs to the gods and goddesses. Imitating the motions of the sea, she let her body be carried by an imaginary wave, then, taking my hand, encouraged me to follow in her steps. In Abuela's world, our hearts beat to the drum song of the thunder god, Changó, *"Cabo e Cabo e Cabosileo . . . Cabo e Cabo e Cabosileo . . ."*

A skinny girl with caramel skin—wide-eyed, wide-eared—I watched and heard and savored it all. As my body recalls my childhood, I journey back to meet family members who live now only in the spirit world but remind me always of who I am and of where I come from. Memories are the musical notes that form the composition of our souls. Feelings churned by memory connect us to the past, help us treasure the present, and can even reveal to us our future. My memories take me on a spiritual, musical voyage to El Barrio.

Mami, can I help Abuela?" I begged.
The herbal and floral aromas coming through our front door signaled that it was Saturday, the day that Abuela,

like my mother, spiritually cleansed her apartment. I knew there would be neighbors gathered at my grandmother's door seeking relief from their daily woes. I knew, too, that she would be cooking my favorite dishes.

Most of the women in our building labored in sweat-shops or as domestics for the wealthy. Their husbands toiled as janitors, factory workers, and doormen, on the docks or as merchant seamen who rarely saw their families. Others worked as messengers, sold furniture door to door, or hustled as numbers runners. My own father worked in an auto body shop and my mother stayed at home with the three of us—Alberto, called Chachito; Socorro, nicknamed Chachita; and me, Cotito. In the evening, like many other families in the building, Mami, my brother, my sister, and I did piecework—gluing small rhinestones to custom jewelry to earn extra money for household necessities, the glue staining our hands and creating a stench. Considering it women's work, Papi refused to glue rhinestones, as did most of the other men we knew.

The families in my building had left behind the countries of their births for the promise of a better life in Nueva York. For the residents of 330 East 102nd Street in East Harlem, the scents drifting from my Abuela's apartment created a climate all our own, a balm that healed heartache, homesickness, and the pain of the week's thankless hard work.

I sat at our kitchen table watching as Mami poured Spic and Span into the plastic pail filled with hot water. My mother was tall, fair, and strong. Even cleaning, she looked beautiful. She added *yerba buena* and *abre camino* leaves, Florida water and tuberose flowers. Ignoring my plea to go to Abuela's, Mami prepared the water to mop the apartment from the back bedroom to the front door. Then my sister or I would take the dirty water out to the sidewalk curb and spill it into the street, throwing out the negative energy it had gathered from our apartment.

"Please let me go," I begged Mami. "Abuela needs me. She gets tired walking back and forth trying to make her altar look pretty." Mami's back was turned, and she couldn't see my sister shooting an angry look at me. I stuck my tongue out at Chachita.

"Mami, she's just trying to get out of helping us," Chachita said, resentment growing in her voice. "Six isn't so young." Chachita was eight years older than I was. "I helped you clean when I was her age. Why can't she?" Mami squeezed and shredded the flowers into tiny pieces. Their sweet fragrance filled the kitchen. My sister tore an old bedsheet into rags to clean the furniture and the miniature glass animals that decorated the top of our wooden television cabinet. Outside on the street below, my father and brother washed our car.

"*Bien*, go and help Abuela, Cotito," my mother allowed. "As soon as you finish come back to clean with your sister and me." Knowing that I would spend the afternoon in Abuela's apartment, Mami said this for Chachita's benefit. Socorro did not think it fair that I escaped my chores and received endless pampering from Abuela, who always referred to me as *la nena*, the baby of the family.

I gave Chachita a look of triumph and opened the front door before Mami could change her mind. Letting it slam behind me, I raced down the corridor to Abuela's apartment—as I did every week—my shoes tapping against the porcelain floor tiles.

I could smell the powerful, enticing fragrances of my grandmother's devotion—Florida water, *rompe saraguey* and *abre camino* plants, Pompeii cologne—wafting from her door down the hall.

The strong fragrance of *las siete potencias*—the incense of the seven powers—signaled that she had finished spiritually mopping her apartment and was now making certain that any *carga*, or heaviness, would be overpowered, driven away by the strong smell. It was her desire that the energy leave not only her apartment but our whole building. I wondered if the smoke was lifting unwanted spirits from around me just as it removed them from Abuela's small apartment.

Today, three neighbors stood around Abuela's open doorway, but she was not to be seen. Their arms full of groceries from the local bodega and laundry they had gathered from the clothing lines in the basement yard, they stood calling compliments and questions inside.

"Doña Luisa, is that jasmine incense you're burning today?" Gloria from apartment 4 asked shyly.

"*Sí, jazmín con myrrah,*" Abuela's husky voice called back from inside. She did not make an appearance at the door. Guarding her privacy and her secrets, she never gave away the ingredients of her ritual mixtures. "Caridad's *botánica* has all the ingredients," she added, trying to dispel the notion that she was holding back information. Abuela knew that neighbors hoped that her spiritual vision would help them solve their problems. She sometimes volunteered information transmitted by the spirits, but she did not like people imposing themselves upon her goodwill.

Jesús from apartment 6 stood quietly and patted my head as I approached. A tall, pensive man the color of a coffee bean, he wore thick glasses and walked with a cane. Abuela was his dear friend, and he put up with her need for privacy. Mami and Papi often took Jesús to the supermarket, or my brother and sister would run to the neighborhood bodega for him. Jesús had no family but us.

Sweet, robust Lula adjusted her overstuffed grocery bags and peered into the doorway, hoping to snatch a moment with my elusive grandmother.

Gloria, a pious middle-aged woman, carried sadness on her shoulders like a shawl. Abandoned by her husband, she worked long hours in a sewing factory to support herself and three children. She was constantly in search of a way, a *remedio,* to get her husband back. The friendly trio formed a semicircle around Abuela's door, talking as if in a comfortable living room, unconcerned that their host had not joined them.

"Doña Luisa, your granddaughter is here," Lula called into Abuela's apartment. Approaching the door, I could hear Abuela's slippers—she called them *mis chanclas*—brush against the floor as she shuffled out to greet me.

Dressed all in white as always, a bright white kerchief tied around her head, my tiny, ebony-skinned Abuela grinned down at me. "I thought you had forgotten your old Abuela," she teased. "I was ready to give away *los dulces de coco*—the coconut candies I made for you."

Abuela waited a moment to see my reaction. I melted into her arms, hugging her tightly. "I'm here to help you, Abuela. Please don't give away *los dulces.*" She kissed my cheek with warm, cigar-tainted lips, looked up at Lula, and said, "When you have children, your heart expands with love. But when you have grandchildren, your heart is an open door."

Laughing, Lula agreed: "That's how I feel about my grandchildren, Luisa. They have a revolving door to my heart." Taking a deep breath, Lula shook her head and said, "The smell of the incense is so heavenly it transports me away. Is this what the mixture is supposed to do? Does it have a special meaning?"

"I was wondering the same thing," added Gloria shyly.

Abuela teased them in return. "No," she said, "it is just to get rid of the strong smell of the bleach the janitor soaks the hallways with."

Laughing in a deep baritone, Jesús commented, "Luisa, you old fox, just tell us your secret."

"Of course the incense has a spiritual meaning," said Abuela, smiling. "Incense can dispel the negative and attract the positive. Burn incense in your home to keep the spiritual energy balanced." Satisfied, Lula, Gloria, and Jesús took their leave.

Abuela ushered me into her apartment. She closed the door, and the flame of a candle danced against the narrow foyer walls. Behind the front door, a red candle for the African warrior gods also stayed lit, protecting her home. On a shelf above the doorway, a glass of water, a piece of bread next to a red apple, an iron horseshoe, and a small golden cross on a piece of red cloth also kept negative forces at bay.

Abuela kept the warriors, the true gods of her home, hidden from public view. I saw that she had placed before their stone and iron objects *eliminate* (a white candle), a dish with assorted candies, a cigar, and a glass of *aguardiente*—rum. I stopped to examine the candies she had set before the warriors. Noting my curiosity, Abuela told me, "I saved some candies for you to take home." She bent down to arrange the plate in a position closer to the wall. "Remember what I'm going to say," she instructed me seriously. "Never tell people what you do to protect yourself because they can always use it to destroy you."

I looked up to Abuela's face, wondering who would want to destroy me. But I knew better than to ask too many questions. If I did, Abuela would grow silent. With a soft chuckle and a mischievous wink she nodded. "This is our secret." From the record player, the high, clear voice of Celina sang, *"Gladiolas blancas para Obatalá, aché para Eleguá, para Yemayá mis flores."* White gladiolus for Obatalá, *aché* for Eleguá, my flowers also for Yemayá.

Abuela emptied the glasses of water on the altar. She threw away the flowers that had graced the altar during the week and replaced them with fresh white gladiolus. Standing on a chair at the kitchen sink, I filled the glasses with cool water, and she placed them carefully in rows on the altar, calling on the Indian, Yoruba, and Congo spirits of old. *"Comisión divina te pido protección,"* she prayed. Divine commission I ask for your protection. Abuela enjoyed playing music as she prayed. "Music is the food of the soul, and the right music calls the spirits," she said. As she placed the fresh items on the altar, Abuela's thin hips kept the rhythm of the music. "Music wipes away sadness and brings joy," she told me, touching my chin.

"Que viva Changó, que viva Changó, que viva Changó . . ." Celina's jubilant soprano evoked the warrior god of thunder and lightning, her voice ringing up and down the

shadowy halls of the apartment. I approached the Victrola and studied the album cover. It featured a petite, light-skinned woman with long black hair. Celina stood on a tropical Cuban mountainside, surrounded by lush green palm trees. Abuela adored Celina's song for Changó, the divinity who, in ancient times, was king of a place even farther away—Oyo in West Africa.

Though she never explained what any of them meant, songs to Yemayá, the sea goddess; Eleguá, the god of the crossroads; and Ochun, the goddess of love filled Abuela's apartment. Abuela danced in the altar room, and taking my hand, she spun me like a toy top.

Abuela's sacred room was covered by large murals of Catholic saints. Shelves were filled with statues of Africans and Native Americans that came alive when she played the special music that called the power of the divinities.

The statues looked to me like people in El Barrio—neighbors, friends, and family members. The large black woman in the red-and-white dress could have been Rosario, the woman who worked in the bodega preparing sandwiches with thin slices of cheese and even thinner slices of salami. The old black wise man had the serenity of Pablo, who lived in the next building. Now that it was summer, his family brought his rocker outside and he spent the whole day out front, swaying patiently and qui-etly watching the movements of the block. Like the statue, Pablo's dark skin shone in sharp contrast to his cotton-white hair and sparkling white clothes. He was a black god in possession of a serene aura that drew people to pause and greet him with a slight bow. Like Abuela, he possessed an invisible power that illuminated the space around him.

Abuela played selections from a collection of old albums

on the ancient, windup Victrola. She changed the record, and nostalgic songs reminding her of Puerto Rico began to fill her apartment.

My grandmother's apartment faced the backs of other gray buildings.

"Le lo lai lo lai, le lo le lo lai, soy un jíbaro del monte." I am a man from the mountains, the slow, melancholy voice of Chuíto, el de Bayamón, crooned, his *jíbaro* songs of praise transporting Puerto Rico's green slopes to our gray tenement.

"Qué será de Borinquen mi Dios querido, qué será de mis hijos y de mi hogar?" What will become of Puerto Rico, my beloved God, what will become of my children and my home? Abuela played the lament of Bobby Capó, creating a mellow atmosphere in the apartment. Like the others, this cherished old record was marked with skips and stutters from the times when Abuela had misplaced the needle, causing the arm to bounce wildly, scratching the record's surface.

Today, as she played music and cleansed the altars in my presence, she provided no explanation of the meaning of the sacred rituals to the divine powers, or *potencias*. Unaware of what it all meant, I happily assisted, knowing that I would get a delicious meal when we finished.

From the kitchen wafted mouthwatering scents of fresh onions, sweet peppers, garlic, *recao,* cilantro, and oregano immersed in the bacon lard called *tocino.* Abuela used this *sofrito* to prepare a succulent *pollo frito*—fried chicken covered with chunks of fried potatoes. My stomach growled in anticipation. Turning and catching my hungry eyes, she laughed. *"Todo en su tiempo,* Cotito," she soothed, patting my head. "All in good time."

Abuela walked into the kitchen to the stove and began pressing the pieces of fried *tostones* between brown paper bags to make them thin and flat before refrying them to a golden crisp finish. She was cooking my favorite dishes— yellow rice with Spanish olives, red kidney beans swimming in thick sauce with pieces of *calabaza,* fried chicken, and string beans.

I sat on the old wooden rocking chair, waiting. My legs didn't reach the floor, so it was difficult for me to sway the rocker back and forth. Bobby Capó's song came to an end and the needle scratched against the paper label. Abuela walked back into the living room and over to the Victrola. She turned the crank and, squinting, managed to replace the needle in the beginning groove of the disc. She scooped me into her arms and settled me onto her lap.

She swayed us in the rocking chair as if in a trance, her head resting on a small blue pillow that hung from the back. I leaned against her chest, and time seemed to slow down. The needle scratched Bobby Capó's mournful voice again. I looked into my grandmother's eyes and thought she might cry.

"Abuela, why are you so sad today?" I asked.

"*Mi hija*, this song brings back so many memories. Some I treasure and some, painful."

"I don't like to see you this way," I protested.

"*Mi nena*, memories are good. They let you know that you are alive, that you have lived a full life." Sensing my fear, she smiled and held me closer. The mellow music soothed me. "Cotito, don't be frightened. Sometimes Abuela needs to travel back to Puerto Rico to relive important moments with family members no longer with us. Abuela plays her music to remember them."

"Where are they now?" I asked her.

"You cannot see them," she answered, "but you can imagine and feel them because they are with us and watch over us." She nibbled pieces of her cigar like chewing gum. Her teeth were worn yellow ivory, stained by the juice of the tobacco she held always in the right side of her mouth. Silvery tin cans that had previously held fruit or vegetables became spittoons, scattered throughout the house and glittering in the light of the candles. Intermittently, Abuela paused the rocker to direct a stream of brown juice into the large tin can she had placed by the chair. She never missed.

But with each sad lyric, Bobby Capó's voice seemed to take Abuela further away. To cheer her, I asked, "Can we look at the picture album?"

"Sí, hija." Reaching into the left side of her bodice, Abuela pulled out the small, handmade cloth pouch in which she kept her money and the key to the wooden cabinet. She took out the large golden key and placed it in my hand. The warmth of her body suffused the metal.

"You know where it is," Abuela told me, brushing off pieces of tobacco that had fallen on her white dress. I went to the cabinet and, carefully turning the key in the lock, opened the doors and pulled out the cherished book. The album's smooth leather cover, polished from years of Abuela's caressing hands, had the casual shine of old worn shoes. Held together with shoelaces, the covers sand- wiched black paper pages crowded with old photographs.

I hold these photographs in my hands today. Through- out my life, loved ones who have joined the spirit world have come to me in dreams, and I have felt their presence in my life. Sometimes the smell of Abuela's cigars permeates a room, and at other times the air fills with Maderas de Oriente, my mother's favorite perfume; though gone from the everyday world, they protect me still.

Photographs are another way to touch these angels. In one picture, taken on Easter Sunday in 1944, my brother wears a stylish dark suit and imitates my father's erect posture. Though he's only eleven, Chachito's mischievous smile foretells the handsome man he will become. My sister, just ten, wears a bubbly expression not yet faded to gloom. Socorro's hair is pulled back, showing off the curves of her full, wholesome face. Her light skin is like Mami's, while Chachito and I share Papi's dark complexion.

In another snapshot my elegant parents stand together on a patch of grass near the East River at Ninety-second Street. In the distance, other families walk with their children. Just two years old, I stand between their tall bodies, protected then as I would not always be later in life from the searing pains of discrimination and machismo. My mother's hair, pulled back into a rolled bun, accentuates her angular face and wide smile. Her left hand rests tenderly on my right shoulder, and I can almost feel it there today. Papi wears a tailored double-breasted suit. His handsome brown face looks boldly into the camera, his right hand proudly holding Mami's shoulder. My parents' faces shine with health and promise.

I was an unexpected surprise for Mami and Papi, who had decided that after the birth of my sister they would not have any more children. "The spirits work in mysterious ways," Abuela told me as we gazed all those years ago at the magic images. "Like Eleguá, you opened the roads to our hearts, bringing more joy and happiness to the family."

Abuela also had photographs of Mami's best friend, Justa, with her two sons, Jimmy and Luis. Justa was a devoted member of the Pentecostal storefront church on One Hundreth Street. Although we were not of her faith, Justa and Mami were like sisters, and her sons, part of our family. Abuela never referred to Justa's religion. Looking at her photograph Abuela commented, "Justa is a good woman. She is truly a child of the Almighty."

Emptying her mouth of a lump of chewed tobacco, Abuela lit up one of her cigars. I blew at the smoke rings she formed, breaking them apart into streams, and a blue-gray cloud rose above our heads.

Abuela turned her attention again to the album. In a large black-and-white picture, my uncles and father showed off their virile twenty-year-old bodies on the rooftop of our building. Bursting with the cockiness of youth, each posed as a young gladiator, defiant and filled with pride. The eldest looked seductively into the camera with a teasing Don Juan smile. The youngest wore a wide fedora hat and wide, large coat, imitating the tough look of Al Capone. Papi, Abuela's middle child and an aspiring prizefighter, assumed a pose as if he were ready to knock out any onlooker.

"Ah, my three kings. How handsome your uncles and father were," Abuela said. "They are still handsome."

"They are not," I responded mischievously, just to hear her argue in their defense. "Abuela, they are very old men." Like Papi, both my uncles were married men, fathers who labored long hours and whose faces and bodies showed their fatigue.

Usually she would contradict me. But that day, her nostalgia threatened to overpower her, and Abuela did not answer. She passed her bony fingers over the faces of her sons as if the images were real. Suddenly, Bobby Capó's record ended. Abuela gently pushed me off the rocker and instructed me to replace the needle on its armrest. I did so, then settled back onto Abuela's lap. We continued to turn pages to the past in silence.

Then I noticed the corner of a picture I'd never seen peeping out from behind another photograph. I grasped its edge and began to pull. Abuela's slim hand covered mine in an attempt to stop me, but my childish curiosity would not be restrained. Before I knew it, I was gripping the image of a young woman.

"Who is she, Abuelita?" I asked, handling the sepia-toned old photograph more carefully.

The photograph, peeling and cracked with age, was framed by a frayed piece of ornate brown cardboard and had the look of a polished amber jewel. I marveled at the elegant young woman who stared back at me, her half smile confident and haughty. Even in sepia, her dark, almond-shaped eyes sparkled. She wore a simple, light-colored dress that fitted her loosely and was cinched at her tiny waist. I studied the picture intently. The woman's formal pose suggested that the photo had been taken in a studio, before a screen painted with the image of a crossroads. A cloudlike design in the background swirled softly, enhancing the quiet composure of the elegant creature whose eyes pierced my soul. Looking into her gaze, I felt an inexplicable uneasiness that made the hairs on my body stand on edge.

Again I asked, "Who is she?" Abuela remained silent.

Heaviness filled the room, and my question hung suspended in midair. I turned to my grandmother for an answer, but her clouded eyes were rimmed with tears. She stared at the photograph, ignoring my presence. I sat quietly, my head resting against her chest, holding my breath so as not to intrude on her thoughts. We sat in silence for a long time. Was this a lost friend, a daughter, a sister?

Looking again at the beautiful young woman in the picture, her long black braid coiling over her shoulder and hanging down her chest, I suddenly knew. "It's you, Abuela, isn't it?" My grandmother nodded sadly, lifting her now gray braid and laying it against her back.

"This was taken the day before I left Puerto Rico, so my children would not forget my face."

"Abuela?" I did not understand.

It was then that Abuela began to wrap me in the arms of a story I had never heard before. She wove it seamlessly, so that it became a part of me, so that I could not tell where I ended and she began. Taking a deep breath, she continued to sway us in the rocker. Her voice detached from her body, and she spoke as if in a dream. I stared at her photograph, and with her words, her younger self seemed to come alive, animating the scenes of her life.

In the years since, I have visualized this story time and again, turning the pages of Abuela's life in my mind's eye. I have filled in missing details and remembered others, and Abuela's story lives on.

Abandoned at birth by her mother, Abuela Luisa was raised in the village of Loíza Aldea by her grandmother, María de la O. María de la O, she said, was a dark, strong-willed woman who, Abuela believed, had been born into slavery. No taller than a broomstick, she had large brown eyes, deep marks on her face, and thick brown hair covered with a white kerchief. She called herself *una africana de verdad*—a true African—and spoke a mixture of Spanish and African words.

When I asked her what this meant, Abuela imitated the deep tone of María de la O. *"Mi kekere da zunga a tu Iya. My child, bring a cigar to your mother."* I laughed at the unfamiliar dialect and Abuela continued. "I would roll my grandmother's cigars for her from fresh leaves I picked from the fields and dried on the front patio," she told me. "Be thankful I only ask you to go down to the bodega for my cigars, *hija,"* Abuela teased. She hesitated, gathering her thoughts before she spoke. *"Todo en este mundo cambia con el tiempo.* Everything in this world changes with time."

Abuela reached back into her past and, with her words, painted me a picture of her childhood.

"My grandmother María de la O's home was a small, one-room wooden hut, *un bohío,* with a roof of dry palm leaves. The floor was the earth, and I swept it at night with a broom of handwoven palms." Absentmindedly, Abuela cleaned the trickle of tobacco juice that formed at the corner of her mouth as she spoke.

"Abuelo Chachito made the few pieces of furniture we had. He carved our cups from coconut shells and our bowls and spoons from dried, hollowed calabashes. *Todas las noches*—every night—Abuelo sat by the door working with his hands to create the things we needed."

"Papi made a coconut cup for each of us, too, Abuela," I reminded her proudly.

Her eyes glinted. She smiled and said, "Yes, but *hija*, we had no other cups at all. You do not even drink from yours!"

Abuela was right. Papi's coconut cups were decorations that sat on our kitchen shelf next to a colorful arrangement of plastic flowers.

"María de la O made all my clothing from scraps of cloth she collected and found," Abuela continued. "Every night I washed my one dress and wore it the next day. When the dress could be worn no more María de la O would make me another.

"When I was your age I did not own a pair of shoes." Abuela raised her thin legs, and her cotton slippers fell from her wide feet. *"Mira mis botes. Puedo llegar a Puerto Rico con estos pies tan grande,"* she laughed. Look at my boats. I can float to Puerto Rico with my big feet.

I looked down at my brown buckled shoes and lacy socks and tried to imagine walking around barefoot every day. Reading my mind, Abuela removed my shoes and socks, carefully folded the socks, and placed them in my shoes alongside the rocker.

"Let me see your little pigs," she said. We laughed as I wiggled my toes in the air, causing the rocker to move more quickly.

"I loved my feet touching the earth. The earth spoke to me, and the sand and ground embraced me," she added, pushing her slippers farther away.

Abuela told me of her village, which was covered with palm trees and infused with the salty smell of the ocean. The azure sky sparkled and the green leaves of the palms spread over the town like large fans in the wind, the smell of fresh coconut filling the air. Young men the age of my brother, Chachito, climbed to the top of the tall, swaying trees with their bare hands and feet, carrying machetes in their mouths, to cut down the ripe coconuts. All day long, the hollow thump of falling cocos sounded out like drums. Vendors walked along the roads selling their wares, hollering in high, melodic voices, *"Vendo, vendo cocos frescos, agua de coco para limpiar los riñones. Tengo pescado fresco, pollos, y mas."* I'm selling fresh coconuts, coconut water to clean your kidneys. I have fresh fish, chicken, and more.

Abuelo Chachito sometimes took my Abuela Luisa fishing in a small boat he had built himself. A small, thin man the color of strong dark wood, Chachito carried the worries of the world on his slumped shoulders. He worked tirelessly trying to earn money to keep the family together. At the end of a day at sea, he often stood by the dirt road near the shack selling freshly caught fish and crabs strung on long strings attached to a wooden pole.

"I must have been twelve years old when María de la O fell ill and could not get up from her bed," Abuela said, her voice somber. "Daily, I cleaned the house and prayed for her to get well. My grandmother insisted that the spirits would cure her, that we should not worry because they were not calling her."

Abuela described how she would take water out of a clay jar filled with stones and seashells that stood by her grandmother's altar and rub María de la O's forehead, chest, and arms as instructed. "María always said, *El agua del mar es sagrada*—water from the sea is holy." At night, Abuelo Chachito worried silently, sitting by the foot of her bed and tenderly rubbing María's feet.

"Every day I placed wildflowers on the altar, praying that María would get well," Abuela recounted. "I prayed to the spirits as I had seen her do, asking them to protect her and make her well. I chose flowers of all colors, hoping that all the spirits would come together and cure her."

Abuelo Chachito worked twice as hard collecting crabs to sell, in a futile attempt to earn money to pay for a doctor's visit. Every afternoon, Luisa stood at his side, calling out, *"Pescado fresco y jueyes"* to the people who passed along the road in horse-drawn carriages.

"Horses!" I gasped with delight.

I had seen horses in El Barrio during the summer, when vendors brought kiddie rides to the neighborhood. Parents paid five cents each for their children to ride around the block twice on a rickety horse-drawn carriage with two rows of seats. The vendor would squeeze seven of us on each bench, transporting fourteen screaming children in a leisurely circle as we yelled out, "Hi-Yo, Silver!" all the way.

"Yes, child, horses." Abuela paused and took a bite of her cigar. Chewing the tobacco, she moved the rocker gently and went on with her story.

"One day, a carriage stopped before the hut and a tall mulatta the color of sweet golden-brown tamarind stepped to the road. Her flowing black hair reached to her shoulders. Her figure was like a beautifully sculpted guitar that played enchanting music with her every movement. María de la O had always said that her daughter's beauty was a burden, like the cross that Jesus carried and was crucified on. I knew right away that this woman was my mother. Tomasa."

Abuela took three deep breaths. I felt her thin chest expand like a soft balloon, lifting me slightly.

"Tomasa did not stay long," she went on. "I watched from the doorway, praying that my mother would hold me. I watched as she kissed her own mother instead, softly caressing María's forehead. She placed a small package of medicines near the cot and moved to the door, looking at me with the eyes of a stranger." Luisa watched her mother get into the carriage. The driver cracked his whip against the tired horse's back, and the wooden wheels of the carriage strained as they slowly rolled away.

"In those days," Abuela explained, "to be the color of strong dark wood was a burden. To be the color of honey like Tomasa was a blessing. Tomasa did not want me because of my color. I cried long into the night.

" 'Don't waste your tears,' María de la O told me. 'Save them for when you really need to cry.' "

The years passed. María de la O died when Abuela was fourteen. Soon after, Chachito passed on, too, unable to live without his companion. The choices my Abuela Luisa made then were marked both by the accidents of her birth and by her own strong will.

"La vida es como los sueños; algunos buenos y otros pesadillas," Abuela whispered. Life is like dreams; some are good and others are nightmares. Then she continued her story.

Abuela left Loíza Aldea for the city of San Juan to find work and soon after became a mother herself. The father of her first two boys abandoned her, and the father of the youngest was killed working on the railroad. Like so many women of color, on their own with no formal education, my grandmother found work as a domestic and a laundrywoman.

It was a hard life. Oftentimes, householders refused to pay wages to hired help of color, claiming after the work was completed that it was of poor quality. Even after slavery was abolished in 1873, racism and discrimination continued, and Americans, English, Spaniards, and others in Puerto Rico still refused to treat *los negros* fairly. A single black woman was prey to the roving eyes of her bosses. If she refused the advances of her white employer, she could be brought to court and accused of being *una bruja*, a witch. In the houses where she worked, Abuela Luisa had to be constantly on guard.

"Me cansé—I got tired of working and not being able to feed my children," Abuela told me.

So she scraped together the money for a one-way boat fare to New York, arranging for the boys, all under ten years old, to stay with different relatives, to be sent for when she could afford their passage to Nueva York.

"Qué dolor—I was heartbroken, leaving my children the same way my mother left me." Abuela's voice faltered.

Papi's older brother was placed in San Juan with an aunt; my father, in Puerta de Tierra with a cousin; and his younger brother was sent to Abuela's home village of Loíza Aldea to stay with family friends.

"The day I left Puerto Rico, the sun shone like gold and the blue of the sky was the color of a gem. The heat and the waving palms wove themselves into my heart along with the tears of my sons, who had begged me not to leave."

The day she left the island, as Luisa stood alone on the dock, crying alongside other seekers of better futures, the freight ship glistened like an enormous metal coffin. Abuela carried an old borrowed suitcase held together by a thick cord.

"The suitcase contained two dresses, underwear, a sweater, a picture of my three sons, and a copy of this photograph." Abuela touched her finger to the snapshot of herself that had launched her tale, the woman at the crossroads surrounded by clouds.

Abuela told me that her heavy, dark brown dress, borrowed from a woman who had recently returned from New York, was too large for her thin body. The tattered brown coat she carried belonged to her friend's husband and draped to the floor like an old sack, the fabric scratchy against her sunburned skin. The old shoes she had bought were too small for her wide feet. Luisa felt imprisoned by the clothing. Around her neck hung a pouch containing dark locks of her sons' hair, seashells, sand from the beach, and *yerba buena* for protection.

Fingering the pouch she still wore around her neck and rocking me in her lap, Abuela began to sing a song. In a soft, raspy voice, she chanted, *"María de la O, que los ojitos los tiene morado de tanto llorar . . ."* Her voice trailed off. María de la O, your eyes are red from crying so much . . .

Tears streamed freely down Abuela's face. "I thought that I would have returned to Puerto Rico by now," she sighed. As an afterthought she added, "Why return if all my loved ones are here now? There is no one left back home. I am so old."

"Abuela, you're still beautiful," I interjected softly.

Affectionately touching my nose, Abuela continued, "Time has a way of passing so quickly. I really don't remember when I became an old woman." She sighed again. Fingering the photograph, she gazed into the eyes of her young self.

I touched the picture too and wondered if María de la O still watched over Abuela and the rest of our family, if Tomasa had ever wondered about her lost daughter. Listening to the song of Abuela's words, I had felt her story lead me into times past, to a long line of family, and to places far, far away.

Hugging me warmly, Abuela spoke. *"Mi nieta,* remember that time is precious." Staring at the old photograph, she said, "Treasure each day. When it is gone, it will never return."

TWO

"Carajo, Cotito, What's Wrong with You?"

Quién soy? . . . Eso me pregunto yo. . . .

Who am I? . . . That is what I ask myself. . . .
— ARSENIO RODRIGUEZ, "QUIÉN SOY?"

There are occurrences from my childhood in El Barrio that echo through my body as if they happened yesterday.

It was a special Monday—my first day in school. The sun shone softly through the plastic curtains in our living room windows. The curtains were covered with large red, yellow, and white roses in a bed of green leaves, and as I watched the colorful play of light through them, I fiddled with the cloth buttons tacked into the cushions of our overstuffed sofa. I was filled with nervous energy and began jumping to entertain myself while Mami was dressing. The metal springs of the sofa strained under my feet as I jumped higher and higher, delighting in the feeling of being momentarily suspended in midair.

"Mami, hurry up! We are going to be late," I hollered, bouncing on sprawling pink magnolias and green vines against a background of Prussian blue. All the colors in the room reflected my festive mood. The cushions let out whistling puffs of air as I landed. I imagined myself sitting in a classroom dressed in the new clothes Mami had placed on a chair next to the sofa. Still jumping, I admired my blouse with its frilly white lace, my socks and their tiny, shiny white ankle bows, my brand-new red-and-blue plaid skirt, and my new black patent leather Mary Janes.

Mami stepped out of the bedroom in a navy blue dress with white polka dots that fit perfectly over her strong body. She wore the black marcasite ring she used only when she wanted to impress. A tall and softly muscular woman, she conveyed a subtle elegance. Most intriguing to me was the gold tooth that shone brilliantly when Mami smiled. Although she had trained as a nurse and wanted to work outside the house, Papi didn't allow Mami to get a job. Her family was her devotion and career.

"Come down from that sofa right now," she said with a frown. "I just combed your hair and the braids are already unraveling. Stop jumping."

I stopped in midair and stretched out my legs, landing on the sofa in a seated position. Mami could not help smiling. "You are a little clown. You belong in a circus instead of school." She laughed and walked to the couch, pulling me to her.

My new blouse was stiff and made me stand up straighter. I didn't want it to wrinkle. The perfectly pleated skirt easily slipped over my head and down my slim body. The white socks were spotless, and the patent leather shoes caught the light and shone like the black jewels in Mami's precious ring. Then Mami pinned a new lacy handkerchief to my blouse. The way it was folded reminded me of a blossoming flower. "This is a present Justa made for your first day of school. Look at how beautifully she wove the lace," Mami said, carefully touching the edge of the frilly lace. "Don't use it to clean your nose," she admonished.

Papi had already left for work very early in the morning, before the sun greeted the day. Chachito and Chachita had gone too, rushing out to get to school on time. But Abuela would see me before Mami took me to school. Before we left our apartment, Mami dabbed a little of her favorite cologne, the heady sandalwood Maderas de Oriente, behind her ears and mine.

Abuela must have heard us coming. She was standing by her door, waiting for Mami and me. *"Qué linda te ves,* how pretty you look in your new clothes," she remarked as I approached. "Turn around so I can get a full view of your outfit. And come in so I can bless you."

Anxiously, I turned to Mami, hoping that she would tell Abuela not to spray smoke over my new clothes. I was afraid the strong odor of her cigar would destroy the fragrance of the sandalwood. "Abuela, do you have to?" I asked.

"Others wish they had an *abuela* to take care of them so," Mami commented, pushing me forward. I stood waiting for Abuela to light a fresh cigar.

"Close your eyes," she instructed. My grandmother sucked on the cigar, taking in smoke until her cheeks puffed like balloons. Then, turning me three times to the right and three times to the left, she breathed the smoke out all over my body. "Now you are really ready for school," she added happily. I nodded, hoping the smell would disappear on the street.

"Flora, our little one is growing up," she told Mami. "You are a good mother to her." Again taking in a deep breath of smoke, Abuela repeated the ritual for my mother. "Gracias, Luisa," Mami said, hugging Abuela. "Now we have to leave so your granddaughter isn't late for her first day." To me, she added, "Give your Abuela a big-girl hug." Abuela received my embrace and watched us descend the stairs.

I was thrilled to be attending school just like my brother and sister. The only difference was that Mami would take me there and pick me up. In my new outfit and with my carefully pomaded, combed braids decorated with blue and red bows, I walked proudly down the block alongside my mother. Mami strutted elegantly. Her black suede heels made her even taller. Her gray hair was pulled back into an elegant roll at the nape of her neck.

The metal taps Mami had put on the toes and heels of my shoes were intended to protect the soles. To me, they were a musical instrument I used to mark the beat of my happy steps against the concrete. *Tap, tap, tap, tap* my shoes sounded as I walked. *Tap-tap-tap, tap-tap-tap* was the beat I made as I skipped along to get to school faster. "Stop skipping, Cotito," Mami gently scolded. "You'll start sweating and your hair will curl up."

Mami held my hand tightly as she smiled down at me, giving last-minute instructions for the day. "Fold your hands on the desk. Listen to the teacher. Don't talk to other children." I tried to pay attention, despite my excitement. "When the teacher speaks to you, bow your head respectfully. Raise your hand to ask permission to go make pee-pee. Do not wait to the last minute to make pee-pee. You don't want to pee on yourself and have the other children laugh at you." I was filled with the thrill of being old enough to attend school. I felt my heart throbbing in my ears, drowning out the last of Mami's words.

As we walked past, I felt disappointed to see that the storefront Pentecostal church, where the churchgoers sang joyous songs to God, was closed. I was secretly pleased, though, that the busybody Julia was sweeping the street in front of her tenement. One of the neighborhood gossips, she was sure to bear witness to how special I looked on my first school day.

We passed the bodega, which was filled with people buying sandwiches and food. Antonio, the owner, had his head buried, as always, in the black-and-white school notebook where he listed the items his customers purchased on credit, along with the date. I wondered if Antonio knew that I was starting school, but he didn't even look up. As I walked along with Mami, the loudspeaker from the bodega blared out the popular merengue, "El Negrito del Batey": *A mí me llaman el negrito del batey porque el trabajo para mí es un enemigo.* (They call me the little black man of the neighborhood because work is my enemy.) *El trabajar yo se lo dejo todo al buey porque el trabajo Dios lo hizo como un castigo.* (I leave work for the bull, because

God made work as a curse.) *A mí me gusta bailar de medio lado con una negra bien preciosa.* (I like to dance leaning to the side with a beautiful black woman.)

The merengue added a sassy pulse to my walk. I felt my skirt flutter around my legs to the back-and-forth sway of the rapid one-two, one-two, one-two beat. At the corner of our block, the school building came into full view.

A monumental edifice painted a dull yellow, it stood out like a gigantic dollhouse. P.S. 121 was wide and took up most of the block. It had a courtyard for playing baseball, hopscotch, and other games, and today the yard was filled with children and adults waiting with them to enter the building. Everyone was speaking at the same time, creating an incessant buzz. A large man stood with a bullhorn at the main entranceway. "Those of you in class one-two, line up here. Those of you in class two-one, line up on that side. Class one-three, line up behind class one-two!" The crowd of children, parents, and teachers scrambled around, trying to follow the blaring instructions.

"Parents, pay attention. Look at the cards I sent with your children's class. They match the numbers held up by the teachers. Line up accordingly. *Por favor,*" he added in Spanish, as if all the information said in English could be understood by tagging on a Spanish "please." Mami hesitated before entering the courtyard. Holding me back, she waited, discerning where class 1–1 had lined up.

In the distance at the other end of the yard she saw the teacher holding up the class card and we began making our way toward my group, navigating through the crowd with our hands linked. Parents gave last-minute instructions to their children in Spanish. "Lupe, hold on to your lunch box." "Miguel, remember to wash your hands after you go to the bathroom." "Gloria, don't walk in the halls by yourself." As we pushed our way closer, the tense voices of parents cluttered the air. "Pepe, here is your lunch. Don't leave the lunch box in school." "Lolita, remember to listen to the teacher. Do not talk." The children nodded impatiently in the affirmative just as I did, all of us anxious to begin our new lives.

Before we could reach them, the man with the bullhorn ordered my class, 1–1, to enter. I was so disappointed tears gathered in the rims of my eyes. I watched the other children file in orderly lines into the building.

"Mami, please let me run. I can catch up with the class."

"No, wait, I will take you in," Mami said, still holding my hand tightly. Her hand was cold. We waited and waited until all the classes had gone in. I thought my stomach would eat itself. Finally, we entered the building and Mami took me directly to my classroom.

Depositing me at the door to the room, she bent down to kiss me on the cheek. In her brown eyes her love was written, along with a reminder of her many instructions. I saw in her expression the pain she felt at leaving me in the hands of strangers, but I ignored the message in her eyes. I wanted to be in school. I kissed her cheek and said, "I love you, Mami," pulling my body toward the classroom. She quickly turned away.

But as my mother walked down the hall, a sudden feeling of abandonment surprised me, and I froze by the door. My brash spirit disappeared. I felt out of place. Timidly, I waited.

The woman in front of the room was tall, thin, and

white. She had light red hair and wore square, black-rimmed glasses. In a black dress with a white collar, her body appeared pencil thin. And with her leather lace-up shoes, she reminded me of a nun, dressed all in black and white. In our family and our neighborhood, black was worn only when someone passed away. Could it be that someone in my teacher's family had died?

The woman acknowledged my presence simply by pointing to a seat without saying a word. In the first row closest to the door, it was at the very back of the room.

With so many children in one place I was surprised it was so quiet. I walked down the aisle to my seat and noticed that the students were all looking to the front of the room, their hands folded on their desks. They glanced at me quickly as I passed, avoiding long eye contact and returning their attention to the front of the room as if pulled by ropes. I noticed three friends of mine from the block. As I walked down the aisle I smiled at Susanna, Ralphy, and Cynthia. But they remained stone-faced and at attention and did not return my smiles. I slipped into my seat, a growing uneasiness in the pit of my stomach. I sat in my chair and looked forward like the others.

The seat was at the back near the closet doors. Screwed to the worn floor, the old desk and chair were filled with splinters that pulled at the threads of my new skirt.

The smell of chalk permeated the room. The chalk dust quickly covered my brand-new shoes with a gray film. Another smell, of old decaying wood, turned my stomach. The dull gray walls looked like those of the Hernandez funeral home on 101st Street, where Mami's friend Anna had been laid to rest last month. The only decorations in the classroom were placards of white letters pasted to the molding around the lower part of the curved ceiling.

The forsaken room resisted the sun and seemed immune to rhythm. In place of the sounds of the candy store, the healthy sounds of family and friends speaking in embroidered Spanish, Miss White's staccato commands took center stage. "Sit up straight. Stop whimpering. Stop talking. Attention. Quiet." She spoke to us in rapid-fire bullets. Miss White had alabaster skin highlighted with a reddish circle on each cheek that matched her lipstick. Her skeletal figure lacked the beauty and grace of the teachers on the show *Our Miss Brooks*, which I had seen on my black-and-white television and which had guided my fantasies about school. Looking around with just my eyes, careful not to turn my head, I wanted to go home.

Miss White began to call out something that sounded like names. After a monotonous list, she read out "Martha Meraino," but I was deaf to the flat noise my name had become in her mouth. When other students pointed to me, Miss White walked to my desk and, looking sternly into my eyes, asked, "Why didn't you respond?" I understood her question—at home we spoke Spanish, but I knew English, too—yet I could not answer.

The teacher's skin burned the color of her strawberry hair as, more and more desperate, she tried to force a response from me. Confused and afraid of being punished, I lowered my eyes and folded my hands before me as my mother had instructed. Staring at the old wooden desktop etched with lines that formed letters, letters that formed words I wished I could read, I hoped this lady would just stop talking to me and go away. Embarrassed by all the attention, shivering inside from fright, I tried to hold back my tears as Miss White loomed above my desk. I prayed that the day would end so I could go home to my mother, to her smell, her voice, and our language.

Although Mami had assured me that she would return when school let out, I cried most of the day, fearing that she might forget to come and take me from this place. María, who lived in the tenement next to mine and was seated next to me, looked just as frightened. Her new pink blouse was wet from the tears that freely flowed down her dark cheeks. Felipe, who lived in my building, looked as if his eyes would roll out of their sockets from fear. His starched white shirt and new bow tie were as stiff as his small body and he sat up at absolute attention for Miss White.

I do not remember how I made it through that first day.

Mami did come for me. Day after day, she and the other parents dropped their children off in the mornings and dutifully picked us up in the afternoons, waiting by the school's somber black fence for us to emerge from the fortress of P.S. 121.

To soothe the pain of separation, Mami made me home-made snacks. In a brown paper bag, she hid the Coca-Cola bottle filled with warm milk and capped with a nursing nipple. Not wanting to be teased and embarrassed, I drank from the bottle wrapped in the paper bag in the school-yard. I fooled no one. But neither did the other kids drinking from similar bottles. It would be two more years before my mother finally stopped giving me the green glass bottle filled with warm milk and drops of coffee at bedtime. Before going to school I drank warm milk mixed with egg yolk, sugar, and Samson wine, Mami's special liquid excelsior, protection from anemia. But at school, I had no such comforts.

After several weeks, frustrated with my silence, Miss White suggested to Mami that I visit a doctor to have my hearing and eyes checked. When the results of the tests came back, they indicated that nothing was wrong. "I knew it," Mami told Papi. "Cotito is perfectly fine. In fact, the doctor said her eyes are like billiard balls—she sees and hears everything." After several months, Miss White decided that I belonged in a special class for slow learners. Upset, my mother requested that she be allowed to observe me in the class before I was transferred out. To get permission, Mami had to confront the administrative bureaucracy of the school. Principals and teachers were accustomed to controlling the lives of students without the input of parents too humble to question them.

After much hesitation, the principals begrudgingly agreed to let Mami sit in on a class. One Monday morning, she entered my classroom. She wore her special Sunday outfit: an iridescent dress that fell below her knees, a smart black Persian secondhand fur coat, black suede pumps, and a gold-studded felt beret.

With great dignity bordering on haughtiness, hiding her fear, my mother sat in a wooden chair by the entranceway. She stoically observed the class, her face devoid of any emotion. The night before I had heard her ask my father, "How can she be retarded? Coty is always talking and in the middle of everything. She has more sense than her brother and sister at that age." My father responded with a deep sigh. "I only have a third-grade education," he said, "but I know there is nothing wrong with my daughter. She is brighter than a light bulb, for God's sake."

As always, Miss White started the class that day by calling attendance. Her even-toned, low voice called out the names of my classmates, and I looked around the cheerless room trying to figure out what Mami was thinking. Did she notice the prefabricated cardboard alphabet letters that we copied daily? The bulletin board that was covered with "A" papers with glowing golden stars for penmanship, mine not among them?

From the corner of my eye, as Miss White's voice droned on, I saw my mother's stern face slowly change from controlled calm to panic. "Martha Meraino," Miss White repeated. I remained silent. Annoyed, the teacher called out for a third time, "Martha Meraino." I looked at my folded hands, wondering why on earth this lady insisted on raising her voice in my direction, calling out the wrong name.

Suddenly, shaking with anger, my mother's voice filled the room, *"Carajo, Cotito, qué te pasa? Respóndele a la maestra."* Cotito, what's wrong with you? Damn it, answer the teacher.

Slowly, the anger on Miss White's face shifted to wonder. She turned to my mother. "Mrs. Meraino, by what name do you call your daughter at home?"

"Cotito or Coty," my mother answered. And both were struck with the answer to the problem at the same time. Mami beamed. Miss White offered her a tight smile in return.

Mami came up and knelt by my desk, as if praying. With

tears in her eyes, she hugged me. Caressing my face gently, she asked, *"Mi hija, cuál es tu nombre?"*

"Cotito," I responded promptly, confused at her emotion, and at why my own mother had to ask my name.

Maybe it was some kind of game. Like when Abuela called the warrior divinity Changó by the name of Santa Bárbara, hiding his African identity, or El Niño de Atoche by the name Eleguá. Like our Catholic saints whose names disguised the ancient gods of Africa, many of us in El Barrio had nicknames that had replaced the names given by our parents at birth. My brother's nickname was Chachito and sometimes Chino; my sister Socorro was called Chachita. And I was Cotito. Justa's son Jimmy had given me the nickname, when he'd seen me for the first time in the hospital. Until now, no one had ever called me anything else.

"Listen to me," my mother said, still kneeling. "At school you will be Marta Moreno and, at home, Cotito." Patting my cheek, she rose to leave and, giving Miss White a firm look, beckoned her to step aside. "Can I assume my daughter will remain in your class?" she asked coldly, in her thickly accented English.

"Yes, I suppose so," Miss White replied, no hint of relief or apology in her voice. Mami looked the woman firmly in the eye, then turned abruptly and stormed down the hall, her heels clicking noisily against the wooden floors. I heard the anger in her steps as the sound of her heels faded.

A cloud of sadness traveled through my body, into my brain. I tried to prevent the sorrow from dominating my emotions. Why was I seated in this hostile room when

Mami was going home to the cradle that nurtured me? I could imagine music flowing through our apartment as Mami cleaned with Pine-Sol and Spic and Span mixed with aromatic herbal plants. I imagined her cooking the daily portion of rice and kidney beans and talking with friends about other friends. Down the hall, Abuela would be doing the same. The hum of melodic voices and the ever-present scent of incense mixed seductively with the rhythms of boleros and mambos, spelling home.

The classroom was a joyless cell where we sat like little mechanical brown toy soldiers with no emotions registering on our faces. We sat, stood, and walked at attention all day long. If we stepped out of line or even left too much space between students, the rapid-fire voice of Miss White quickly attacked us.

What became painfully clear as the year progressed was that Miss White did not like me. She did not have to say the words. Her face and body movements spoke of her disdain and her displeasure at having me as a student. At home, when I did a task correctly, I received praise. So when the teacher asked me to clean the blackboard, water the plants, empty the garbage can, or collect papers, I did so dutifully, with great care. I strove to perform perfectly, hoping for a compliment from Miss White. None came. Not even a thank-you.

Before I understood what an education and the important role of an educator were, I grew to hate school. "Mami, please let me stay at home with you," I pleaded. "Let me help Abuela instead of going to school" was my next argument. Faking sickness was not an option, because Mami's remedy for any illness required the disgusting ritual of several tablespoons of cod-liver oil or Emulsion de Scott, followed by sucking on a peeled orange.

Miss White made me feel inferior and unintelligent. I was unable to articulate these feelings because they had not been part of my reality until I'd attended school. The best explanation I could provide my mother was "Miss White does not love me."

Mami's response was simple: "I love you. Papi, Abuela, Chachito, and Chachita love you. Miss White is supposed to teach you. Not love you."

Holding my face between her warm hands, my mother looked deep into my eyes. "Let me tell you how much I love you," Mami said, laughing as she rubbed the tip of her nose against mine. I held Mami's face between my small hands and rubbed my nose against hers, insisting, "I love you more." Sweeping me up in her arms and pressing me against her chest, she twirled me around the kitchen, my legs swinging out into midair, until she was breathless. "Cotito, I love you *mucho, mucho, mucho*." Mami nuzzled her nose against my neck, tickling me until I could not stop laughing. Gasping for breath, I gave in. "Mami, you win. You love me more—swing me again."

When I looked into Mami's eyes, I knew by any name who I was.

But I did not understand why I could not be both taught and loved by my teacher, too.

THREE

Usted Abusó

Usted abusó, sacó provecho de mi . . .

You abused me, you took advantage of me . . .
— CELIA CRUZ, "USTED ABUSÓ"

I dressed quickly as the beads of perspiration formed on my forehead. With the summer heat unbearable, I picked a sleeveless T-shirt and blue skirt to accompany Abuela and Mami to the *botánica*. I did not want to be left behind.

On Thursdays fresh *plantas* were delivered to Caridad's at one P.M., and Abuela insisted on leaving early to get the first pick of the fresh leaves and medicinal herbs she used to protect the family.

"In Puerto Rico all these plants grow wild. I just went to the hillside and picked all the plants I needed for free. To pick the sacred plants I prayed to Ochun Osayin for permission." With a huff she added, "Plants grow freely. I do not understand paying for the gift of the spirits." Even though Abuela protested, she made it her business to be the first one at the *botánica*. But she hardly had to do so. Caridad always waited for my grandmother before opening, allowing her to get the first pick. The owner of the *botánica* had the utmost respect for Abuela's spiritual knowledge and her elder status. Abuela was almost eighty.

My grandmother was ready at twelve-thirty. "Why would I want leftover plants that have picked up the energy of others?" she explained to Mami. My mother smiled. She enjoyed accompanying Abuela and helping her pick the special sacred plants. We walked down the block slowly, and I positioned myself between Abuela and Mami, begging them to swing me back and forth.

"Pull your skirt between your legs," admonished Abuela. "Keep your legs tightly closed so that your panties don't show."

"Cotito is so different than her sister was at her age," Mami complained to Abuela. "She's always jumping, running, and dancing. I can't keep her still."

"Change-of-life babies are different. They come with spiritual sight," Abuela reminded Mami. "Cotito is your Eleguá. She'll open doors, you will see." Mami remained silent.

As we walked, the street came alive with summer sounds and summer games. Bouncing rubber balls crashed against windows, walls, and cars. The sharp pop of the Spalding connecting to broomsticks defined El Barrio during these warm months. Young men divided themselves into teams, transforming the street into a baseball stadium from morning till night. Cars honked, trying to pass, but the players ignored the horns until the inning finished. The shouts of the drivers, players, and onlookers reverberated off the buildings.

The players mocked the drivers trying to get through. My brother shouted, "Damn it, hold your horses."

"Watch your mouth," Mami reprimanded him half-heartedly. She smiled, proud of his athletic prowess. Abuela waved to my brother affectionately as he ran from a manhole cover to a trash can lid, scoring a run. The young players' brown skin glimmered, covered with sweat, which seeped through the soaked T-shirts that hugged their tense, muscular torsos.

Jimmy, too cool to sweat, stood by our stoop freshly groomed, admiring the young women who strolled seductively by. The young women hoped to be noticed and singled out with a romantic compliment from one of the young knights. Always willing to please, Jimmy offered a slick comment that sent the young women into uncontrollable giggles.

His clear, light tan skin, chiseled features, and tall, slim body tantalized women, who went out of their way to walk in front of him. One of his smiles was enough to send a young girl into a babbling frenzy. Jimmy let his cigarette dangle from his lips as he flirted.

Stickball, music, the flirtatious language of the street. This pattern of sounds floated all around me, penetrating my skin with rhythm, awakening my young body to motion. Change-of-life child that I was, I could not be still. Rather than walk, I wanted to skip, run, and jump down the street, but Mami held my hand tightly so we could match Abuela's slow pace.

Caridad was just opening the doors when we arrived. She crossed her arms across her chest and then hugged Abuela, first on the right side and then on the left, honoring her status as a high priestess. Caridad always wore a white cotton dress and a white kerchief on her head, like my Abuela. Around her waist she had a large yellow ribbon that matched the beaded bracelet on her left wrist. The color of dark cinnamon, she had sympathetic brown eyes like my grandmother's. They could have been sisters.

"Luisa, wait till you see the fresh *plantas* brought in from Miami. They are strong and healthy, with large green leaves and strong branches. Perfect for *limpiezas*."

Abuela's wide grin displayed her cigar-stained teeth. *"Mi hermana*, you say that every week about the puny plants you insist on selling. Let me see them."

As we walked farther into the *botánica*, the coconut palm growing by the door brushed my face. I pushed away the leaves. Caridad had smuggled in the plant and beach sand from Pinoñes, her hometown in Puerto Rico. "Be good to my palm, Cotito," she said to me. "I need a reminder from home or I'd go crazy in this city."

"These palms grow higher than a building, and they are all over the roads of Puerto Rico," Mami added. "Wait until you visit Puerto Rico, Coty. You'll fall in love with these palm trees and all the shades of green that cover the hillsides."

Ahead of us, Abuela had worked her way to the middle of the store, where the large bundles of plants and herbs lay wrapped in brown paper. She carefully broke off a piece of a leaf and put it to her nose. Addressing Caridad, she asked, "Why is this bundle labeled *abre camino?* This is *yerba buena*. Here, smell." Caridad took the piece of leaf and held it to her nose. Standing next to Abuela, I tore a small piece of the leaf and rubbed it on the tip of my nose, too. The minty juice of the leaf filled my nostrils with its pleasant scent.

"Luisa, you're right. It is *yerba buena,*" Caridad remarked, surprised. "How careless of the packers."

Abuela volunteered to check the other bundles, which also allowed her to inspect and select her plants at leisure. Caridad offered her a cup of espresso. "It's black and strong like us," she tempted Abuela.

Abuela laughed but refused. "I just had a cup. *Gracias, mi hermana.*" Caridad then offered the cup to Mami. "Flora, freshly brewed."

"*Gracias,* Caridad, I also had a cup before leaving the house," Mami replied with a gracious smile. Shrugging her shoulders, Caridad drank the coffee in one gulp. Abuela was very strict about our eating or drinking in other people's homes, even friends'. *"Quién sabe lo que ponen en la comida?"* she would say. "Who knows what people put in their food and drink? The most harmful and ill-intended preparations are done with food and drink."

The *botánica* was filled with candles stamped with healing prayers, dry hanging leaves, many types of incense, and the perfumes that cleansed our home. Sweet-smelling *siete potencias* rock incense, tuberose flowers, sunflowers, *yerba buena*, *abre camino*, and *albahaca* plants filled the air with their sweet scent. In the corner of the shop, the strong plants used for dispelling negative energy were neatly labeled: *yerba bruja, espanta muerto, rompe saraguey;*

they sent out their own powerful aromas. Caridad's cigar smoke also contributed to the strong mixture.

Other customers began filtering in. A cloud circulated, filling the *botánica* with a bluish haze. Standing next to Abuela and Mami, waiting for them to make their purchases, I looked up at the ceiling. With its cover of dried brown leaves and twisted knotted branches, it was like a giant puzzle. The smooth, spotted skins of leopards and striped tigers hung like fancy shawls on display, and shiny tin amulets carved to resemble hands, eyes, legs, torsos, and feet glittered in the flames of candles. On the highest shelves, a line of statues of Catholic saints stood at attention with red, blue, and yellow votive candles burning before them. Every week Caridad added to the assortment of objects.

In the *botánica*, I felt like Alice in Wonderland, as if I'd stepped through the mirror into a world filled with curiosity and marvel. I loved seeing the familiar objects that were also on Abuela's altar, and I carefully studied the newer, unfamiliar objects. Today, it was a tiger's head—a whole head! The big black eyes were wide open. The open mouth, filled with jagged teeth and two long fangs, roared angrily at me. My heart pounded, and as the store filled with people from the neighborhood, I imagined myself on a jungle expedition.

Women and men crowded around the counter to purchase plants for spiritual baths. All were seeking health, love, better jobs, and mended relationships. They bought fragrant leaves for spiritually energizing their homes and beckoning luck. Poignant plants kept enemies from their front doors and out of their lives.

Margarita, a sassy, attractive middle-aged woman dressed in tight clothes, lived in the tenement next to ours. She hustled up to Abuela and demanded, *"Vieja,* what do you see. Tell me."

Old though my grandmother was, no one called her an old lady.

"A woman with little manners," Abuela replied, filling small brown paper bags with the colored powders she used to make *desahumerios.*

Caridad admonished Margarita: "Learn how to speak to your elders."

Angry and embarrassed, the woman stormed toward the door exclaiming, "I'll take my money somewhere else."

Caridad shouted back, "Leave the five dollars you owe me first!"

Margarita slammed the door. The *botánica* rang out with laughter.

Abuela ignored the scene and continued collecting her powders for incense. My grandmother possessed the knowledge of generations before her. In the *botánica* she selected her products with intent, knowing what each was used for. Unlike the other customers, she did not ask Caridad for assistance.

Abuela was the elder not only in age but in spiritual knowledge. Caridad respected Abuela's experience and friendship and often sought my grandmother's advice. Mami, unlike Abuela, knew little of the religious traditions and just watched and tried to learn.

"Están frescas las plantas?" our neighbor Pedro asked. *"Qué precio tienen?"* Are the plants fresh? What is the price?

When Caridad answered, he asked, teasing, "Why so expensive?"

"Están al mismo precio de la semana pasada," Caridad shot back, not missing a beat. Same price as last week and the week before that.

Caridad turned her attention to Abuela. "Luisa, remember I told Roberta to take spiritual baths? Well, she didn't and yesterday she lost her job." Caridad shook her head and Abuela sucked her teeth with the unique sharp slurp of Caribbean women. Caridad added, "That's what happens when you don't listen to the messages of the spirits. I wonder why people ask for help, then don't follow instructions?"

As the bustle went on all around me, I studied the statues behind the counter. Like those on Abuela's altar, these also looked like people I knew. The strong African woman was Provi, the robust, tobacco-skinned woman who lived at the end of our block. Solid and stoic, Provi never hesitated to scold and punish children who littered in front of her tenement building or made too much noise when they passed. The warrior Indian statue with the solid bronze chest and strong determined face was Gregorio, a tall, handsome, flirtatious man who lived on the top floor of our building. With his smooth raven hair and succulent reddish-brown skin, he was an object of desire for all women who set eyes on him.

The battles between Gregorio and his wife, Alma, often punctuated life in our building. They were their own soap opera and the neighbors their audience. "It is not my fault women follow me and offer themselves to me. Blame God for making me so handsome!" he once shouted to his wife, running out of the apartment as she sobbed and screamed in the doorway.

Gossip had it that Stella's son, Bertha's daughter, and Elena's twins were Gregorio's children. "Look at their faces," I had heard Mami comment to her friend Justa. "Look at the color of the skin and the raven-black hair of those children. *Son indios puros*—pure Indians. Who else on the block has those features?"

As if called by my thoughts of her troubles, in that instant Alma walked through the door of Caridad's shop. A small, thin woman worn beyond her years, Alma always came to the *botánica* looking for *un trabajo*, a magical remedy that would make her husband faithful, or *un amarre*, a treatment that would stop his wandering and help him find a job to support their five children. Alma's large eyes were filled with sadness, surrounded by dark rings. Her light brown hair was straggly and uneven. Jittery with nervous energy, she ran her fingers through her hair. Alma's clothes hung from her thin body like an oversized coat.

"Caridad, please help me," she begged, after greeting my grandmother and mother. "I need something to control my husband."

"*Hija*, why do you want a philandering husband? You can never trust him. Find yourself a good man."

Caridad did not reveal that Gregorio had already come to the *botánica* the week before seeking a *trabajo* to blind his wife's vision to his messing around. He had no desire to find a job and had asked for a remedy to help him get on public assistance. Caridad had refused to help him. Like Abuela, she was a spiritualist who believed in working for good—*con las manos limpias*, with clean hands.

"Alma, my child, I have told you time and again that he is a child of Changó," she said now. "He is a born ladies' man. His destiny is written. He won't change. Most of all, he loves his destiny. No amount of *remedios* will change that."

Unwilling to accept Caridad's observation, Alma pleaded, "He's the father of my children and the love of my life. He's the only man I've known. What will I do with five children and no husband?"

Abuela and Mami stood quietly, listening to the conversation. Mami looked down at me with a concerned glance to see if I was listening, too.

Abuela reassured her. "Flora, do not worry. Cotito doesn't understand what's going on. And even if she does, you can't keep life away from her forever." Displeased, Mami didn't respond. I remained still, trying to figure out the drama that was unfolding before me. I was nine and had survived two years of P.S. 121, but still I had a lot to learn.

The shop was full now, and Alma had an ample audience for her concerns. Pedro could no longer bear Alma's whining and dryly suggested, "Caridad, why don't you stop her from having a sixth child?" Other clients muffled their laughter and commented among themselves about Alma's inability to accept the truth about her husband. "*Coño*," Pedro said, growing impatient and wanting Caridad to attend to *his* problem. "Damn, Alma, open your eyes—Gregorio will never change."

Caridad frowned and shot an angry glance toward Pedro and the others. Then she turned to Alma and said, "Gregorio was already here asking for remedies. I cannot reveal what he wanted, but I must warn you that he does not have your best interests at heart. I work with clean hands, but there are other spiritualists that do not. Beware."

Alma's pitiful expression caused Caridad to reconsider. Studying her customer's tortured face, she declared, "If we cannot change him, we will change you. Take these *yerbas*. One is called *mal de amor*—it will lessen your love for him. The other, *ver bien*, will open your eyes and allow you to see into the trifling spirit of Gregorio." Like a mother scolding a child, Caridad added, "They say love is blind. But you don't have to be stupid." Tearing off a piece of brown wrapping paper, Caridad wrote down the rest of her remedy and handed it to Alma with the plants wrapped in newspaper. "Do as I have told you," Caridad implored.

Suddenly pretending not to listen, Pedro and the others made idle conversation about the high cost of food. Mami joined in. The *botánica* was our community center, the place to catch up on neighborhood gossip. I held Mami's hand and listened to the music the adults' expressions made, while in the background Caridad played her favorite recording of "El Yerberito Moderno" by Celia Cruz and La Sonora Mantancera.

Celia's rich, husky voice filled the *botánica*. *"El yerberito llegó. Traigo yerba santa para la garganta, traigo abre camino pa tu destino, traigo ver bien, pa el que no ve.* The herb man comes. I bring *yerba santa* for your throat, I bring *abre camino* for your destiny, I bring *ver bien* for those who do not see." Against this background music, the growing drama with Alma held my attention.

"Caridad, I promise you I will follow your instructions exactly," Alma said. *"Que Dios te tenga en su gloria siempre."*

May God have you always in his glory. Alma reached into her dress pocket and pulled out several crumpled dollars to pay Caridad for the plants and her services.

Caridad stopped her, dramatically holding her hand up to her forehead. *"Hija,* my child, if this works then we will discuss your *derecho.* You need this money to feed your children. Promise me that you will stop letting your husband steal your beauty and dignity," Caridad sternly instructed. "Fix yourself up. Wear makeup and clothes to show your body. Take pride in yourself and your appearance. Stop being a *pendeja*—an idiot.

"Remember what you did to attract him. Do it again. This time, use it also to attract other men. Gregorio needs to be reminded that he's not the only man that's good in bed." Again, laughter filled the *botánica.*

"When you come in next week," Caridad continued, "I want to see another Alma, not the one I am seeing now. I want to see the seductive daughter of Ochun." Caridad smiled and touched the yellow sash at her own waist.

"You will," said Alma as she timidly prepared to leave. Caridad shook her head, unconvinced. Turning, Alma came face to face with my Abuela. She stopped abruptly, trapped by the riveting spiritual energy emanating from Abuela's eyes. Alma remained transfixed and then, like an actress in the movies, fell to the floor and curled up like an injured kitten.

Customers immediately rushed to pick her up. Caridad quickly stepped out from behind the counter.

"Don't touch her." Abuela spoke in a calm, commanding voice, looking down at the tiny bundle on the floor. Everyone stopped moving, and silence filled the room.

Stunned and frightened, I pressed closer to Mami. The warmth of her body was reassuring. I glanced up at my Abuela and then down at Alma spread out on the floor. She looked like the parishioners of the Pentecostal church when the Holy Spirit possessed them.

My friend Myrta and I would stop playing our games whenever we heard the songs, tambourines, and piano playing in the storefront church on our block. We gathered at the open door and looked curiously into the front window, as did others on the block, watching as the practitioners sang, jumped up, danced, and fell to the floor, ecstatic. When I'd first seen it, I'd been shocked and frightened by the invisible power that made people collapse this way. Over time, I had grown accustomed to watching how practitioners pleaded with the Holy Spirit to possess them.

When the parishioners fell to the floor, others danced around them with their eyes and hands raised to the heavens, praising the glory of God and begging to be filled by the Holy Spirit.

Myrta and I would hold our hands over our mouths to stifle the giggles and laughter we knew would burst out as we witnessed people being possessed. We didn't feel disrespectful. It was almost a game to us, and we watched out for church elders moving toward the door, then ran away before they could shoo us.

Today in the *botánica* it was different. Alma looked dead. There was no singing or rejoicing. Just absolute quiet. My heart began to pound against my chest as I reached for Mami's hand. "Don't be frightened. Alma is okay. Abuela will take care of her," Mami assured me. My body trembled but I stood silently, holding Mami's comforting hand. I watched my grandmother carefully. This was the first time I saw Abuela attend to someone possessed by a spirit, though I knew it could happen because Mami often saw Abuela's spirits visit her and would report to our family so we could carry out the remedies.

"Spirit that has taken over Alma's body, stand up and speak to me," Abuela demanded in a steady voice. "Stand up."

Slowly, Alma started emerging from her dream state. She moved her head from side to side, trying to wake up.

Abuela demanded, "Spirit, why do you throw your child to the floor if you love her?" Alma's eyes remained shut. Alma stood up slowly, staggering from side to side like a child taking its first steps. She stood in front of Abuela. Then, swaying back and forth, she spun around and jumped. Spinning in midair, she came down before Abuela on the floor of the *botánica* and bowed with her hands and arms crossed against her chest. Abuela also crossed her arms and then hugged Alma, welcoming the sacred spirit.

Alma's expression and tone were transformed. Before Abuela stood a young warrior woman acknowledging her elder.

"Spirit, why do you allow your host to live through such torture?" Abuela asked.

From deep within Alma's chest, the spirit spoke as if its host weren't there. "She loves that good-for-nothing more than she loves her children, more than she loves her spirits, and more than herself. He cheats on her and beats their children. This cannot be. Tell her that she can't allow her children to be punished for behaving like the children they are." The words spilled into a stuttering barrage that became difficult to understand, then became clear again.

"She must not allow herself to be disrespected. I will not tolerate it any longer. Alma has been warned many times that her behavior is unacceptable to her spirit guides. She continues to ignore the message. Tell her that now she either heeds the message or I will take her to the spirit world."

I shivered. Mami placed her hands on my shoulders to calm me. I covered my eyes with my hands. But curiosity got the better of me, and I spread my fingers and peeked.

"Alma must respect me, Ochun, the guardian spirit that she carries. I do not allow the abuse of children or women. Alma knows this. Yet she tolerates disgrace. No love can be greater than her love for me."

Abuela took a white kerchief from the display on the counter and covered Alma's head. Blowing into Alma's ears, she removed the kerchief quickly from her head with a snap.

Then she sprinkled Florida water all over Alma's head and body. I felt a few cold drops fall on my face, which I quickly cleaned off with my hand. Looking down at me, Mami smiled. *"Agua Florida* is good for you. Don't worry." Awakening from the deep trance, Alma looked around, disoriented, trying to figure out what had happened. She shook her head.

Without hesitating, Abuela spoke sternly: "Alma, your guardian spirit, Ochun, has left you a message. If you don't follow a new path, she will take you. Ochun said that you have been warned before—this time she will take you to the spirit world for disrespecting her. The children will be left behind without a mother. Is this what you want?"

"No, no, no, I love my children more than life itself," Alma said through the flood of tears that suddenly covered her face.

"My child, the spirit is saying that this is not true, that in spite of what you say you love Gregorio more than the children, your spirits, and yourself. Your guardian spirit will no longer permit this. Ochun is ready to take you away if you do not heed her. She will not tolerate another act of disrespect."

Alma started trembling like a leaf caught in a windstorm. Publicly shamed, she shrank within herself and buried her head in her chest. "What must I do?" Alma whimpered, avoiding Abuela's eyes.

"You know what to do," Abuela responded without compassion.

Alma thanked Abuela and left without saying another word. When she was gone, the atmosphere of the *botánica* slowly returned to its normal hectic chatter. I wondered if the spirit was still in the store or if it had gone with Alma. If Ochun was in the store, could she possess me or someone else?

Abuela and Mami gathered and paid for the plants we needed in silence. As we left, Mami placed a few coins in a glass bowl filled with blue detergent water, for luck. *"Uno nunca sabe,"* Mami said to Abuela, who nodded her approval. One never knows.

"Es mejor precaver que tener que remediar," responded Abuela, who always felt it was better to prevent a problem rather than deal with its consequences. As we walked, more slowly than before, Abuela noticed my preoccupation and unusual silence.

Abuela turned to me and said, "Spirits are good, *mi*

nieta. Remember that they come to solve problems. Never be afraid of them." Then she and Mami continued talking as if nothing extraordinary had happened. But I knew it had.

My uneasiness and questions began to fade as we walked along the *marqueta* on 116th Street. The smells of mangoes, melons, bananas, tropical vegetables, sweet sugar candy, and spicy Puerto Rican food replaced Alma in my thoughts.

"Mami, can I have a *piragua de coco*?" I begged. We stopped by the snow-cone vendor's stand, made from an old shopping cart. As he scraped the surface of the ice, small slivers flew everywhere. Mami paid the *piragüero*, and we continued walking. The street was filled with housewives arguing with vendors to lower the price of items. Bargaining was part of the excitement of shopping at the *marqueta*.

Mami asked a vegetable vendor, "How much for three *plátanos*—green plantains?" When he answered, she hollered, "You crook! I can get four *plátanos* for the same down the street."

The vendor screamed back, "Then go down the street." Mami faked walking away, and the man promptly changed his mind, letting her have her price. Abuela and I laughed, enjoying Mami's performance.

In the crowded *cuchifrito* store, *pastelillos* and *pollo frito* sizzled. The window, filled with deep-fried meat and crab patties, blood sausages, spicy oxtails, and fried pork rind, was a feast of colors for the eyes that made my stomach gurgle with desire.

Mami stopped to buy the pork rinds that opened up like

large twisted hand fans. They were fried to a crisp in bubbling fat the color of thick molasses. At home, my brother, sister, and I would fight over every crunchy piece doled out by Mami. The crackling sound made by biting the deeply fried pork rinds was part of the fun. Almost everyone in El Barrio carried a brown bag covered with large grease spots.

Walking closer to our building, I sensed a heightened tension flowing through the block. Conversations were louder, and people stood around agitated, waiting for something to happen.

Miguel, our super, was sitting with a group of old men playing dominoes and drinking beer. "Give it another minute. You'll see more clothes flying out the window," he laughed. As we walked by, he shouted to Abuela and Mami, "Your building is hot with excitement, ladies." He ignored my presence, as most adults did when addressing their peers. In our community, children were to be seen and not heard unless directly spoken to.

"Alma just caught Gregorio with Teresa in her bed. She's all fired up. Alma threw all his clothes out the window— she kicked him out! She was like a madwoman, throwing out clothes, shoes, and then Gregorio and Teresa down the stairs of the apartment building."

Mami asked about the children. Miguel did not know.

Los espíritus son muy fuerte," Abuela remarked. The spirits are very strong. *"Con los espíritus no se juegan*—you can't play with the spirits. Alma has finally faced reality." My attention had already shifted from Alma's drama to the other kids playing in the street.

As the women of the block reviewed the new chapter in

Alma's life from their windows, their children played hop-scotch, ring-a-levio, Coca-Cola, *cebollita,* and stickball. The buzz of adult voices mingled with the staccato sounds of these games.

When my best friend, Myrta, saw me walking down the block she called out, "Cotito, come play double Dutch with me and Rosa."

Myrta's black burst of hair surrounded her rich brown face. Her tall, reed-thin body seemed barely able to hold up her ballooning mane. From a distance, she looked like a human lollipop.

Rosa, my other best friend, was closer to a cuddly bear. Her warm, light brown hair and round body bore witness to her constant munching. Rosa always had crumbs around her mouth from the pieces of Italian bread she kept in her dress pockets. Myrta and I constantly competed for who could jump for the longest time, while Rosa tangled the rope as soon as she jumped.

"Cotito, come. We have the good jump rope today. It is the right weight—it doesn't tangle like the other one," Rosa called out. She and Myrta were twirling the rope rapidly, creating a *ta-ta, ta-ta-ta* beat as it hit the pavement.

I turned to beg permission. With a smile Mami said, "You can play for one hour and then come straight upstairs. You haven't had lunch."

Breathlessly, I ran down the street. Myrta and Rosa began the swirling turning of the two ropes. The sharp snapping tempo against the pavement invited me to jump to the exciting beat of the dancing double Dutch rhythm.

I took a breath and studied the cadence, trying to absorb the exact timing of the crisscrossing ropes into my body.

Ta-ta-ta, ta-ta, ta-ta-ta, ta-ta, they called me, and I leapt into their center, picturing myself as a flamenco dancer, my feet ablaze with sudden movement. My body moved smoothly between the ropes as they whizzed over my head and swooshed under my feet. In sync with the cadence of the revolving clotheslines, I jumped on one leg, turned, and danced, defiant and free of all restraint.

Myrta counted my jumps—101, 102, 103, 104—and the ropes kissed my calves. Blood was rushing through my veins, my heart pounded with excitement, and my head spun hard. When the ropes tangled and fell at my feet, I came to an abrupt stop. My dizziness cleared.

I wondered if this was how Alma had felt when the spirit came and went, leaving her so different.

FOUR

Negrita Linda

Aunque la Virgen sea blanca, píntame angelitos negros,
que también se van al cielo todos los negritos buenos.

Even if the Virgin is white, paint black angels. All the
little black angels also go to heaven.

— XIOMARA ALFARO, "ANGELITOS NEGROS"

In the summer of 1953 when I was eleven, my family ventured for the first time to Rockaway Beach, in Brooklyn. Generally we went to Orchard Beach, in the Bronx, but Papi saw a trip to Rockaway as a special adventure, a break from the ordinary. At the advice of one of his coworkers at the auto shop, he decided we should "discover this new beach." When Mami protested, he insisted, "What is the purpose of having a car if we don't go to different places?"

Mami invited Justa to enjoy our venturesome trip. Justa refused because her youngest son, Jimmy, had not come home again. Jimmy was disobeying his mother more frequently, claiming embarrassment at her "Holy Roller religion." Jimmy used this excuse for cutting his classes. He didn't dare disrespect Papi or Mami when they spoke to him about his disobedience toward Justa and his increasingly delinquent behavior. Jimmy just bowed his head and listened, but he eventually stopped visiting us.

We set out in Papi's 1948 sky-blue Dodge at seven A.M. on a Sunday to avoid the *tapón*, the summer beach traffic. We could get to Orchard Beach—which we'd unofficially renamed the Puerto Rican Riviera—in less than forty-five minutes, but the trip to Rockaway Beach took us twice as long. The heat and humidity made the drive uncomfortable. Squeezed together in the back seat, my brother, sister, and I found every excuse to argue.

"Stay on your side, Chachito. Keep your big feet on the mat," my sister complained. When my brother ignored her, she pleaded, "Mami, stop him from leaning on my shoulder."

I fidgeted, sweat soaking my blouse. Mami, annoyed by the long trip herself, had made a fan of Papi's newspaper and ignored us. To relieve our growing irritation, Papi said, "I hear that Rockaway has enormous waves at least four stories high. We can have more fun than going where the water's so still."

Mami didn't swim and was afraid of the potential danger. "You're always tempting the water to drown you," she told Papi. "I don't want you taking the children out too far," she added with a shiver. "They might be devoured."

On the first trip to the beach each summer, Mami would enter the water backward until it reached her knees. Then she'd scoop water in her hands and throw it over her shoulders three times. She would say a prayer and insist that we do the same.

Chachito, Chachita, and I were always embarrassed, but we followed the yearly ritual. "My guides and protectors, take away all the evil that has been wished upon me. Take it to the bottom of the sea. Protect my family and bring us health, happiness, and prosperity. Protect my family as they enjoy your home," Mami would say. Only after uttering these last words would she allow us to go all the way into the water.

Today, Papi missed the exit, making the long trip even longer. Finally we arrived. Stepping out of the car, our legs were wobbly, our clothes wet from the humidity, and our patience at the point of exploding. The chore of carrying our usual assortment of boxes and pans, generally an unpleasant task, was particularly bothersome today.

Forming a caravan, Mami, Chachito, Chachita, and I followed Papi toward the area he decided had the highest waves. Mami had a special set of old utensils, pots, dishes, and old blankets that she took to all beach outings and family picnics. Papi had built a five-piece metal contraption he used as a portable stove. We would heat our food over lit Sterno cans, leaving a burnt black residue on the bottoms of the pots that later needed scrubbing with steel wool. The assortment of objects formed a sorry lot, one step away from being tossed in the garbage. But Mami thought them perfect for the wear and tear of the beach.

At the age of eleven, I was already studying magazines

and newspapers to see how people outside El Barrio presented themselves in public. Chachito and Chachita accused me of being uppity, while Mami identified my fantasies as envy and jealousy, traits that had to be crushed. "Appreciate what you have," she was always saying. "Your father works very hard to provide a home, the clothes on your back, and food."

As we trekked over the hot sand, I looked around, noticing that the people here were very different from the crowd we were accustomed to at Orchard Beach. Orchard Beach looked like El Barrio on the sand. Rockaway Beach resembled a television commercial. Most of the people looked like my teachers. Their checkered red-and-white blankets held tidy baskets filled with food. Their color-coordinated umbrellas and chairs appeared picture-perfect. My brother, sister, and I looked at one another with uneasy glances, wondering why Papi had decided to bring us to such a place. Finally, our convoy came to a stop near the shoreline and we unpacked. What a relief to finally put down the heavy bag filled with a *caldero* of fried pork chops.

We spread out three worn, colorful blankets. Under Mami's direction, we loaded the green blanket with an assortment of blackened pots packed with potato salad, rice and beans, and chops. A deep dish brimmed with *escabeches*, codfish salad marinated with bay leaves, black pepper, and olives, and saturated the air with the pungent smell of onions, vinegar, and fish. Immersed in a large aluminum pail overflowing with chunks of ice floated a jug of Kool-Aid and cans of Rheingold beer.

The yellow blanket, reserved for eating, had on it a cardboard box with old plates and spoons and forks neatly wrapped in napkins. The red blanket functioned as the closet, piled with sweaters and socks in case it got cold toward evening. We also placed our shoes and towels there. Mami made sure that we kept the areas organized according to the categories she had designated. To my embarrassment, the blankets now seemed to have become an apartment in El Barrio.

Leaving the arrangements to Mami, Papi, a powerful swimmer, bounded immediately into the water. Mami cautioned him not to go out too far. Looking up to the sky, she asked God to protect him. *"Cuidalo por favor,"* she implored, much to Papi's amusement. It was not that my father held different beliefs from his wife and his mother, but in general he seemed to feel that spiritual matters were too "emotional" to be manly, and thus better left to women.

He went out as far as the lifeguards allowed and returned riding the rough crests of waves that descended with cascading roars to the shore. Mami instructed us to remove our clothes, and then Chachita and I were assigned to help her finish arranging the blankets and food. Mami's bathing suit was a short version of the pinafores she usually wore around the house. Big white and pink flowers decorated the skirt that covered her thighs, almost reaching her knees. Chachita's orange two-piece showed off her ample body. Her large breasts struggled to stay in her bra, her stomach bulged over her waist, and the bottom part of the suit packed in her large bottom. But my sister's sullen and harsh attitude canceled out her body's sensuality.

Like Mami, my sister would only go in knee-deep, afraid

that the water would sweep her away. Approaching the ocean, they held hands like children, trying to protect each other from waves they saw far in the distance. My embarrassment reached a new height as I watched them screaming and tripping, trying to avoid the weak waves that lapped the shore.

Chachito, always the adventurer, was enthralled by the large waves. He followed our father into the water, his slim, strong torso diving deep. My brother had been trained by Papi to love and challenge the water. I enjoyed the water, too, and followed my brother farther in. In a white-and-red two-piece, my body was very thin. I tightened the top and then caught up with Chachito, buoyed by his fearlessness to approach the thunderous waves as well.

Behind us Mami screamed, "Did you say a prayer?" Chachito and I made believe we did not hear her.

I shared Papi and Chachito's love for the roaring strength of the water, and I stayed out, floating and riding the waves, for a long while. After about a half hour, having decided to join Papi, who was swimming much farther out, my brother told me to go back to shore. From the water, I could see Mami and Chachita hiding from the sun underneath a rented rainbow-striped umbrella. My mother's and sister's light skin was shiny with the lotion they used to protect their bodies from the intense rays of the sun.

Mami gestured for me to join them. I refused. I loved the feeling of my body in action and the strength and force it was capable of achieving. Papi and Chachito had shown me how to swim, and I struggled to perfect my strokes so I could one day join them in the deeper waters. For now I kept close to the seashore, reveling in the cool spray of the salt water while testing my abilities as the surging tide occasionally overwhelmed me.

I stayed in the water long into the afternoon, trying to imitate Chachito and Papi and also to avoid the comical "camp" created by Mami. I couldn't understand why Mami and Chachita spent most of the time under the umbrella instead of enjoying the thrill of the tide. Again and again, it pulled me back into deeper waters. But as the day progressed, I grew tired. A strong surge sent me tumbling like a rag doll in its foam. Screaming, Mami ran to the shore and, followed by Chachita, dragged me out of the water. Shaken, I did not protest, but I hoped that Papi and my brother had not seen my disastrous retreat back to the blankets.

"That is what you get for competing with your father and brother," Mami scolded.

"You're not a boy," my sister added, dusting off some sand sticking to my shoulders and arms. "Look, she scraped her elbow, and it's bleeding," Chachita said to Mami.

Mami pulled me around to see the damage. "If your sister and I weren't watching, you could have drowned," she said dramatically, pulling a bottle of hydrogen peroxide from the first-aid bag. "Neither your father or brother were watching you," she said angrily. I could see their little heads in the distance and envied them their freedom.

My brother was the first to return from the long swim. "Look at what happened to your sister," Mami admonished, showing off my scraped elbow.

"It's not my fault Cotito forgets she's a girl," he laughed as he dried off, drained from his long swim. Looking out into the sea he added, "I can't believe Papi's still out there." My brother walked to the water's edge to watch our father.

Finally, toward the late afternoon, exhausted, Papi lay on his back and let the water hold him afloat, ignoring the calls of the lifeguards. Through a bullhorn one of the young men called out, "We're leaving for the day. Come in closer to the shore."

Everyone on the beach seemed to turn toward Papi's floating head in the distance as the lifeguards cautioned him. Frightened by his daredevil antics, Mami kept her attention focusd on our father. When he disappeared behind a wave, she quickly stood up and prayed for his safety, *"Dios mío, por favor cuídalo."* Ashamed by our attracting so much attention, I wanted only for us to leave.

With the sun beginning to set, Chachito went out again to rejoin Papi. I followed, but Mami called me back. "Are you crazy? You already got hurt once—are you looking to get hurt again?" asked Mami. "Sit down and relax like your sister."

My sister tried to take a nap, but I kept her awake, mumbling in my embarrassment. "Why do we have to look like a circus troupe coming to the beach?"

Mami was heating up the food in a large burnt frying pan. The black smoke of the ignited Sterno cans drew more unwanted attention to our area. Plates were spread out, waiting to be covered with food from the assortment of old dented pots she set out on the blankets. "We look like a poor carnival," I complained, trying to get my sister's sympathy.

"Look at those people," I continued, indicating the few

remaining families around us. "They bring sandwiches neatly packed in plastic bags and picnic baskets with fruit. They have an ice storage bucket especially made for keeping things cold. We have a big old aluminum pail with big rocks of ice with beer cans and old plates. We're the only family heating up food on the beach."

Her back turned, Mami ignored me. "We shouldn't be eating pork chops and rice and beans here," I continued. "This is a picnic, not a kitchen." I went on and on, making myself more miserable.

Annoyed, my sister raised her sun-blushed face and hissed, "Shhhh. Stop wasting your breath. Think of us as the *cuchifrito* store on *la playa*," she added, ridiculing me as her face disappeared back into her folded arms. I turned my back on my sister and mother, trying to distance myself from the festive spectacle.

"Since you're too embarrassed to eat our food, I won't heat any for you," Mami responded calmly. "I suggest you go to the people with the nice sandwiches and ask them for one."

Snickering, my sister interjected, "Yeah, go and ask for food. Since when would you rather eat salami and cheese instead of creamy potato salad and crisp, crunchy pork chops?" Papi and Chachito were walking toward us as Mami began to serve my sister food. After they dried off, they sat next to each other, waiting for Mami to serve them. Noticing the growing tension, Papi asked, *"Qué pasa?"* as he reached for his plate.

"Your daughter is too good to eat our food," Mami answered. Papi rolled his eyes, amused.

Angry, I refused to ask for anything. Chachito laughed and asked, "Mami, can I have her pork chop?"

Chachita joined in. "Yes, Mami, I want it too. Split it for us?" Ignoring me, they both continued to beg for my portion of the food. "Divide her portion," proposed Papi. Teasing, my brother and sister sucked with exaggerated gusto on the bones of the chops as they consumed my food.

"Mmm, mmm, mmmm, delicious. Mami, these are the best pork chops you've ever made," Chachito said, laughing. In an earsplitting, high-pitched tone, my sister imitated what she thought rich people would say. "The potato salad is sooo divine," she breathed, holding a pork chop with her pinky finger in the air. I sat in the glare of the sun while my sister and Mami stayed hidden under the umbrella. Enjoying the sun, Chachito sat next to Papi, who was sipping a beer after having devoured his pile of food. Baking, I refused to join my family on the yellow blanket, where they ate. With a stray stick I played with the sand, trying to ignore my brother and sister. Amused, Papi and Mami allowed them to continue teasing me.

Finally, after what seemed like forever, we packed up and, weighed down with stuff again, headed for the car. My stomach grumbled.

On the way home, my brother's and sister's pestering continued. Chachita rubbed her stomach. "Those pork chops just melted in my mouth." Laughing, Chachito joined in: "Mami fried them perfectly tender on the inside and crispy on the outside."

I looked out the window, drowning out my brother and sister by imagining myself in the lovely houses that whizzed by the car window. Two-story brick houses with pristine white-and-tan shingled roofs looked like homes in postcards. Front yards and picket fences danced before my covetous eyes. Some had mailboxes in the front yard. Others had little wooden benches or children's swing sets. I wondered if families like ours could live in such beautiful homes. What food did the people eat? Who kept these places so clean? The teasing voices of my brother and sister disappeared into the background as I admired the beautiful houses that didn't look anything like our gray tenement.

"Thank God," I blurted out when the car finally stopped in front of our building. But I was only half happy to be home.

"Don't use the Lord's name in vain," Mami responded curtly. Unloading the supplies and trudging up the stairs, our family tumbled into the apartment, exhausted. Papi brought in the large aluminum basin, Chachito the shopping bags filled with dirty dishes, Chachita the assortment of blankets, and I the bags of sandy utensils.

Chachita turned on the kitchen radio, which was set permanently on the Spanish station. The jubilant dance beat of "Mambo No. 5," accentuated by Pérez Prado's signature groaning in the background, didn't lessen my anguish. We piled everything as neatly as we could on the kitchen floor, trying to keep the mess contained before Mami came in. She was always the last to enter. She took her time climbing the stairs and always checked in on Abuela before entering our apartment.

Papi walked into the bedroom. Chachito tried to bribe Chachita with the promise of a record of her favorite singer, Billy Eckstine, so he wouldn't have to help clean up the mess. Mami entered the kitchen. *Con qué dinero?* With what money are you going to buy your sister a record?"

Mami demanded, bursting my brother's lie. Chachita and I laughed at his surprised expression. "Help clean up," Mami ordered as she sat down by the kitchen table.

The atmosphere thick with irritability, we unloaded all the blankets, pots, pans, and dishes. Papi came back into the kitchen in clean clothes and sat down at the table. Exhausted, he began assigning tasks. "Chachito, clean the aluminum pail. Use soap and make sure it's completely rinsed out. Chachita, hang out the blankets." Despite their fatigue, my brother and sister sprung into action. Chachita opened the kitchen window and began pulling the clothesline, leaning out the window with her arms full of blankets. "Use a lot of clothespins," Papi ordered. "Don't let the blankets fall into the yard. Careful, don't lean out too far or you'll fall."

He turned to me. "Cotito, you are old enough now to do the dishes, pots, and pans." I looked at him, startled, not believing my ears. My usual chore was to throw out the garbage. Mami, Chachito, and Chachita always cleaned up the beach mess.

"What?" I snapped, momentarily forgetting I was speaking to my father. "You're mistaken, Papi."

"No," he said, fixing me with an even stare, "I did not make a mistake. You heard me." He sat calmly like a giant sculpture, frozen and expressionless. Rattled, I looked at Mami to help me. She sat next to Papi, her face also carved in stone. Ignoring my pleading eyes, she announced that she would take Chachita to help her carry pizzas home. Stunned, I looked into my sister's surprised eyes. When it sunk in that she was miraculously liberated from cleaning, her face filled with glee.

Papi dug into his pants pockets and pulled out a small pile of neatly folded bills. Taking his time fingering the money, he counted out the amount needed and gave it to my mother. Stretching his arms to the ceiling, Papi stood up slowly and said, "I am going to rest in the living room."

I watched Mami and Chachita exit without looking back. Still sure that Mami wouldn't leave me to do the dishes, I stood waiting for her to return and say she had been kidding.

"Cotito, the dishes are not going to wash themselves," Papi called out from the couch. "Start working on that pile." I stood in the middle of the kitchen, stunned, refusing to move. After several minutes Papi called, "I don't hear the water running."

Like a robot, I walked to the sink and turned on the water. My anger mounting, I shook my head in disbelief. My braids began to unravel, and my frizzy dark brown hair billowed around my head. Sweat laced with ocean salt ran down my forehead into my eyes. The sting of the salt made my eyes tear.

Angry, I turned the water on full force. I poured too much soap into the hot water and the bubbles turned into a thick blanket of foam. Suds multiplied quickly and floated around me. The spume was like soft snow. I distracted myself by cupping the lather in my hands and blowing shiny globes into the air, creating a mobile of transparent rainbows around my head.

Positioning himself at the kitchen table, my brother called out spitefully, "Papi, she's playing with bubbles instead of washing the dishes."

"Cotito, finish those dishes before your mother returns," Papi responded. "Make sure you leave no grease or sand."

I turned to my brother, daggers shooting from my eyes, and silently mouthed out the word "Idiot."

Chachito continued, "Papi, she's still not doing them." Our father remained silent. With nothing to do himself, my brother sat at the table, put his hands under his chin, and stared at me.

Chachito's dark, toast-brown skin shone with the lotion he had lavished on it at the beach. His dark brown, wavy hair was pomaded, resembling Mami's Persian wool coat, and his dark brown eyes sparkled with the glint of a trickster. Above his lips, a sparse moustache was beginning to grow, and he patted it with the tips of his fingers as if to reassure himself that it hadn't disappeared. Watching me slump before the black greasy pots, a sly smile crossed his face.

I turned away. Looking at my arms and hands under the warm water, I admired their deep bronze color. I let my thoughts drift back to the ocean, the intense heat of the sun, and the crashing waves.

Miguelito Valdez's voice flowed out of the radio. *"Babalú, Babalú Ayé,"* he sang, addressing the Yoruban god of healing, the rhythmic beats of Afro-Cuban drums in the background. *"Yo le quiero pedir que mi negra me quiera."* I want to ask that my black woman love me." I hummed along and allowed myself to dream, imagining myself in the kitchen of one of the houses we had seen on our drive home.

Tapping his foot to the music, my brother seemed not to hear the words.

"Look at the woolly hair and dark skin you have," Chachito started in. "Cotito, you look like an African. Here, let me get you a spear." Thrusting a fork at me, my brother made monkey sounds. I tried to ignore him, but Chachito would not let up. Something inside me began to curl into a tiny ball.

Chachito's words inflicted a painful wound. I was only just becoming aware of my thin, blossoming body. Self-conscious yet elated that my nipples were beginning to show through my shirts and that soon hair like my sister had would be appearing magically on different parts of my body, I felt sure that I would soon leave childhood to become a ravishing young woman.

"African!" Chachito scoffed.

He laughed at my puffy hair and brown skin until finally a spark of rage ignited in me. Holding a glass filled with water, I threatened to throw it at him. "Leave me alone," I shouted, nearly crying. "If I look like an African, so do you."

Giggling, Chachito started jumping around the kitchen, imitating the ridiculous movements of the "Africans" we had seen in Tarzan movies at our neighborhood theater. I threatened him again with the glass filled with sudsy water. "Stop, stop!" I shouted. "Or I'll throw this at you!"

"Bug-a, bug-a, bug-a," my brother responded, jumping around the kitchen. Annoyed by the noise we were making, Papi appeared at the door.

"Brothers and sisters don't argue or fight," Papi scolded, rooted firm like a giant tree. His expression stern, my father told me to put the glass down. "I'll punish your brother," he promised me. But despair engulfed me. I knew he wouldn't. Chachito always got away with his pranks.

My brother continued to jeer. Annoyed, Papi stood in the doorway. Why wouldn't he come to my rescue? Finally,

I could take no more. I faced my brother and let go of the glass. As it floated through the air, Miguelito Valdez's plea to Babalu played on. The glass moved in slow motion, a stream of shimmering water arcing out.

Missing my brother, the glass crashed against the old radio. The voice of Miguelito Valdez abruptly went silent, replaced by a long moment of nothing. I froze in my spot, wishing I could melt into the linoleum. My father looked from me to the crackling radio and back again.

With water seeping in, the glass tubes of the old wooden radio suddenly exploded. Gray smoke formed a plume that extended straight to the ceiling. The stench of burning wires quickly filled the air. Shocked, none of us moved. Then Papi raced to the wall and disconnected the cord.

Slowly shaking his head, my father looked at me, dismayed. Then he walked back to the doorframe that held the rubber strap he called the "Enforcer." Chachito dropped his eyes and leaned against the kitchen wall, his arms folded across his chest. My father moved toward me.

"Please, Papi, don't hit me, please, *por favor,*" I begged. My father shook his head and readied the strap. Before he ever touched me, I could feel the flame of anger rise inside me as I imagined the sting of rubber against my bare legs. A former amateur boxer, Papi never hit his children with his hands. On my older brother and sister, he always used the Enforcer. Me, he had never hit before.

I quickly measured the distance from the sink to the front door and, without a second thought, bolted. I pulled opened the door and dashed out, running down the stairs like a scared rabbit. Catching my breath at the bottom landing, I went through the front door and started sprinting down the block. I heard Myrta calling from her stoop, "What's wrong? Wait for me. Wait!" I ignored my friend and kept running, dodging between pedestrians, pushing others aside. The smooth pattern of the block had become a maze with no exit.

I headed toward the pizza shop, frantic. My heart knocked against my chest, blood pounding in my ears and head. I had no breath, and as I neared the door to the shop, I collapsed in a fit of coughing and choking.

I was afraid of being hit by my father, but my brother had caused the real hurt. This wasn't the first time he had called me an African. Why did he always tease me about my color and hair? Papi, he, and I all looked alike. We had the same coloring and the same textured hair. So why was I the target? If girls my color were not beautiful, not desired, why did Miguelito have to beg for a black woman's love?

Crashing through the door into the crowd of waiting customers, I reached Mami, who had just finished paying for the pizza. Crying hysterically, I wrapped my arms around her waist and buried my head against her warm stomach. Mami almost dropped the pizza and nearly lost her balance. She turned and gave the box to my sister. Assuming the worst, that someone at home was hurt, she began to cry as she pulled me away from her asking, *"Qué pasó?* What happened?" I could not talk. Realizing that when I got home I'd be disciplined even more severely for having run away, I only cried harder. One of our parents' rules was that we were not allowed to run or hide when we were going to be punished. We had to stand before them and accept our penalty.

Frightened, Mami ran out of the pizza store. Squeezing my hand, she beckoned for Chachita to follow. She rushed us home, holding her hand over her weak heart. Gasping for breath, Mami entered the front door of our tenement and climbed the stairs as quickly as she could. *"Qué pasó?"* she hollered into our apartment. When she saw Papi and Chachito walk out of the living room, she cried out in relief. *"Gracias mi Dios!* You're all right?"

My father reassured her and motioned for her to sit on a kitchen chair. Standing without the protection of Mami's body, I grew scared all over again, shaking with fright and fully exposed. My parents were strict disciplinarians, and I knew that I would be reprimanded. I caught the full impact of my father's steely stare as he spoke to Mami. "Your daughter forgets that she is a child and must listen," he explained with his usual eerie calm.

"Look at the radio," Papi said, directing Mami's attention to the disaster still smoking on the small table. I stood just inside the door, ready to run again. Stunned, Mami looked with disbelief at the mess. Her hand moved from her heart to her mouth, magnifying her shock. Her eyes turned to mine with a questioning gaze that was answered by Papi. "I told her not to throw the glass of water at her brother," he said. "Come here," my father ordered, turning his full attention to me.

Shivering with fear, I slowly walked toward him, trying to sense if Mami would protect me. Papi picked up the "Enforcer," which he had left on the kitchen table. I thought my head would explode. Papi moved in slow motion, taking each step carefully. No one spoke. Chachito remained silent, standing next to the sink. Chachita, still holding the pizza, stood next to the kitchen table. Their eyes shifted from Mami to me and then to Papi.

"Stand in the middle of the kitchen," Papi ordered. I

stumbled over myself with fear. Chachita called out, "Don't hit her! You know how Chachito likes to tease." Ignoring her, Papi gestured for me to come forward. Sobbing, I stood before him, praying that he would pity me. Mami interjected, "Clemente, don't hit her too hard. Remember, you're very strong."

Not responding to their comments, Papi said, "You'll receive five lashes. One for not listening to me. The second for throwing the glass. The third for running away. The fourth for frightening your mother, and the fifth to remember not to disobey me again. Do you understand?"

I forced my head to nod my agreement, closed my eyes, and waited. "Open your eyes," my father admonished. "I want you to remember this moment."

I did as he said.

Papi raised his hand over his head and counted out the lashes slowly. Each lash made a snapping sound as it hit my calves. The rubber strap curled around my legs like a snake. Papi had frayed the tips of the rubber hose, exposing the inner wires, which caused a stinging sensation when they struck my tender skin. An ocean of pain washed over me.

When he finally counted the fifth lash, I felt that my legs would buckle. I could no longer stand. Papi told my brother and sister to take me into my room. Collapsing onto my bed, I sobbed until no more tears would come and my hollow gasps filled the room. Rubbing my legs, I felt the swelling lumps under my hands. The heat was unbearable. I cried myself to sleep.

I did not know how much time had passed when a voice woke me.

"Here, drink some cool water," my brother said, holding out a glass. Dazed, I turned to him and then turned my head to the wall without saying a word. "I'm sorry I teased you, Coty," he added in a low whisper. I refused to turn around. The painful throbbing in my legs reminded me of my powerlessness and of the injustice that my brother had not been punished. I started sobbing again.

Chachita came into the room and sat at the edge of the bed next to Chachito. Stroking my hair, my sister tried to console me. My brother sat silently for a while. Finally, he spoke. "You have a beautiful color and your wild hair is lovely, really pretty. That's the truth. I was just playing. I didn't mean for you to get hit."

I refused to respond. I didn't care what he said. I was the one who had been beaten. Chachito had escaped, as usual. I resented that Mami and Papi allowed him to get away with his pranks and provided him freedoms that Chachita and I would never have.

Handsome and athletic, attractive to girls, and an excellent dancer, Chachito was a younger image of my father and took full advantage of the privileges our father and mother bestowed. His growing manhood allowed him to go out in the evenings and date, and Papi was filled with satisfaction when the phone calls from women started coming at all hours of the day. "Chachito is a real man. Look how the women are after him. He is just like me at his age—a ladies' man."

Now my brother perched on the edge of my bed, looking like a little boy.

Chachita tried to smooth ointment over my legs. When she touched the welts, I recoiled from the pain. "It hurts too much. Go away!" I screamed. Instead, my sister cradled me in her arms. Swaying back and forth, she sang a soothing lullaby that Mami had sung to us when we were little: *"A dormir, a dormir, pichón del monte, a dormir a dormir, pichón del monte . . ."* Sleep, sleep, my little pigeon from the mountain, sleep, sleep, my little pigeon from the mountain . . .

Chachito turned to our sister. "I didn't mean for her to get hit," he whispered. Chachita did not respond, but kept singing the soothing lullaby. Chachito looked at the two of us girls, Chachita's light arms wrapped around my darker ones.

As if excluded forever from our embrace, Chachito stood up and walked solemnly away without saying another word.

FIVE

Camina Como Chencha
la Gamba

*El ritmo no se canta, se dice 'Cha-cha-cha.' Listen,
listen, honey, que sabroso está.*

*This new rhythm is not to sing, you just say 'Cha-cha-
cha.' Listen, listen, honey, how delicious it is.*
— GRACIELA, "OYEME, MAMÁ"

At twelve, my body was out of control. Different parts
were exploding, creating a new me. I would sneak
into my bedroom, remove my clothes, and examine
myself with the intensity of a scientist. My flat chest
had begun to sprout small breasts, and a new kind of
hair covered my underarms and pubic area. "Finally
I'm growing up," I thought. In my mind at least, my
body was no longer a straight ruler. I hoped I would
not become *el truck de carne*—so big that the men on

the corner called me a meat delivery truck. But I thought I was filling out nicely, that I stood a good chance of growing into a beautiful young woman who could dazzle young men whenever she passed.

My ideals of beauty were formed by the young women my brother dated. Sometimes they met him at our home, flaunting extravagant dresses, sexy high heels, and haughty attitudes. I imagined myself at the Palladium, the popular dance club downtown where Chachito and his friends had started going to dance and hear the gods of Latin music. At the Palladium, my sexy new hips would move to the rhythms of mambo and merengue as I tossed my curly hair around, mesmerizing any man who came under my spell.

Taking as my model the Catholic Santa Marta la Dominadora on Abuela's altar, who sat cross-legged on the ground and held in her hands a large serpent that she had subdued with her charm, I dreamed of placing the handsomest guys at the club in a trance. The seductive image of La Dominadora, with her hypnotic eyes and defiant posture, danced in my head. Her youthful, sensual body was always adorned in bright green, her breasts and hips full, healthy. I imagined her voice as mysterious and enthralling, one that drew her prey nearer with each word. I posed for the mirror in my bedroom with my hands on my slim hips.

My vision of La Dominadora was a composite of the statue and of actresses and women in the neighborhood that I thought beautiful. My imagination created a perfect image, eliminating Rita Moreno's irritating accent in *West Side Story,* which did not sound like anyone I knew, adding the powerful legs of Katherine Dunham dancing in the movie *Mambo*, including the swaying hips and enticing smile of Dorothy Dandridge, and encompassing even the piercing eyes of Abuela as they had appeared in that sepia photograph of her as a proud young woman and the elegant strut of my mother.

Like La Dominadora's, my skin was infused with warm caramel. Her lips were a rich bright red, and I wished I were allowed to wear lipstick. I reasoned that if La Dominadora was on Abuela's altar, there was nothing wrong with me wanting to look like her. I admired and wanted to emulate the saint's unapologetic strength.

Posing in front of the mirror one day, I heard my mother walking around and quickly put on my clothes, afraid she would scold me. Sometimes I would hear her complaining to Justa, *"Cotito ya parece una mujer"*—that I almost looked like a grown woman. Although a gross exaggeration, this comment reflected her concern. Justa, always caring and nurturing, laughed and remarked, "How I wish we had the power to keep them children. This way we could control their actions. But the Lord did not will it that way," she added with a tinge of sadness. "Look at my son Jimmy, an intelligent, strong, healthy young man insisting on becoming a man before it is time. They want to grow up too fast. Why?"

I yearned to share the discovery of my new body with Mami and my sister, but in our home we never talked about sex, menstruation, boyfriends, or dating. We were not Pentecostals like Justa—like us, Pentecostal girls were not allowed to use makeup, but they also had to wear long dowdy dresses, and they went to church all the time. My mother was strict, and seemed to feel that if she avoided certain topics, they would never come up or grow into problems.

That spring, proud of my little breasts, I held my chest out in the hopes it would be noticed and that Mami would buy me a training bra. But without saying a word, she got me several tight vests instead. By summertime, I still had to wear the ugly plaid things over my blouses and dresses, my blossoming treasures contained. One day I overheard Mami explaining to Justa, "If I buy Cotito a bra, she'll think she's grown. Imagine! She's only twelve and already I have to worry about her friend coming."

I wondered who this friend was that Mami didn't want to come. I knew she loved my very best friend, Myrta. With our long, thin brown bodies and dandelion-shaped hair, we looked like sisters. And she had never found any fault with Rosa.

"That hair," too, was a source of constant battles. Mami kept it in braids and tried to control it with Vaseline and big pastel butterfly bows. I released it in fat curls that quickly transformed themselves into puffs of dark brown cotton. Once a week, Mami sat me between her legs in the living room, turned on her new radio—the replacement for the one I had destroyed the previous summer—and attacked my head.

As she worked on my head Mami hummed to the recordings of the brilliant Puerto Rican composer Rafael Hernández. One of her favorite tunes, the lively *"Buche y Pluma No Más,"* ridiculed people who boasted of skills they did not have. Mami loved the song, and the ferocity of her attack on my hair subsided as, out of tune, she sang along with its lyrics. She encouraged me to join her, and though

I did not know the words, I tried my best. Inevitably, Mami started laughing as I mixed up the Spanish words with English words. *"Yo que conozco el elemento pà yà, pà yà,"* sang Mami, while I stumbled along with "You *nosco el hombre ya ya.*"

"Cotito," she laughed, "your words have nothing to do with the song, or with anything. You're making up words that have no meaning. Are you inventing a new language?" Mami enjoyed teasing me as we both sang out of tune and she waged war on my hair.

One day as she tried to pull my rebellious hair into shape, a catchy tune by Mirta Silva came over the airwaves. I had heard everyone, Mami included, singing this song on the streets and in the halls of our tenement. *"Camina como Chencha la gambá. Ay, camina como Chencha la gambá."* Mirta Silva sang the risqué lyrics in a low, raunchy voice.

Though I did not fully understand it at the time, Mirta's words implied that her sexual prowess had bowed her legs, that her legs were open so wide a "train" or "truck" could easily pass through them. Mami giggled, singing along as she worked the comb through my hair, looking for lice. But when I opened my mouth and tried to sing too, Mami shushed me with a ferocity I did not understand.

"No daughter of mine has a mouth like that," she spat, attacking my scalp with newfound zeal. Before I could ask her what she meant, she poured a thick, smelly liquid all over my head to kill *piojos,* lice and the eggs she suspected of growing on my scalp. In the midst of the onslaught I asked, "Well, why are you singing the song?"

"I'm an adult and you are a child." Her response was the

usual tactic she used for not answering my questions. She wrapped my head tightly in a thick white kerchief so that I wouldn't stain the bedsheet when I went to sleep. The odor of the lice killer was very strong and smelled up the house. That evening my sister refused to share our double bed. "That *piojo* stuff smells like shit. I'm not sleeping with her," she announced to Mami, tossing blankets on the floor to make a makeshift nest for herself.

"Shut your mouth before I shut it for you with a slap," Mami responded angrily. "I do not allow cursing in this house."

Under her breath, my sister growled, "It still smells like shit."

"You're right," I whispered back. "Mami keeps putting that stuff in our hair even if we don't have lice."

"Yeah, but this time you have *piojos, piojosa*. I don't want any sneaking into my head," she teased.

"Next week is your turn to smell like shit, and I'll sleep on the floor," I told her. Happy to have the bed to myself, I spread out fully. This was my private time. Shutting out my sister's presence, I asked myself questions and had conversations in my mind that I couldn't share with any-one else.

No one seemed to understand that I was growing up. In a year I had grown so much I'd reached five feet. Each time I looked in the mirror I saw another version of myself. The tip of my nose was too round. My legs were too long. One breast was bigger than the other. Sometimes my hairstyle pleased me. Other times my hair could not be tamed. Tonight my major concern was my weight. I put my hand on my protruding stomach, which felt strange and sore.

In the morning I ran to the bathroom, thinking I had wet myself. When I looked down, I saw my panties covered in blood. I wiped myself with toilet paper, and more blood appeared. Sitting on the toilet seat, I felt my heart begin to race. The closetlike bathroom contained only a toilet. The bathtub and sink were in the kitchen, the center of traffic in the apartment. The tub had a white enamel cover that sometimes served as a drainboard for freshly washed dishes. Mami had developed a rotation system to allow each of us private time to take a bath. When it was Socorro's or my turn, everyone left the kitchen and went into the living room or one of the two bedrooms until we finished. (My brother slept in the living room on the sofa, which pulled out.) Privacy in our home was never easy to find. How could I clean myself up now?

Suddenly, to my horror, there was a knock on the bathroom door.

"Hurry up! I have to go," my brother yelled.

"I'm not finished," I hollered back. How would I get out of the bathroom without my father and brother seeing the stains on my nightgown? It was Saturday. Papi and my brother were already sitting at the kitchen table making plans to clean the car. Chachita remained asleep in our bedroom. Mami, still in her room, was unaware of my dilemma. I sat on the toilet for what seemed like forever.

"Cotito, come out of the bathroom. Your brother needs to use the toilet," Papi called out.

"I'm not finished," I responded, hoping Mami would come into the kitchen and rescue me.

"Are you okay?" asked Papi.

"Yes, I'm fine," I answered nervously.

"I can't wait any longer!" my brother called out, annoyed.

"I'm not finished," I repeated, close to tears.

"Flora, come see what's wrong with Cotito," Papi shouted. "She doesn't want to come out of the toilet and Chachito's about to pee on himself."

After an eternity, I heard Mami coming out of the bedroom.

"What's the problem?" she asked me through the door.

Not knowing how to explain my situation, I tore off a small piece of toilet paper and wiped it against my panties. Opening the door slightly, I showed Mami the stained paper. She pushed my hand back in.

"Chachito, ask your grandmother to let you use her toilet," Mami instructed my brother. "Clemente, why don't you clean the car?"

I sat frightened and quivering on the toilet seat, not knowing what was happening to my body. I wondered what had caused the bleeding. Was I sick? Would I be taken to the hospital?

"Don't worry," Mami whispered through the door. I heard the front door slam twice, as Chachito and then my father left our apartment. "Stay there and I'll be right back," Mami told me gently. I heard her footsteps as she walked to her bedroom. She quickly returned to the kitchen and ran the water in the bathtub. Then she opened the door. I sat on the toilet, frightened, awaiting instructions.

"*Hija,*" she said in a calm, gentle voice, "your friend has come to visit. Your friend will visit every month for a week and then go away." Mami explained this with a slight smile on her face. "Don't be afraid. This happens to all young girls. It is a sign that you are growing up. But don't tell anyone. This is our secret." Suddenly I remembered the conversation Mami had had with Justa; "this" was the friend they'd been talking about.

Rubbing her eyes, my sister suddenly appeared at the bathroom door. When she looked in and saw my panties she smiled. "Cotito has her period already? I was fourteen when I got mine."

"What does this mean?" I asked my mother. "Is it a friend or a period?"

Mami ignored my question. "Wash yourself good with soap. I've torn up a clean white sheet and folded it to fit between your legs," Mami explained, holding the limp folded rag in her hand.

Chachita chimed in, "You need to change at least three to four times a day and wash yourself good in the morning, afternoon, and before bedtime."

Mami added, "I'll fold twenty-one of these strips for the week, as I do for your sister. If you need more I'll tear up another sheet."

Mami pulled an object from her dress pocket. "Here's a safety pin to secure it to your panties. Here are paper bags to throw the soiled ones out. You have to take the garbage out every night when your friend visits. Blood stinks if left in the garbage overnight. Understand? Remember to wash thoroughly."

Bewildered, I followed all of the instructions. I climbed to the edge of the tub, my butt hanging close to the faucet. The soap and warm water quickly washed away all evidence of this change in my body. "Mami, can I take a bath now?" I asked.

"No, no, no, it's dangerous to bathe when you have your friend," Mami responded, uncomfortable.

"Why?" I asked.

"Because it can cause *locura*—craziness," she said. "Remember, don't talk to anyone about having your friend," Mami continued. "This is a private matter."

I looked at my sister. Chachita shrugged her shoulders, winked, and walked into the bathroom, closing the door. I kept washing myself, frightened by the idea of going crazy due to my "friend." I thought of Leocadia, a neighborhood lady who spent her days sweeping the sidewalk in front of the Pentecostal church, talking to herself in a loud voice and even addressing God directly, as if He were floating right above her head. I wondered if her "friend" had caused this craziness. Though the water from the tap was warm, I shivered.

When I was done washing up, Mami decided to remove the lice medicine from my hair. Hanging my head over the edge of the tub where I had just finished cleaning myself, she continued her instructions. "Normally you don't wash your hair when your 'friend' visits. It is easy to catch a cold during this time." She poured shampoo over my head and vigorously scrubbed with warm water. Mami's tone indicated I should not ask any more questions but simply accept what she said.

But my mind was filled with questions. Why the secrecy? Did my friend Myrta have her period? Should I be ashamed or happy? Did I look different? Would my schoolmates notice a difference on Monday when I went to school? How was I supposed to wash up in school? An A student at Junior High School 99, I was a monitor during lunchtime, as was Myrta. I couldn't leave my post without an explanation to my supervising teacher. I wondered what I would do. If my "friend" caused all this trouble, why was she called my friend?

I helped my sister clean our room as I waited for my hair to dry. I didn't know what to say, so I remained silent, hoping she would speak first.

"So, my baby sister is a *señorita* now," Chachita murmured, smiling. "Welcome to the club. It's filled with mysteries and secrecy reserved just for us," she whispered. "Our friend has so many names that it will drive you crazy. *La regla, el periodo, la amiga,* the friend, the curse, time-out. I can't even think of them all. Silliest is *cantó el gallo*—the rooster has sung."

"I'm scared," I responded, wishing there was a place I could hide to figure out what was happening to me. To my mother in the next room, I called out, "I'm finished. Can I visit Abuela?"

"No, not today," she called back. Appearing in the doorway, she added, "When you have your 'friend' you can't help in the altar room or the spirits will stay away."

"Why?" I asked, annoyed and even more confused. Was this blood so powerful it could keep away the spirits? I wanted to talk with Abuela and could not imagine that the spirits would care if I had my period. Her apartment was always a welcoming, safe space for me. And with her uncanny intuition, Abuela always knew when something was on my mind.

"That's just the way it is," responded Mami, turning her back and returning to the living room with no further explanation.

Chachita stood next to me and whispered in my ear, "I'll explain everything to you tonight, after Papi and Mami go to sleep. Don't worry. Mami's telling you what her mother must have taught her in the old days. It's hard to believe she got training as a nurse! In hygiene class I learned the truth about menstruation."

"What is menstruation?" I asked, confused by all the terms.

"Your 'friend,' your 'period'—it's all the same thing. Didn't I tell you, 'it' has many names. The real name is menstruation, or *la menstruación.*" Obviously enjoying the role of my new counselor, my older sister took on a more adult tone.

I looked up into Chachita's face, then hugged her, filled with gratitude at her willingness to explain what Mami would not. But I was frightened, too. The maze that Mami was constructing had me confused. Chachita was a help. For the first time, she was treating me as her peer and not only her little sister.

Once I had pinned the strange new bedsheet strips to my underwear and dressed, I asked my mother if I could go outside to play. "Air is good for you. Go outside, but no jumping," she admonished.

"Why?" I wanted to know.

"Not good for you. Wait until the visit from your 'friend' ends," Mami responded curtly.

"Then what'll I do outside?" I asked.

"Turn rope or watch others play," she said.

"Watch others play?" I was shocked. My mother strode into the kitchen as if she wanted no more of my questions.

Helplessly, I turned to my sister, who had come into the living room with the mop bucket. "Am I sick?" I whispered.

"Welcome to becoming a *señorita* in our backward El Barrio world," she hissed, rolling her eyes. "Go downstairs and play. Just make sure Mami's not at the window," Chachita cautioned. "Don't let Mami know I said so," she added with a frown, knowing that if Mami found out she would be punished.

Feeling a little guilty, I shouted, "I'm going downstairs, Ma," and left the apartment. I walked slowly down the stairs, afraid to run because I didn't know what could happen. Did jumping make the blood come faster?

Standing by the stoop, I tried to calm down. The gentle breeze of the early afternoon was soothing and refreshing. I watched Myrta and Rosa twirl the double-Dutch rope for Rosa's cousin Mercedes. Mercedes lived in Brooklyn and was visiting for the weekend. She didn't know how to jump. I watched as Mercedes tried and failed to catch the tempo of the doubled-up rope as it spun and crisscrossed in the air. Her round, pear-shaped body couldn't capture the beat. Her feet would not dance to the rhythm. My own heart beat to the cadence of the turning rope, and my feet were anxious to join in. I was miserable just standing and watching. Myrta noticed me and called, "Cotito, come show her how to jump double Dutch."

My body wanted to move in the direction of my friends, but I recalled Mami's words: "Not good for you." I shook my head, approaching the other girls slowly.

Myrta noticed my uneasiness. "What's wrong?"

"Nothing. I don't feel like jumping," I lied.

Rosa, teasing, responded, "You must be near death."

Myrta stared at me in disbelief. "What is it?" she asked.

"*Nada,* leave me alone," I pleaded. "Or I'll go back upstairs," I added angrily. Myrta, surprised at my response, fell silent and kept turning the empty rope. Sulking, I stood against the door of our tenement and watched as Papi and Chachito finished cleaning the car. The surface of the Dodge was like a mirror reflecting the mellow blue of the sky and the brilliance of the white clouds. They carefully gathered the pails, rags, and sponges and started walking toward me. My heart skipped a beat, my face and hands grew cold, and my feet remained rooted as I wondered if they could see a difference in me.

"Cotito, are you okay?" asked Papi, gently rubbing the top of my head.

"Yeah," I answered, trying to act normal and wondering about his casual question. Did he know or not?

My brother's attention was drawn to a beautiful chocolate-skinned woman prancing toward us. Her name was Dolores, and her jet-black hair, tied in a ponytail, swayed back and forth in countertempo to her sexy gait. Dressed in a gray flared skirt and baby-pink sweater, she naturally drew male attention. To my relief, Chachito was fascinated by Dolores and totally ignored me. I guessed that if he knew about my friend, he didn't care.

With his brightest smile and most enticing voice, Chachito called out, "God, turn me into a pink sweater so I can wrap myself around Dolores forever." He laughed as she approached. "Dolores, *mi amor*, you have me hypnotized. I'm yours. Take me." Papi stood by, proudly watching his son.

Arrogantly, Dolores lifted her head even higher, acknowledging the compliment and accentuating her strut with even more swing to her hips. She didn't say a word. Her body spoke for her. I wondered if this was how I needed to be now that I was a *señorita*.

Dolores passed. Papi went upstairs and Chachito lingered, watching her walk away. He sang out his parting words to Dolores: *"Si caminas como cocinas, me como hasta la raspa."* If you cook like you walk, I'll even eat the scrapings from the pot.

Myrta put down the rope and stood next to me. Whispering in my ear, she said, "I bet you got a visitor."

"What are you talking about?" I responded.

Realizing my confusion, she clarified her remark: "You got a visitor, a visit from the 'friend,' didn't you?" She dragged out the word *friend,* teasing me. "Your period, stupid."

Remembering Mami's words about secrecy, I remained silent, lowering my eyes. "I got my visit last week," Myrta continued. "My mother said not to tell anyone that *me vino la luna*—the moon came to me. I bet your mother said the same thing." Amazed, I stared at her. The moon? I nodded in agreement.

"We're grown now. We can even have babies," Myrta added proudly. "I told all my girlfriends. I didn't tell any of the boys."

"Why didn't you tell me? I'm your best friend," I accused, suddenly hurt.

"Because I knew you didn't know about the visit yet," she answered.

I said nothing. Rosa and Mercedes, oblivious to our conversation, continued turning ropes. Rosa tried to get Mercedes to feel the rhythm made by the syncopated ropes hitting the pavement. Mercedes tried, but her stiff movements made her look like a wooden puppet. Why was it so difficult to get an explanation about what was happening to me? What was so mysterious? And why did this friend have so many names and now another, the moon? What was the point of keeping the moon, the friend, the visitor a secret, since everyone knew about it?

When nighttime came, I was so glad. I couldn't wait to talk more with my sister about what was happening to me. As I was gathering my nightclothes, Mami came into the room.

"Well, how are you feeling?" she asked. Before I could respond, she said, "See, it's nothing. You're fine." She walked out just as quickly as she had come in. I hadn't had a chance to say a word.

Disappointed, I looked to my sister. Animated by my dilemma, she began to share more information, her ears tuned to Mami's footsteps. We knew that Mami had the habit of leaving and returning without warning.

"Cotito," Chachita whispered, "don't be afraid to bathe, play, or wash your hair. My hygiene teacher said that it is safe to do all of these things." My sister went on: "When you take a bath, your period stops." I listened, fascinated by the amount of information she possessed.

"Mami makes us wear old torn-up sheets instead of the cotton pads they sell in the drugstore," Chachita said. "But I buy the pads on my way to school and store them in my locker. Mami just wants us to stay her babies. She's trying to stop us from growing up. Don't worry," Chachita whispered, "I'll share pads with you if you promise to keep them hidden and not to tell her." I agreed. Glad to get rid of the nasty rags, I reasoned that since Chachita had not gotten caught, neither would I. And if she didn't feel guilty about deceiving our mother, I would try not to either.

"Do you bathe in the tub or just wash like Mami wants us to?" I asked anxiously.

"I listen to Mami, but I know she's wrong," my sister sheepishly responded.

"Why is Mami so secretive about the friend?" I wondered aloud. "Is it a bad thing or is it good?"

"Shhhhhhh, the big secret is that guys aren't supposed to know we're young women and are ready to have babies," Chachita told me with a knowing smile.

I had been afraid to react to Myrta, and now I didn't know what to say to my sister, who had just mentioned men and babies in the same breath. I was beginning to figure out that there was a relationship. But since no one ever spoke of sex or having it, I didn't exactly grasp how they related.

The opportunity to talk openly about my changing body with my sister provided some release. But as soon as I'd worked up the nerve to ask more questions, I heard her snoring. Disappointed, I lay awake wondering about this unexpected visitor all women received. Without knowing exactly how or why, I understood that the unexpected "friend"— this rooster's song, this moon—had changed my life.

SIX

Una Mujer en Mi Vida

Al fin tú eres mujer y no tienes alma para querer.

In reality you are a woman and lack the soul to love.
— TITO RODRIGUEZ, "ALMA DE MUJER"

When I was thirteen, my brother began to spend his evenings at the Palladium. The popular ballroom, known as "the home of the mambo," was located at Broadway and Fifty-second Street, at the pulsating center of Manhattan, and had mambo dance nights Wednesdays, Fridays, and Saturdays, and dance matinees on Sundays.

One Wednesday night, my sister and I huddled under a cave of blankets, praying that our parents wouldn't hear the phone ring. The moment it did, we grabbed the receiver and pressed it as close as we could to our ears. The smooth voice of our brother accompanied the rhythms of Tito Puente's sizzling mambo band. "Listen to the timbales rip the place apart," Chachito crooned. "Puente is swinging and the place is rocking! The timbales smoke from the force of his drumbeats."

From a public phone at the Palladium, our big brother placed us smack in the middle of the dance floor, bringing the pulsating rhythms of Tito Puente's magical solo to us live. Chachito loved the sound of his own voice, and on these nights when he called us from the Palladium, so did we. "I am not kidding. Puente's on fire. The floor throbs with the movement of the dancers. Listen! Listen! Tito is playing with all his heart." In the background we heard the roar of the audience as they pushed the master musician, encouraging him to reach the highest of heights. *"Toca, Tito, toca, toca, toca."* Play, Tito, play, play, play!

The rapid beats of the timbales flowed through the telephone, speaking directly to the rhythm of our hearts. Puente's "Hot Timbales" had the audience exploding with excitement. The crowd clapped to the *clave* beat—*ta-ta-ta, ta-ta, ta-ta-ta, ta-ta.* As Puente's solo intensified, the clapping grew louder. The people raised their voices and shouted, "Tito, Tito!" Shaking with joy under the covers, Socorro and I could hardly breathe. Straining not to make any noise that would wake our parents, we couldn't help but rock to the sound of the *clave.* The old springs of our mattress squeaked. Sweat dripped down our bodies. Trembling with excitement, my sister and I each tugged at the receiver.

I wished that somehow I could squeeze through the

telephone lines and appear at the other end wearing Rita Moreno's flamboyant, strapless red dress from *West Side Story.* My imagination swam with a picture of Tito's timbales literally on fire, smoke whirling around him and onto the dance floor. I saw him as a young musical warrior, dressed meticulously all in white as he was on his album covers, swinging his drumsticks like swords. The music grabbed me and held me with an entrancing force, a mysterious spirit that touched me at my core.

Music was love, pulsating with romance and dreams of what I desired. Rita Moreno's sensual fire and Dorothy Dandridge's smoldering sexuality as the songstress Carmen Jones were the images that spoke to the beauty I dreamed of being. The color of their skin was the color of mine, and their bodies held out a promise of what I could become. They were the epitome of the everyday sensuality I saw in the women who walked down the streets of El Barrio. I was intrigued by the power they held over men.

But not all of these real-life beauties were powerful. One example was Teresa, a Dorothy Dandridge look-alike, who let the man in her life sell her beauty for his own profit. Myrta and I loved her charm and grace, the way she dressed, and the attention she drew. *"Esa es una puta*—she is a prostitute. I don't want you talking to her," Mami constantly reminded us whenever I spoke of Teresa's beautiful clothes. Yet other women on the block looked at her with eyes filled with envy, wishing they had the power and command over their bodies that Teresa possessed.

The "good" women were like my godmother, Carmen, and like Mami, never using their beauty to provoke or entice. Good women showed their virtue by dressing attractively but not too sensually. Carmen, a caramel beauty, hid her voluptuous body in oversized cotton pinafores and her Rita Hayworth hair in twisted braids on the crown of her head. Carmine, her Italian husband, constantly accused her of looking like a prostitute. His jealousy kept her prisoner. He stalked her, trying to catch her with one imagined lover after another. And this, I supposed, was love.

Like Carmen, Mami dressed in cotton pinafores. This uniform changed only for special occasions, when her special clothing would come out of the heavily mothballed closet to air out. Mami enjoyed looking elegant and commanding. Her strut when she was dressed up often attracted flirtatious remarks from men on the street. Enjoying the compliments, she would blush, unaccustomed to being the center of male attention.

As a *señorita*, I had begun to wonder about boys. I attended an all-girls junior high school, and boys from the neighboring school would surround the fence of the yard when we were dismissed. The whistling and noise they made when school let out was staggering. Guys would follow behind us as we walked home, wanting to talk and even cop a quick feel. Two in particular, Manuel and Geraldo, were always tailing Myrta and me as we made our way home. Both of us knew that our mothers often showed up unexpectedly at our school, so we pretended to avoid the boys. At the same time, we encouraged them with coy glances and smiles. Beyond that, we didn't know how to react to such outrageous flirting.

I never heard my mother or father talk about love. Neither do I remember being taught what love was. Mami and Papi never expressed their affections openly. They never held hands, embraced, or kissed in our presence. I do not remember seeing them share tender touches or loving words. And in that thirteenth year of my life, their relationship changed in a way that would never be repaired. What cracked their marriage was a seemingly insignificant desire of my mother's. She wanted to learn how to drive.

Papi's '48 Dodge was a showpiece that he and my brother faithfully cleaned and simonized each Saturday in full view of all our neighbors. Everyone on the block knew not to go near this car. A serious, muscular man, Papi immediately aroused fear in those who did not know him. What's more, he had instructed us to holler at anyone who even leaned on the vehicle for so much as a second. If they refused to get off, we were to tell him or Mami.

She also watched over the car from their first-floor bedroom window. From this window, Mami kept abreast of all the goings-on of the block. She had a network of friends that extended to 116th Street and would keep her updated with the latest gossip with a mere telephone call. Carmen lived on 103rd Street, next to the Lexington Avenue subway, and would call Mami as soon as my brother and sister stepped out of the station. Mami then timed them to make sure they hadn't stopped along the way. Chachito teased her, saying she was the Puerto Rican Sherlock Holmes.

Early afternoons, everyone hung out their windows, waiting for the numbers man to come. The conversations from window to window were unscripted dramas.

Juanita, an almond-colored, pear-shaped woman who lived on the fourth floor, hollered down to Mami, "I know today is my day. I played 783. I had a dream with *la diosa*

Yemayá rising from the sea under the watchful eyes of Obatalá. Seeing her beautiful sensuous body emerge from the sea, Obatalá immediately fell in love with her. They got together, *ya tú sabes, chingaron,* and gave birth to Eleguá. *Tú sabes que* Yemayá is seven, Obatalá is eight, and Eleguá is three. Flora, Olodumare gave me the numbers in my dream."

Laughing, Mami responded, "What you need is a man. That's what the dream is telling you. *Te hace falta la chingadera.*" Enjoying their spicy conversation, Juanita, Mami, and the other women waited patiently for Juan, the numbers man, to stroll down the block.

He walked by casually, holding up his fingers to let the ladies know the three numbers that had come out in the horse races. Hiding his hand with his straw hat, Juan might raise his index finger to let a lady know that the first number of the day was one. He'd raise four fingers to let her know the second number was four, and, finally, he might put his hat on his head and hold up two hands with sufficient fingers to let her know the last number was eight.

Juan was a short, chocolate-skinned man whose trademark was a large straw *jíbaro* hat and a guayabera shirt. In the winter he covered his guayabera with an oversized black-and-white coat that was too long for his short body. A cigar stub perpetually protruded from his thick lips, but it was never lit. His warm friendly eyes matched his chiseled smile and engaging charm. His gold tooth, inlayed with a small diamond, shone in sharp contrast to his deep, dark skin.

Sitting alongside Mami in the afternoons after school, I

loved watching Juan's antics. I laughed at his pantomime, not realizing he was trying to hide from the police. There was no state-sponsored lottery, so *la bolita* held the neighborhood's only promise of wealth and the money to return to Puerto Rico. For us, it was not illegal, exactly. Everyone we knew played *la bolita* openly. Juan's public performance could fool no one. Mami said that probably the cops on the beat also played the numbers, which is why he never got picked up.

Papi didn't want Mami playing *la bolita.* He felt it was a waste of money. As soon as Papi left for work, Juan knew to come by the house to collect Mami's list of numbers written on a long, narrow sheet of folded paper. Next to each number she noted the amount she wanted placed, either five or ten cents. She would have the exact change ready so he could complete the transaction quickly and move on to his next customer.

Mami would respond to Juan curtly when he called, making certain that she projected no level of friendship to this man who was not her husband. Mami's objective was to "hit" the numbers so she could enjoy the small necessities and the freedom that having her own money allowed. She approached playing the numbers as if she were studying for a class. The *Daily News* ran a particular cartoon, "The Chinaman," which, according to neighborhood lore, hid the winning numbers somewhere in the drawing each day.

With a large magnifying glass, Mami would sit at the white Formica kitchen table carefully examining the *chino*'s hat, black braid, kimono, slippers, and hands. "I found it." She called me over to show me her discovery.

"Look, his braid is shaped like a seven, his left hand another seven. His shoes are shaped like zeros. The number for today is 770." If that day the number did not hit, she added it to the expanding list of numbers she had played, dropping some of the oldest ones.

Sworn to secrecy about her numbers playing, Chachito, Chachita, and I were sometimes allowed to select a combination of three numbers. My brother played numbers that related to his birthday, as did my sister. I played 303, a variation of our house number, 330, which was Mami's favorite number. She played this special number daily in addition to the ones she found in the cartoon.

That fall, 330 finally won and Mami was thrilled. She floated around the house on a cloud, deciding how she would spend the money. When Juan handed her the wrinkled brown paper bag filled with cash, Mami giggled like a young girl. My brother and sister each received five dollars, and I was given one.

With her winnings she decided to take driving lessons, in spite of Papi's refusal to let her drive the car. Adamant in his belief that women were not supposed to drive, Papi had long ignored Mami's requests for lessons. Though she'd nagged him constantly about how it would come in handy for shopping, he'd refused to teach her. "I take you shopping and everywhere you want to go. Why would you need to drive?" he'd say, putting a stop to the conversation. Driving was only one of many things my father did not allow my mother to do. Papi felt that a woman's place was in the house, caring for her man and children. It was the man's responsibility to look out for his family. He thought that a woman outside of her home would get "ideas," implying that it provided the opportunity for her to *pegarle los cuernos al marido*—"put horns," or cheat, on her husband.

Mami's response always silenced him. "Do you roam when you're away from me?" He'd ignore her. The pain of doubt would leap into her eyes, as his dismissal provided no answer.

When she asked to take driving lessons Papi scolded her like he did us. On the day after her number had come in, as Papi prepared to leave for work, she again expressed her desire to learn to drive. *"Coño, para ya,"* he said, turning angrily away from the door and throwing his words in her direction like thunderbolts. "What is wrong with you? Have you lost your head? Is it screwed on backwards? Women are too careless and stupid to drive. Only men are good drivers. Get rid of the idea of driving right now, do you hear me? Don't mention it again," he insisted.

With her secret cache of money, Mami worked up the courage to break the rule imposed by Papi. She enrolled in driving school. When she announced her covert decision to Chachito, Chachita, and me, we were overjoyed. But later, Chachito worried. He told Chachita and me, "I hope none of the neighbors see Mami driving and tell Papi." Being a conspirator in keeping her decision a secret particularly excited me. I was thrilled when she brought me with her to enroll.

The storefront on 100th Street had bright golden letters that read "Burgos Driving School." As Mami opened the door, bells jingled loudly, announcing our presence. We saw Mr. Burgos sitting behind a large desk piled with magazines and overstuffed files. There were magazines tossed all over the sofas and chairs. Piles of driving manuals were stacked in the corners of the large room. On the freshly painted walls hung certificates and photos demonstrating the excellence of the school and praising the teaching skills of its sole owner and teacher. Mami held my hand tightly as we walked farther into the office, and she continued to hold it nervously throughout the interview with Mr. Burgos. Mami's hands were cold. Even when filling out the information on the application form, she held my hand for support.

"When do you wish to start your lessons, Mrs. Moreno?" asked Mr. Burgos in a deep, rolling voice. A powerful, handsome man with a solemn presence, he could have been my father's brother. But Mr. Burgos looked very official in his dark gray suit, white shirt, and blue tie. He stared directly into Mami's eyes, amused by her nervousness.

Mami hesitated and then suddenly released the words she was so afraid to utter: "Immediately. How much is the deposit?"

He told her and she dug into the brown bag of money, quickly pulling out the right amount. Mr. Burgos studiously counted the deposit and said, "Each lesson takes one hour. Is tomorrow around four okay?"

"Can we begin at three-thirty instead?" Mami asked nervously.

"Fine, no problem." Mr. Burgos stood up and extended his hand toward Mami. "Would you like me to pick you up?"

Mami was stunned by the question. She knew that if a man picked her up in a car the block would be buzzing with neighbors wondering if she was having an affair. Trying to gather her composure, she shook his hand quickly and told him, "It's best that I come here."

Walking home, she shivered even in the lingering,

Indian-summer heat. Mostly talking to herself, she mumbled along the way. "Imagine if someone told your father that I was picked up by a man. You know all the gossips on the block. They love to turn something innocent into something dirty. Cotito, say absolutely nothing about the driving lessons. Do you hear me?" Nodding my head in agreement, I tried to understand why Mami was so agitated.

A battered black Chevy with a large yellow handwritten sign on the hood announcing "Student Driver—Burgos Driving School" served as the training car. During Mami's first lesson, I sat in the back seat behind Mr. Burgos. Mami sat stiffly behind the wheel, determined to learn to drive with as few lessons as possible. Her hands gripping the wheel tightly, Mami glowed. Even Mr. Burgos commented, "You look so elegant behind the wheel." Unaccustomed to compliments, Mami appeared startled and embarrassed. Noting her discomfort, Mr. Burgos immediately started the class.

"Turn the key and step on the gas slowly," he said.

Mami complied, and the old Chevy roared to life.

"Now step on the gas gently," he continued, "and shift in one movement to the first position." The car jerked and stalled. "Don't be so nervous," Mr. Burgos cautioned Mami. "Calm down and let the car do its job. Just set the car in motion and gently guide it."

Her first lesson was a disaster. But by the fourth lesson, Mami had gained significant confidence and was rewarded. She drove us out along the East River Drive. In front of the driving school Burgos had her parallel park between two cars. She swooped right into the spot the first time. Mr. Burgos was very pleased.

On the way home after each class, we would celebrate her successes. She usually bought me an ice-cream cone even though it was just before dinner. "I will tell your father tonight that I have been taking driving lessons," she declared after about three weeks, proudly adding, "I am a damn good driver."

That night after dinner, Papi was sitting quietly at the kitchen table reading the paper as he sipped from the small cup filled with freshly brewed espresso. When he got to the sports section, we knew to leave the kitchen and sit in the living room. At this time, Papi and Mami usually discussed the events of the day and adult matters in low voices, purposefully making it difficult for us to hear.

That night, a few minutes after Chachito, Chachita, and I had left the kitchen, all hell broke loose. We heard dishes crash to the floor, along with the kitchen table and the chair Papi had been sitting in. "*Cálmate*, calm down, calm down," Mami repeated, trying to control Papi's anger and her own growing fear. The three of us dashed into the kitchen to see what was happening.

Usually calm and unflappable, my father had erupted like a volcano. His fury distorted his face and body. "I told you that women should not drive. Women do not have the intelligence." Drawing his face dangerously close to hers he shouted, "How dare you disobey me?"

Belittled in front of her children, Mami found the courage to respond. In spite of her fear, quivering words came out of her mouth. "I'm smarter than you," she said. "I finished high school, you did not. You never finished third grade. How dare you speak to me as if I am a child? You are the stupid one."

Papi's fury overwhelmed him. He clenched his fists so

tightly that the blood drained from his hands. His strong, muscular arms, molded by years of body and fender work, were massive. He swung his right arm like a sword toward Mami. My brother, sister, and I cringed, anticipating the impact. Flabbergasted, she stepped back, and we watched, stunned, as his fist grazed her face. Her hands protectively jumped to her cheeks as her eyes drowned in tears.

Chachito, Chachita, and I sprang into motion without thinking. Chachito tried to hold back Papi's arm. Without realizing it, Papi lifted Chachito as he tried again to swing at Mami. I grabbed Papi's leg in hopes of holding him back. He dragged me effortlessly along the floor.

I panicked, crying and screaming at Papi to leave Mami alone. My brother, hanging like a rag doll from our father's arm, tried unsuccessfully to bring it down. Chachita, screaming and sobbing, was the first to regain her composure. She boldly stood before Papi and screamed, "Are you crazy? Stop, right now. I'll call the cops and have you locked up." Papi looked at his daughter with disbelief. His eyes filled with flames, then suddenly closed.

Chachita started to cry. My brother realized his helplessness and held on to Papi's arm because he didn't know what else to do. Mami, crying hysterically, screamed out, "You're not even a man. How can you hit a woman, your wife, in front of your children?" My father's temper was again ignited, and he launched forward again. I held on to Papi's leg, afraid to let go as the tears and mucus flowed down my nose and into my mouth, choking me.

Papi's anger exploded. He reached for Mami as she ran into the bedroom. But, surrounded by his children, he was confused and disoriented, not wanting to hurt us. He stopped in midmotion in the living room. Chachito cautiously let his arm go. Chachita pulled me from his leg. Trembling, I wrapped myself around her waist. We held each other as we fought to catch our breath.

My brother, bewildered and powerless, looked on, not knowing what to do. His eyes brimmed with tears that refused to come down because men were not supposed to cry. In spite of this madness, he had to show my father that he was a man. I clung to my sister, afraid to move. Chachita tenderly stroked my head to quiet me.

Then she inched us to the living room doorway, blocking our father's path to the bedroom. We were three frightened soldiers, standing like the warrior gods Abuela kept by the entrance of her apartment for protection. Confronted by his children for the first time, Papi didn't know what to do. In the background, Mami's sobs could be heard through the thick plastic curtain that served as a gateway to their bedroom.

Papi turned away from us and walked to the refrigerator. He paused, then opened it, pouring himself a glass of water. But anger again overtook him, and he slammed the door shut with all his strength, sending the tray of decorative glasses on top of the refrigerator crashing to the floor. He walked slowly to the front of the apartment. Hesitating, he looked back at us dazed, without expression. As he walked out he slammed the front door so hard its hinges sprung loose from the frame.

Jolted by my mother's disobedience, Papi, we later found out, stormed out to confront Mr. Burgos. Although I was never given the details of this encounter, we heard tidbits as Mami told the story to Carmen in a telephone conversation. Apparently, Papi met his match with Mr. Burgos. Mr. Burgos told Papi that as a married man with a wife and children he had great respect for Mami and all the women who took lessons with him.

With an added sense of intrigue, my mother lowered her voice and murmured into the receiver, "Clemente is jealous. He knows that I'm an attractive, light-skinned woman. You know that dark men are attracted to women of my complexion. Clemente is a good man. He just loves me too much. That's why he doesn't want me to work or go out." The thrill in her voice suggested that somehow my father's anger was an expression of his love.

Against my father's wishes, Mami stubbornly continued the lessons. For weeks, Papi refused to speak to her, and she to him. This frozen silence was broken only by messages relayed through us children. Mami's clanging pots marked her anger, while Papi's silence conveyed his. Dinnertime was painfully long and uncomfortable as we all sat around the kitchen table silently eating our food.

Mami and Papi had never openly expressed their love by kissing, holding hands, or embracing each other, yet we had always known they loved each other. Now they scarcely touched in our presence. They acted like strangers.

One night, after weeks of tension, my father walked into the living room, where Mami sat reading. He pulled a record from its jacket, which featured the Puerto Rican *jíbaro* vocalist Ramito smiling out from under his straw *pava*. Ramito held a rooster in his hands and stood against the backdrop of a wooden country farmhouse, lush avocado-colored mountains, and a sky the same blue as the Dodge. Papi placed the album on the record player and

Ramito's high-pitched voice sang out the melancholy bolero "Una Mujer en Mi Vida."

Papi began to dance, holding his hands around an imaginary partner and smiling, his eyes downcast. Swaying slowly as if caught in a fanciful dream, he barely moved his feet. His body spoke volumes. Sculpted by the romantic music, his muscular frame curved softly, as if enchanted.

He cast a tender glance at my mother. She turned her head, pretending to ignore him, but he extended his hand. Softly, he coaxed, *"Ven, vamos a bailar."*

"You know I don't know how to dance, Clemente," my mother remonstrated. But the gold tooth in her smile shone like the rays of the sun as my father continued to encourage her. "What about the children? They're watching," she protested. Laughing, he responded, *"Mujer,* I am just asking you to dance. How can you resist when Ramito helps me serenade you? You are *la mujer en mi vida,* the woman in my life."

My father's dark, handsome face appeared unusually gentle. His smiling lips traced his strong white teeth, and his eyes twinkled with mischief. Finally, he coaxed Mami from the sofa. Sliding into Papi's strong arms, she laughed like a little girl. Her light blue floral housedress floated around her body in a slow, spiraling stream. She responded to the pleading voice of Ramito and the smooth movements of my father.

Slowly, the two of them swayed back and forth in the same spot. Ramito's tear-filled voice sang, "The woman in my life has decided to destroy me. Before I die, God will punish her. She responds with disloyalty to the love that I give her." Papi's actions feigned forgiveness, but the bittersweet lyrics of the song conveyed his true feelings. Flushed and resigned, Mami rested her head on my father's shoulder as he tenderly caressed her back with his large, callused hands. Watching from the doorway, I did not understand how my parents—he in his soiled uniform, she in her worn housedress—could look so much like movie stars. Then it occurred to me. My mother, Flora Cruz Marcano, and my father, Clemente Moreno, dancing their romantic dance to the simple tune, were not only my parents but lovers, too. But how could Papi love Mami and still try to hurt her?

Though my parents made up that night, the rhythm of our home was never the same after my mother learned to drive. There was always a level of tension that could rear its head unexpectedly when our parents' views clashed. My brother, sister, and I had to learn to protect our mother from our father's "love."

I wondered if accepting this kind of love was what it meant to be a woman. And, if so, what kind of woman would I become?

SEVEN

What Was Changó Doing at the Palladium?

Changó ta veni, Changó ta veni, Changó ta veni, con el machete en la mano tierra va temblar.

Changó is coming, Changó is coming, Changó is coming, with his machete in his hand the earth will tremble.

— MACHITO AND HIS AFRO-CUBANS,
"CHANGÓ TA VENI"

One spring evening in 1956, Chachito called Socorro and me from the Palladium, as always. First, he told us to hang on. There was an extended pause. And then the blaring trumpets of the orchestra heralded the voice of Machito. *"Changó ta veni, Changó ta veni, Changó ta veni,"* his voice roared over the microphone. *"Con el machete en la mano, tierra va temblar,"* he sang.

Machito sent lightning bolts with his voice as the sound of the maracas roared like thunder through the telephone lines from Fifty-second Street and Broadway into our bedroom in El Barrio.

"Machito said Changó. Did you hear, Chachita? He said Changó, like the records in Abuela's house," I whispered to my sister.

"Shhh, Papi and Mami will hear. Just shut up," she snapped.

The Changó I knew from my Abuela's was the warrior divinity, handsome and valiant. He won wars by throwing thunderbolts and lightning to destroy his adversaries. Abuela had explained that Changó was also a ladies' man and enjoyed dancing to the sacred *batá* drums that were his domain. Abuela's altar to this powerful orisha, or saint, was decorated in red and white, the colors that symbolized him. When the powerful sound of the thundering drums and the chants to Changó were played, Abuela would lift her hands to the sky, slash the air as if looking for enemies, and dance with bold steps like roaring thunder. With fire in her eyes, Abuela danced and the room itself seemed to take on an electrical energy and vibrate with power. But Changó's fierce warrior spirit had a soft, romantic, passive side, too, symbolized by the coolness of white.

"The dance floor is packed, everyone is dancing," Chachito screamed into the phone over the blaring music of the orchestra. "Marlon Brando is at the Palladium tonight. I was sitting at a table close to him," he boasted. Listening to Machito's mellow voice, I felt stirrings of power in my own body and dreamed of finding my own warrior on the dance floor of the Palladium one day.

"Got to go," Chachito's voice broke my reverie. He hung up abruptly, leaving Socorro and me to imagine his adventures.

My brother had grown into a young Latino Billy Eckstine, the handsome African-American vocalist whose records Chachito loved and whose good looks and smooth voice made women of all colors swoon. With skin like soft caramel and soulful brown eyes, a neat mustache that caressed his sculpted lips, and glistening white teeth, Chachito knew how to take full advantage of his looks. His relaxed yet elegantly upright posture made him appear taller than five foot nine. His studied, debonair manner resembled the poses of the leading musicians of the fifties on their album covers. Tito Rodriguez, Tito Puente, Machito, and Mario Bauza were always dressed in dark suits or tuxedos, standing proudly, their fresh haircuts smoothed with pomade, their nails buffed to a soft shine, and their shoes highly polished. Like them, my brother drew women like bees to honey, projecting a self-confidence and manliness that was even more attractive than his physical appearance. Chachito's pride, spiritedness, and leadership qualities made him the center of attention.

Mami and Papi celebrated his manhood. But Chachita, just a year younger, was not encouraged to be a woman. Our brother was also protective of us, making certain that his friends didn't disrespect us. When his friends visited, he never left the room. Chachita and I were always reminded that we were young girls, which meant we must contain our sexuality and our desires.

Unlike my sister and me, my brother had free rein to go anywhere and do almost anything he wished. Music, dancing, women, and stickball were his passions. The four were intrinsically connected in his mind. He attended college and had a part-time job, but Chachito's life was really devoted to following the best orchestras. He even tried learning to play the trumpet. My brother reasoned that the best dances drew the prettiest women, those who were worthy of his looks, fashion sense, and dancing prowess. Enjoying competition of all kinds, he excelled at stickball, which also attracted an audience of women.

Papi saw his younger self reflected in my brother. "I was the same way," he said. "Women were always after me because of my good looks, the expensive way I dressed, and my dancing style. *Coño,* when I walked into a club women asked *me* to dance." When Papi saw Chachito dressing to go dancing, his eyes shone with pride. His son was *un macho*.

The first time my brother came in drunk, Papi celebrated. "He is truly my son. *De tal palo tal astilla*—like father like son." The mark of a true man was his ability to hold his liquor, and both my father and my brother did. Over time, my brother and father became drinking buddies as they watched sports, washed the car, or played dominoes. To others, they appeared sober. I learned to detect when they were not.

My brother's womanizing quelled the greatest unspoken fear of all parents in El Barrio. It proved he was not *un maricón*—a homosexual. Mami, too, encouraged Chachito's philandering, claiming, *"Mejor mujeriego que maricón."* Better a flirt than a homosexual. His coming-of-age impacted the whole family. Mami's deferred dreams of being a nurse were projected onto Chachito. "Imagine Chachito becoming a doctor in a white coat, taking care of patients in a hospital," she said. Papi wanted him to eventually be a responsible man with a family and a job. Papi felt that his son could fool around now, until the time came to settle down.

To please Mami, Chachito had enrolled in a community college, but he rarely attended. He worked part-time at a neighborhood cleaner's to earn money for his clothes and the entrance fee to nightclubs like the Palladium, Hunts Point Palace, and the Park Palace. With his natural charm, he always managed to convince Mami that "the next semester" he would do better and get passing grades. Mami would then persuade Papi to pay for another semester of classes for Chachito. "Imagine our son being a doctor. It will make us so proud," she pressed. Both Papi and Mami brainwashed themselves into believing that their dreams were also Chachito's.

At twenty-two, my brother was interested simply in having a good time and looking the part. On weekdays, he splashed on Old Spice aftershave, purchased at the local drugstore, but on Wednesdays, Fridays, Saturdays, and sometimes Sundays, he used Varón Dandy. His wavy black hair was always freshly cut with a close-cropped, super-precise hairline, and it shone with the sweet-smelling Yardley pomade favored by young Puerto Rican men of the fifties. Yardley pomade was so popular that the guys who wore it were called *negritos Yardley*. The name announced that, although black, they were young, handsome, elegant, attractive, and full of irresistible charm.

Chachito took special care to acquire his slick Palladium style. His gray silk shantung suit glistened like polished steel. The narrow collar and wide cuffs of his gray-and-white shirt were stiffly starched. His golden cuff links shone brightly. Razor sharp, the creases on his suit pants could have cut through butter. Once dressed, Chachito refused to sit or bend, lest he wrinkle his clothes and lose the all-important crisp, just-pressed look.

His preparation for Palladium nights was extra special. He sent his shirts to be starched and pressed at the Chinese laundry, insisting that the launderer place them on hangers rather than folding them. Walking through the door with a bundle of plastic-wrapped clothes from the neighborhood dry cleaner's, he would hang each item up and then carefully select his outfit for the evening. He would allow Mami to press only his handkerchiefs. Placing his clean suits on the sofa alongside his shirts, he played mix and match until he was satisfied. Next, he decided on his socks and cuff links. Last came the shoes. He lined shantung shoes up next to leather loafers and wing tips. With his newly buffed, manicured nails, he refused to do any task that would destroy his look.

At the last minute, he would beg me to spit-shine his shoes to a mirror finish. For this, he offered to pay me twenty-five cents. Because he was in a hurry, without too much haggling I could usually drive up the price to fifty. If I tried to go beyond that, Chachito would complain to our parents, and they'd make me shine his shoes for free. It was their opinion that, as brother and sister, we should not charge each other for favors. "Today he needs a favor. Tomorrow you may need a favor," Mami would say, adding that selfless deeds were always bountifully reciprocated. I knew better—in my brother's case, favors were rarely returned.

But I looked forward to Chachito's nights out. For one thing, I got to help him practice the dances cherished by the young kings and queens of the Palladium, who, by day, were just regular people like me who lived in our neighborhood. On Wednesdays my brother took a particularly long time to get ready. This was show night at the Palladium, when the best dancers and famous movie stars went to the club. Before dressing, Chachito rehearsed the new dance steps he would showcase at the nightclub.

With its intricate, rhythmic call and response steps between male and female dancers, mambo required someone to practice with, and Socorro objected to anything that had to do with helping our brother. For me, the opportunity to practice with Chachito was a dream come true. I craved mastering the dances, and to be as beautiful and graceful as the Palladium girls who sometimes came to our apartment to meet Chachito. If dancing created the incredible bodies and style of Palladium women, then I would commit to dancing mambo, cha-cha-cha, *pachanga*, and *charanga* in our living room every day of the week. The challenge was to mirror my brother's quick, skilled steps, to spin smoothly, twirl gracefully, and fall effortlessly back into the beat, two bodies swinging in sync, responding to an internal *clave* tempo. "Don't move so fast. Listen to the *clave*. You are not in a horse race," Chachito cautioned earnestly. "Dancing is not jumping rope. It is the body responding and playing with the music."

Our living room became the Palladium nightclub. When the music played, I was transformed. Again and again, I repeated the steps my brother wanted to perfect. Stretching my neck, I tried to hold my head up high and to coordinate my skinny body with my constantly moving feet.

To rehearse, I wore my poodle skirt with tons of crinoline slips. Chachito thought I was crazy. "Why don't you just wear your jeans? You're not going out anywhere." But in my imagination, as we danced to the pulsating rhythms, I saw myself not as a schoolgirl but as a Palladium queen.

One night, I twirled too fast and stepped on the toes of my brother's shoes. He stopped me and laid his hands on my shoulders. "Stop stomping, Cotito, you look like you're killing roaches. Feel the music, allow the rhythm into your body. Hear the *clave, ta-ta-ta, ta-ta*. Move with the rhythm, not against it." His instructions sounded like lessons for life. "Hold your head high. Have pride in your body, and move gracefully. Be smooth. When you dance mambo at the Palladium you have to be smooth."

Standing before me, he listened intently to the rhythmic order of the music. My body was overanxious to move, and too often I'd start a step before the right moment. His dark brown eyebrows knitting together, my brother admonished me, "Listen to the rhythm. Feel it. How can you dance if you don't hear the music in your head and body?" Although my heart was racing at top speed, I took a deep breath and tried to relax. "And follow my lead," he added. "The man leads, not the woman. Remember that."

His shoulders loosened. He took my right hand in his left and held it high, near the height of my head, placing his right hand lightly on my waist. Letting the music travel through his body like slow-moving lava, he took a graceful step to the right, hesitating slightly before his left foot followed. "Hear the beat of the music," he said softly, as if speaking to himself. My feet and body followed his. His face relaxed. To my brother, dancing was like going to church.

Gliding right to left on every downbeat, he turned me and swung me out. We turned in opposite directions, our steps mirroring each other's as we followed the beat of the music. Chachito bent his knees slightly and gently moved his shoulders to the strong *clave*, his hips kneading the air slowly with the rhythmic rise and surrender of his legs. I softened my steps, moving my narrow shoulders, tossing my head back and looking up to the ceiling with my eyes almost closed. We faced each other at the same instant. Then, spinning me counterclockwise, Chachito stopped us just as the music ended. My forehead was covered with sweat. Chachito's was dry. "If you dance as if you are floating, you won't sweat. You have to remain calm and collected."

Leaving me to repeat the steps on my own, Chachito went into our parents' bedroom and brought out a full-length mirror. Placing it strategically, he started the record again. We repeated the dance while Chachito studied his every move in the mirror. He smiled seductively at his own image while he moved gently and swayed to the music. His body glided as confidently as a shark's through the musical waters. Leaving me to watch, my brother spun and stopped again with a flair, his arms securely resting at his waist. He smiled confidently at his reflection, a young warrior ready to dazzle and conquer his prey.

"When I show off these steps, people are going to form a circle around me. I'll dance right in front of the band so

I can be seen," Chachito declared confidently as he looked at himself in the mirror. With a smooth, slow turn he came to a climactic stop in a dramatic pose, then slowly turned again.

We had one phone with a long cord, but Mami, unaware that Socorro and I took it into our room for dispatches from the Palladium, insisted that the phone stay in the living room. This way Mami could eavesdrop on all the calls. The phone rang incessantly. Mami and Chachita were always on the line with friends, and they answered a growing number of calls for my brother. Papi sat in the kitchen, reading the newspaper. He hated talking on the phone. "People only use that thing for gossiping. I don't gossip," he said. Even if the phone rang right next to him, Papi refused to answer.

Women were always calling Chachito. He wouldn't come to the phone unless the caller was the woman he was currently interested in. Mami lied for him. She would mention the woman's name and he would signal if he wanted to speak. "Lola?" Mami asked. If my brother waved no, she said, "Sorry, he just left. I don't know when he'll be back." Mami's favorite line was "I'll give him your message."

Chachita enjoyed teasing him and would invent different scenarios. "Your name? Let me see if he is in." She would step away from the phone, and my brother would beg to find out who was calling. He even offered money: "I'll give you a dollar. I'll give you two." Taking the bills, she would tell him the name of the young woman she knew he wanted to hear from, not the one who was really calling. In this way, he'd be stuck talking to a woman he was trying to avoid. Chachita would give the money to Mami and run into our bedroom to hide. We all enjoyed Chachita's tricks. Mami and Papi would howl with laughter as my brother lied his way out of whatever the situation was.

I refused to lie for him. Papi and Mami always insisted on our telling the truth, and I resented Mami lying for our brother when she was adamant about our honesty. I rarely picked up the phone. If my brother was there, I would say so. "I won't teach you how to dance," he threatened. But I wasn't worried. I knew that he had no choice. Mami and Chachita didn't enjoy dancing. I was the only one he could practice with.

Chachito's male friends—Reynaldo, Willie, Hector, and Harry—stopped by our apartment on Wednesdays before going to the Palladium. Young and handsome, they brought a pulse of strong energy to our apartment. From my room, I loved to eavesdrop on their conversations. Like a flock of birds, they stood in the living room bragging of their latest conquests and their passion for stickball. Their loud voices spilled out, making it easy for me to listen in. "Riding that girl was like going to the moon and back," Willie bragged. "You got some of that stuff? Wish I had gotten there first," added Hector. They all laughed and kidded, enjoying Willie's latest conquest. "The way she danced I just knew she would be perfect in bed," continued Willie. "Who was she, the one with the blue dress?" asked Chachito. "No, no, no I was dancing with that one early on. The one with the tight black dress," he responded. "She moved like a bitch in heat." Again they all laughed, talking without mentioning names. The women were faceless, meaningless, with no identity. The conversation, held out of her earshot, nonetheless reinforced Mami's warning to Chachita and me about men. They bragged the same way about their ability to make spectacular catches and home runs playing stickball. Listening to them, I wondered if they were telling the truth or just trying to impress one another.

Increasingly often, Mami admonished my sister to keep her legs closed and not believe everything guys told her. "Remember, men lie. They tell you they love you until they get what they want. Once you drop your panties they will dump you like a hot potato. Use your brother as a lesson. Look how he treats the girls who are in love with him."

Annoyed, Chachita responded, "My legs are nailed shut."

Recently my mother had started telling me the same things. "Don't worry, Mami" was my constant response. Both my sister and I would look at each other, irritated by the innuendo and angered by Mami's double standard. While she encouraged my brother to behave like a "man," she warned us against the behavior of such men. I hardly dared to notice my growing interest in one of his friends, Reynaldo, whose dimpled chin and quiet grace and dignity made him stand out from the other *negritos Yardley.* But I was only a child, I knew. He probably hadn't even looked at me twice.

And what if, like my brother, Reynaldo kept many girls spinning around him like tops?

One evening, Chachito invited a new girl home before taking her out. This was unusual, and Mami, Papi, Socorro, and I studied the young woman with interest from the moment she walked through the door until the moment she left with Chachito on her arm.

In a tight-bodiced, strapless black taffeta dress, Laura looked exquisite. Supported by layers of stiff black crinoline, the dress billowed out from her tiny waist like a beach umbrella, reaching just below her knees. Her open-toed, four-inch stiletto mules were straight out of the fashion drawings and designer magazines Chachita brought home from school. For added panache, Laura wore a small black sequined pillbox tilted to one side of her head. Its blue-black netted veil was sprinkled with rhinestones that reflected glimmers of light and reached to the tip of her lovely broad nose. Fire-red lipstick showcased her expertly applied makeup, contributing drama to the already glamorous outfit.

She floated into our living room, moving her hips sensually. Her bell-like skirt rippled back and forth. The intoxicating fragrance of Chanel No. 5 filled our apartment. Laura's scent shouted, *"Caro!* Expensive!"—a definite contrast to the Evening in Paris my sister and I were allowed to buy at Woolworth's.

More elegant than any other date of Chachito's we'd met, Laura didn't seem as lost in my brother. None of us could recall her having phoned him. When Chachito presented her with a glass of soda, she accepted with a warm smile, holding herself proudly. My sister and I were dazzled by Laura's sophistication. When we learned that she had attended the University of Puerto Rico and was a schoolteacher, we were elated. Here was hope that we, too, might continue our education and achieve our dreams and still be alluringly beautiful. Our parents also approved of her manners and her looks.

After Chachito and Laura left, my sister returned to our bedroom, my parents to theirs. I danced in the living room to the music of Machito. It filled the room, and my limbs. *Zarabanda Changó ta veni, Zarabanda Changó ta veni . . ."* My body melded with the music as I practiced the steps my brother had taught me. An image came to me of Abuela dancing; it combined with the intricate mambo steps I was practicing, inspiring my movements. I played the record again and again and kept dancing until I felt the movement of my body become one with the music.

I positioned the mirror to see myself dance. Finally I stopped, drenched in perspiration. I told myself that I had to move more conservatively to stop sweating, that Changó's blade cut both ways. The self-assured sophistication of Laura reminded me that in order to dance at the Palladium, and to attract a man, I could be smooth as well as fiery.

EIGHT

Amiga Mia

Amiga mía, nadie como tú me ha comprendido.

My friend, no one like you has understood me.

— TITO RODRIGUEZ, "MY FRIEND"

On a warm day in June, the summer before I entered high school, Chachita sat in front of the vanity in the room we shared while I lolled across our bed. In a week, she would be leaving for camp and I'd have the room to myself. A part-time student at the Fashion Institute of Technology during the year, my sister was to spend the summer working as a counselor at a children's camp sponsored by the local Protestant church. The minister had convinced our parents that it was a wonderful opportunity for the young adults of the block to experience working in a totally different, safe, rural environment upstate. The church sponsored neighborhood children from ages ten to sixteen to attend the camp. The minister felt that they would make an easier transition if their counselors were young adults from the neighborhood. Surprisingly, he had convinced Mami, who'd then convinced Papi to allow my sister to take the job.

I stared at Chachita's reflection in the mirror. Her usually pale and morose face was flushed with excitement today, her eyes bright. Her mouth full of bobby pins, she asked me, "Do you like my hair up or down?" Patting the high, flat braid on top of her head, without waiting for my answer she told herself, "Up is sexier." She rose to try on different outfits, hardly able to contain her energy. "How do these blue pants look?" she demanded, showing them off. "Are they too tight?" When I nodded my head yes, she ignored me. "What about this blouse? Does it match?"

From under the folded camp clothes in her suitcase, Chachita pulled a lipstick, a shiny powder compact, and fake pearl earrings surrounded by rhinestones. "Don't tell Mami," she warned, testing the coral pink on her full lips. Parting her mouth, imitating a movie actress, she carefully applied the color and formed an imaginary kiss. Looking coyly into the silvery glass, Chachita moved her head from side to side, checking her reflection from all angles. Smiling approvingly, she held the earrings up. The rhinestones shone in the light. Her eyes sparkled, too.

"How do I look?" she asked. Stunned, I could not answer right away. All year long, Chachita had hibernated, moping around in the loose dresses Mami had forced her to wear since she'd started taking classes outside our neighborhood, her pale skin sallow, her chubby face devoid of expression. With freedom in sight, she was suddenly transformed.

"Beautiful," I told her, amazed by the new person who stood before me. Raising a finger to her pink lips, Chachita dug deeper into her suitcase. Slowly, she pulled out a light pink bra and bikini set embroidered with lace and imitation pearl beads and handed them to me for examination.

"Oh, how soft and silky," I said breathlessly, running my hands over the lingerie and trying to contain my excitement. "I wish I had a pair like these." When Chachita pulled out a fancy bottle of Maja perfume and dabbed some on her neck, I blurted, "How did you get those things?"

"Shhhhhh," she hissed, placing her finger on her lips again. Her eyes opened wide, filled with a mischievous liveliness.

Taking my hand and laying it over her heart, she drew close to me and, swearing me to secrecy, whispered, "I have a boyfriend. He works in a delicatessen across the street from my college." Chachita's skin was alive. She was blushing and giggling. "His name is Joe, really Joseph. He's *un negro*, but light," she added, acknowledging without even thinking about it our culture's ingrained prejudice against dark skin. "He's the same color as I am."

Papi and Mami were not ready to accept that their eldest daughter was growing up. Chachita knew that having even a Puerto Rican boyfriend would be unacceptable to our parents. Having *un negro* for a boyfriend would cause her major problems with Mami and Papi, who felt that it was important to *"adelantar la raza."* "Advancing the race" by marrying someone with a lighter complexion was an unwritten law. Mami somehow ignored the fact that she had married our father and had two children that were the color of rich brown cinnamon. She never hesitated to remind us of the importance of color whenever she could. Whether Chachita's boyfriend was lighter than us or not would not matter as much to our parents as *"que era un negro."*

Chachita glowed, admiring her clandestine gifts. She fluttered around the room, reveling in the joy of her secret, then hiding her treasures again in case Mami walked in.

Chachita's excitement totally transformed her. She had uncovered a part of herself that, like her hidden gifts, was new to me. All I could do was stare. She packed and re-packed her clothes in an old suitcase Abuela had lent her.

The first week that she was gone, I nearly forgot Chachita's secret, so happy was I to have our room to myself. At fourteen I wanted some privacy to dream and fantasize. I was five feet, four and a half inches tall. My size-twelve clothes fit snuggly against the rapidly developing curves of my adolescent body. When I let my hair loose and bit my lips and pinched my cheeks to get them red, faking lipstick and blush, people thought me older than my age.

Occasionally, my thoughts returned to my sister's secret, and I worried for Socorro. Nothing could be hidden too long from our mother. Openly and without apology, Mami often inspected our possessions. She checked our books, drawers, clothes, and pockets without giving it a second thought. In our home there were no secrets. My brother, sister, and I knew that Mami could be relentless when her suspicions were aroused.

Mami could read our facial expressions, tone of voice, and body movements. There was no doubt in my mind that Chachita was going to get into deep trouble with our parents when they discovered she had a boyfriend. The explosion would be even greater when they found out he was *un negro*. Our parents, despite the difference in their own skin tones, were clear and unified in their desires for our marriage partners: "They should be light skinned, have good hair, come from a good family, and be Puerto Rican." There was no thought, for us girls, of having a boyfriend that we would not marry. To remind us of the importance of getting ahead in our lives, Mami would often ask us, "Where are the balls of a dog?" Then she would answer her own question: "Always in the back. Do you want to be like the balls of a dog?"

But my immediate concern in Socorro's absence was enjoying "my" room and cherishing my growing crush on my brother's friend Reynaldo, who filled my thoughts day and night. With my brother working full-time for the summer and Chachita in camp, I had the living room to myself during the day. I played my brother's records constantly and danced before the mirror in the room until my legs buckled from exhaustion.

The first Wednesday my sister was away at camp, my brother invited his friends to rehearse a routine they wanted to show off at the Palladium that night. I was resting on the bed in my new, all-to-myself room when I heard Mami open the door and welcome them. Their laughter and conversation filled the apartment. I immediately eavesdropped, wanting to know who was visiting. The familiar voice of Willie, my brother's best friend, greeted my mother adoringly: *"Mi madre, cómo estás?* You look beautiful today."

"Hijo, you say that all the time," Mami laughed. Willie always profusely complimented Mami, reducing her to girlish giggles.

"Mami, Harry and Reynaldo are also here." When I heard Reynaldo's name, I sat up on the bed.

"How are you, Mrs. Moreno?" they responded respectfully. I listened, hoping that Reynaldo would ask if I were home. In his deep, smooth voice he added to Willie's compliment: "You always look *bella.*"

"Bienvenidos—welcome as always to our humble home," answered Mami. "Come in."

"Is Papi home?" my brother asked as they walked from the kitchen into the living room, wanting to make certain he was respectful of Papi, the head of the household.

"No, he went to buy windshield wipers for the car. He should be back soon. Cotito's the only one here with me," she continued. "Since Chachita left for camp, Cotito lives in that room," she added.

"Good. Let her stay there," my brother commented to his friends. "My sister is a little brat," he called out, knowing it would upset me.

Willie yelled through the door, "Bratty sister, how are you doing?"

I didn't answer but, heart beating fast, continued looking at the fashion magazines I had found under the mattress, which my sister had hidden from me. Mami thought the magazines expensive and a waste of money, but she would occasionally buy them for Chachita.

Chachita would not allow me to read the magazines unless she was present to turn the pages. She felt I was careless and creased and smudged the pages. I lounged on the bed, able to enjoy the fashions free of her control. I envisioned my own image replacing the thin, long bodies and colorless, haughty faces of the models with vacant eyes. None looked like anyone I knew.

In a teasing, whiny voice, Chachito called out, "I'll play the music loud so you can dance in your room. That way you won't step on anyone's toes."

I refused to answer, but I fumed with resentment at my brother and Willie's comments. Teasing and joking, they were purposefully belittling me when I was on a crusade to appear sexier and older for Reynaldo. I could tell they were moving into the living room. My brother's voice rose over the others. "Wait until you hear this recording. Your feet will dance by themselves."

Dressed in an old nightgown, I put my sister's fashion magazines aside. Quickly, I changed into a snug pair of jeans and a T-shirt. I combed my hair, trying to think of a reason to come out of the room without appearing overly anxious.

Mami provided the perfect excuse when she offered the guests freshly made guava juice. She always tried to bond with all our friends, feeling that in doing so she could keep better track of us. Chachita had a few girlfriends who came to the house. Mami would sit at the kitchen table and in a friendly manner interrogate them about school and their families. "Tell me, does your mother work? Who is at home? Your father, does he live at home?" My sister hated it. When they left she demanded of Mami, "Why do you question my friends and not Chachito's?"

Mami's answer was constant. "Because he is a man. You

are a girl. Girls get pregnant, men don't. This conversation is over." Our friends respected Mami and would relate to her as if she were also their mother. She made them feel part of our family. Mami was of the opinion that your circle of friends spoke volumes. "Tell me who you walk with and that will tell me who you are" she was fond of saying.

"Cold and delicious, and just made by Abuela," she tempted, calling out, "Cotito, do you want juice?"

"Okay, I'll be right out," I shouted, trying to sound casual.

Suddenly the walls of my bedroom trembled as the breathtaking orchestral music of Tito Rodriguez rushed through the apartment like wildfire. Tito's mellow voice exploded over the swinging brass riffs: *"Mama Güela, Mama Güela . . ."* My brother always bought the latest records, keen to learn the newest dances before anyone else. The *montuno* caught my immediate attention. This mambo had a different sound, and I was sure that my brother was about to show his friends the new step that accompanied it.

I couldn't hold back my curiosity any longer. The overwhelming desire to see Reynaldo *and* the new dance steps overtook me. I opened the door to my room slowly and walked out, as the voices of my brother and his friends competed for attention.

"Rodriguez outdid himself with this arrangement. Do you believe the swing of this?" asked my brother, talking over the music while his hands moved to the beat of the *clave.*

"Damn, to dance this mambo you have to be in top shape," hollered Willie. Willie was slow-paced, the exact opposite of my Chachito, though people assumed they were brothers since they were always together. His comment was typical. He would rather dance a slow bolero than swing to an energetic mambo. His voice strained over the music as he said, "By the end of it we'll be drenched in sweat. It'll ruin my cool."

When she saw me come into the hall, Mami's eyes opened wide, surveying my outfit suspiciously. *"Nena,"* she said, offering me a glass of guava juice. I took it and walked to the living room doorway, watching from a distance as, reluctantly, she returned to the kitchen to make dinner.

"Just take it in stride," my brother told Willie.

"Don't give it your all until you get toward the end of the record," Reynaldo suggested.

Harry's deep, husky voice interjected, "To dance this mambo we need three clean handkerchiefs. One for our sweat, the other for our dancing partner, and the third for the rest of the evening.

The young men laughed.

My brother replayed "Mama Güela." Their feet slid, stomped, and skated along the floor as they continued rehearsing.

The air filled with excitement and anticipation.

"Let's rehearse the steps one more time," requested my brother. "I want us to out perform everyone with our routine. Line up. Let's move perfectly in sync."

I couldn't contain my interest any longer and walked in to get a closer look at their movements. My living room had become the Palladium ballroom, ablaze with the thundering presence of four virile warriors. Cutting through the air with their accentuated arm movements, their attractive bodies moved gracefully, ready for battle. In their immaculately pressed suits and highly shined leather shoes, with slicked-down, dark, wavy hair, they danced in intricate patterns as their hands moved through the air like swords. Reynaldo, lean and taller than the rest, moved with smooth authority, knowing that his physique was as engaging as his suave steps.

Their freshly shaved faces and trimmed mustaches highlighted their brilliant white teeth and generous smiles. They were attractive, and they knew it. Rich shades of deep tan to delicious chocolate, their youthful, muscular bodies glided effortlessly through the dance routine, evoking the sexual energy of Changó, the divinity of manhood.

Their arms moved above their heads like the open wings of eagles suspended in midair. Tito's voice encouraged them with his throbbing words: "Mama Güela, Mama Güela, Mama Güelona," he sang. The vibrations of the music and their dance steps trickled from the floor into my feet and up my legs. I watched with envy. I, too, wanted to dance the steps of the young warriors.

I studied Reynaldo. His high cheekbones, his cleft chin, and his height, together with his nonchalant elegance, pulled like a magnet. When the record ended, he leaned carefully against the wall, trying not to wrinkle his jacket and to keep the crease in his pants.

My heart stirred, and my body swelled with desire. But I felt uncomfortable, embarrassed by my physical reaction to him. An uncommon feeling of shyness dominated my normal exuberance. I sneaked peeks at Reynaldo, then redirected my eyes to my brother.

Reynaldo's lips parted slightly as he exhaled, trying to catch his breath. Careful not to disturb his hair, he patted his forehead with a handkerchief he pulled out of his gray shantung jacket. The suit glistened softly.

"How will we end the dance? We need to look for a unique ending," he told the others, smiling with excitement.

Chachito suggested waving their handkerchiefs from side to side over their heads. Willie felt they should just bow and leave without ceremony.

"Harry, what do you think?" asked my brother. Harry's complexion was the lightest, closer to what African-Americans called high yellow and Puerto Ricans termed *Jabao*.

"I agree with Willie. Let's just bow and make our exit," said Harry. "I don't want anyone throwing eggs at us," he kidded.

"Reynaldo, any thoughts since you raised the question?" Chachito asked, with all the efficiency of a coach directing a baseball game.

A warm sensation flowed through my body as I heard Reynaldo's name spoken. My brother and his friends, wrapped up in their world, had not noticed me standing quietly in the corner. I shifted my weight to my left foot. Reynaldo caught my movement from the corner of his eye and turned unexpectedly. He looked directly at me. Transfixed by his gaze, I said nothing and remained motionless as his eyes wandered slowly and approvingly over my body.

"Chachito, your little sister decided to join us," he said, turning back to my brother.

"I knew she couldn't resist the music," Chachito answered, absentmindedly returning to the discussion on how the dance should end.

Reynaldo gazed at me even more intently, with a questioning look. Then he nodded his head ever so slightly. Staring directly at me, he walked closer. Reynaldo's movements were graceful and deliberate, like those of a panther.

"I am Reynaldo Mora—do you remember me?" he said with a mischievous twinkle in his eyes. *"Soy el hijo*—I am the son of Reynaldo Mora Sr., and my mother is Morales de Mora. They own the *cuchifrito* restaurant at 116th Street and Lexington." I laughed at his formal introduction. Of course I knew who he was. And the glances we had exchanged tonight had already formed an unspoken bond.

Reynaldo's large, soft hand covered mine. With a debonair bow he asked, "Share your name with me again?" He was playing with me.

"You know it," I told him, blushing as I sensed that this act was an excuse to touch me.

I felt the warmth of his hand caress mine. I do not know if he held my hand a bit longer or if I held his longer than was necessary. My hand felt nestled in his, safe as a bird. There was a moment of awkwardness as we let go.

"Rather than call you a brat," he asked, looking more deeply into my eyes, "may I call you Coty?" My face felt as if it had caught fire. His eyes teased and danced. He said, "I am not as lucky as you. I have no nicknames. Just call me Reynaldo. Okay?"

I nodded yes. I couldn't think of what else to say. Flames ripped down my body. He turned and walked back to the wall and leaned against it again. As the others discussed the ending of the routine, his eyes kept wandering in my direction. When our eyes met, he smiled and shyly looked away.

"Reynaldo, what do you think?" Chachito asked again, turning to face him.

Drawing himself upright and shifting his attention, Reynaldo thought for a moment. "Toward the end of the number we should pull out some of the women we know to dance," he proposed. "That will encourage others to join in."

"What if they don't dance well?" remarked Harry, confused by the suggestion.

Reynaldo responded, "Chachito always dances with Gina, Willie with Margo, and you with Lorraine. They are tremendous dancers. Why would you select anyone else?"

"And you?" asked Willie, turning to Reynaldo. "You float from girl to girl without deciding on a partner. Tonight you have to decide."

Chachito started teasing him: "What about Sonia with the big butt. She follows you like a puppy dog."

Harry chimed in, grinning: "Erica is the better dancer, though she's not as glamorous. Her dresses look like she bought them in kiddyland. So who will it be?"

I was overwhelmed with unexpected anger. My ears were burning. I felt a stab of jealousy pierce my heart. I held my breath as I waited to hear the name of Reynaldo's partner.

"Someone will show up," he said. Quickly changing the topic, he focused on the dance. "We have to decide at exactly what point to end our routine and select our dancing partners."

My brother played the record again. The four young men surrounded the phonograph, listening intently and spinning, extending their hands to no one and wrapping their suspended arms in the air around an imagined waist. Individually, they danced around, practicing steps.

They would never have considered dancing with each other to test the ending of their routine. Suddenly relaxed, I burst out laughing as I watched their solo pantomimes. "Watch out, Chachito, she is going to step on your spit-shined shoes!" I called out. Mami appeared in the doorway. "Look at your son's new girlfriend," I told her.

Mami started laughing too. "Besides Laura, that's the best-looking girl he's invited to the house," she said in between her loud chuckles. "I like her. *Es muy bonita.*"

Both of us kept laughing until our stomachs hurt. "How ridiculous you all look dancing with your arms in the air," I said, forgetting my shyness.

Mami walked back into the kitchen, saying, "They bring more tears to my eyes than the onions." She returned to her work peeling and chopping fresh onions and garlic for the *sofrito*.

At first the four men were startled by our outburst. Their faces registered embarrassment. Just as quickly, though, they began laughing at themselves and started kidding around. "Look at my girl. She's got what it takes," Harry said, gazing romantically into the air. Laughing hysterically, Willie responded, "Man, she looks like a skunk and smells like one. My girl is the one." Carving the shape of an hourglass in the air with his hands, he started blowing kisses.

The living room filled with laughter while Rodriguez's orchestra again played "Mama Güela."

"We're wasting time. Let's finish this," my brother re-marked, all business. Turning my way, he called out, "Okay, brat, come and show us what a good dancer you are."

My emotions high, again I felt a surge of anger and blurted out, "Call me by my name or dance with your air-head girl." I turned, ready to walk out of the living room, but my brother implored, "Cotito, my little sister, *please* dance with me." I looked his way and hesitated.

Willie joined in, fooling around. "Okay, okay you're growing up. We won't call you a brat. Just our baby sister."

Mami, listening keenly from inside the kitchen, came to my rescue, calling out, "Stop teasing her. You don't like it when she teases you." In her voice I heard satisfaction—I was still her *nena,* her baby.

"Sorry, Ma," Chachito responded, loud enough for Mami to hear. Then, in a softer voice, he said to me, "Come, little brat, let me show you this new mambo step."

Although still angry, I wanted so much to stay. I walked over to Chachito and stood next to him to imitate his moves. I quickly learned the slide-and-skate step that gen-tly shifted my body from side to side. My shoulders and hips moved with ease to the rhythm. This joyful, energetic mambo was less complicated than I'd thought. As soon as I learned the step, my confidence swelled, and I happily partnered up with Willie and Harry, perfecting the move-ment and flow of the dance.

But when it came time to practice with Reynaldo, I grew nervous and tense. I stumbled over the steps that had not been a problem when I'd danced with the others. The more I tried, the more mistakes I made. I felt like a clod.

"I don't want to dance anymore," I said, embarrassed.

"Relax, you're a wonderful dancer." Reynaldo smiled as he wrapped one arm around my waist and took my right hand in his left. He whispered into my ear, "You're a beautiful dancer. I love watching you. Don't be nervous. I don't bite." I giggled at his comment and tried to compose myself as he hesitated and then spoke to my brother.

"Why don't we do a slight bop and then slide into the mambo, then bop, ending with mambo?" Like Cesar Romero, the suave, romantic movie star, he spun with a dramatic flair and reached out his hand for me to hold.

"Too complicated!" my brother said. The others agreed.

"We all mambo. This is just another rhythm that we can play with and enjoy," Reynaldo encouraged them. "Let me demonstrate. Coty, will you help me show them?"

"I'm not sure I understand," I responded, afraid to make a fool of myself and be ridiculed by Chachito. I was nervous, yet anxious to feel the warmth of Reynaldo's hands in mine again and that fire in my body.

"Just relax and follow my lead," he encouraged.

Chachito started the record again, seemingly oblivious to the current passing between his friend and me. Reynaldo started dancing at the beginning, not waiting for the section that would end their routine. He enjoyed his mastery and used his body as an accompanying instrument to the music. He teased and challenged me into trying more complicated steps and patterns, moving seamlessly between the bop step and the mambo.

I enjoyed the provocation but controlled my movements, so that I was slightly behind. This let me study him, complementing his motion and experimenting with my own. We moved around the living room with ease. A wide smile covered his face as I returned his challenge.

When we stopped, Reynaldo asked Chachito, "Where did your sister learn how to dance like this? I need a dancer like her tonight."

"I taught her how to dance so I could practice with her. That's why my moves are so clean and precise," he boasted. Then, in a cooler voice, he added, "I don't want any sister of mine going to the Palladium, though."

Reynaldo looked down and smiled. "I enjoy dancing with you," he said softly.

My face was burning. I was terrified to look up and let him see the fire. I couldn't fathom what to say. I responded in a whisper, "I love dancing mambo."

With his hand still around my waist, he whispered seductively, "So do I. And I still hope that one day you'll dance with me at the Palladium."

I smiled and remained silent. The record ended. Reluctantly, I tore myself away from his body and walked back to the doorway of the living room. I hadn't noticed, but Mami had been watching us dance. Her face stern, she motioned for me to go into the kitchen. My joy was quickly trapped in panic. I wondered if my attraction to Reynaldo was apparent to Mami or my brother.

I stood next to Mami in the kitchen as my brother and his friends finished talking and gathered their things to leave. Amid other bits of conversation, I heard my brother tell Reynaldo, "My sister is fourteen years old." My heart sank. I didn't know if Reynaldo had asked or Chachito had volunteered the information to make a point. But how could he want me now?

Mami walked them all to the door. I remained by the kitchen sink. Each of them hugged Mami and said good-bye. Reynaldo, the last to exit, thanked my mother for her hospitality and then looked toward where I stood.

"Coty, thank you very much for dancing with me," he said formally. Disappointed that he was leaving, I nodded and smiled.

Mami addressed him sharply: "I want her to study, not to be one of those Palladium girls."

"I understand," Reynaldo responded in a hushed voice. He left with the others.

Dejected, I said nothing and quickly went into my bedroom. Tears streamed down my face.

That night I wasn't able to sleep. My mind replayed Reynaldo's words and our dance. "I hope that one day you'll dance with me at the Palladium" was an invitation to all that I dreamed of. Did he mean it? And if he did, how could it be possible for me to accept?

During the middle of the night I got out of bed and put on the night-light.

I looked in the mirror and started dancing with an invisible partner, imagining that Reynaldo was holding me. I repeated in my mind all the words he had said to me, and the heat I had felt burned again through my body.

NINE

Voy a Apagar la Luz

Voy a apagar la luz para pensar en tí . . .

I am going to turn off the lights so I can think of you . . .

— VICENTICO VALDÉS, "VOY A APAGAR LA LUZ"

One Saturday morning toward the end of that summer, I lay in bed half awake, my mind filled with romantic images and hazy dreams. I heard the muffled sound of the phone ringing in the living room and wondered who could be calling so early. I glanced at the clock on the night table. It was only eight-thirty. Suddenly, I heard my mother scream out, "How is that possible?" Mami's anxious words pierced the morning silence. "No, no, she must be there," she cried. "You're mistaken."

Startled by my mother's tormented words, I began to get out of the bed. From the doorway, I heard her trembling, insistent voice speaking into the phone. "Why do you ask if she is better?"

Listening to half of the conversation, I pieced the whole together. In a disbelieving, hesitant voice Mami asked, "Are you sure you are talking about Socorro Moreno? No, she wasn't sick when she left." There was a silence while she listened.

"What do you mean she's not in camp? Why are you telling me this now?" Mami asked, her voice trembling as she tried to stifle tears. "She's due home tomorrow from your camp."

I listened, waiting for the long pause to end.

Incredulous, Mami said, "It can't be—*no puede ser*."

Suddenly she shouted to the person on the other end, "My husband and I saw her climb into the bus with the other camp counselors. Where is she? Where could she be?"

With each question Mama's voice had risen to a higher octave, and now she was sobbing and screaming hysterically into the phone.

"How is it possible she is not there?" Mami kept repeating, even as she replaced the receiver in its cradle.

I stood watching her, stunned.

"Where is she? Where? Where?" Mami gave an impassioned wail and rushed into the living room. I followed.

Lowering herself onto the sofa and burying her face in her hands, Mami cried, choking on her tears. My brother was playing in a stickball series game, and he and Papi had left the house early. Alone with her, I felt powerless and scared. Mami's hair, now completely white, was disheveled from sleep and hung to her shoulders. Her once aquamarine nightgown was a faded gray. Against the festive patterns and rich colors of the sofa, my mother appeared disoriented, exhausted, and worn.

"Mami, what's wrong?" I asked gently, already suspecting the answer.

Without raising her head she said, "Your sister never went to camp. How could she deceive us? Where could she be?" I sat next to Mami and embraced her, leaning my head on her shaking shoulders. Frightened, I held on tight. Enjoying having the room to myself during these past seven weeks, I had barely thought of Socorro.

"Mami, maybe something happened to her?" I said, feeling my stomach cramp up from fear.

Shaking her head, Mami said, "We would have heard something by now." Nervously she rubbed her arms and hands.

I was lost. I had no idea how to comfort my mother. Mami was uncontrollable. She rambled and repeated the same phrase over and over: "Where could she be?"

I also began to cry. The warm, salty tears entered my mouth and made me cough. I felt I was choking as Mami's question resonated in my mind. "Where could she be?" I remembered how thrilled my sister had been over the presents from her secret boyfriend. A sudden chill made me quiver as I realized she was probably with him.

Mami cried, "She should be back tomorrow. But who knows?"

"Everything will be all right," I said, knowing that my words were meaningless, that nothing would relieve our mother's pain. I felt my stomach grow tense and my head throb with fear as the thought of my sister having deceived us penetrated my mind.

Mami curled up on the sofa and sobbed. I walked to the kitchen, trying to gather myself as I got a glass of cool water to help calm her. There was no one to call. I didn't know where the stickball game was being held.

Through her tears, Mami managed to direct me: "See if you find any telephone numbers of Chachita's friends in your bedroom." I rushed from the living room and searched under the mattress, in the drawers, in and behind the night table, and in the closet. I found nothing. Chachita had few friends. She kept their telephone numbers and addresses in a small notepad that was always with her. She rarely brought friends home or used the phone. Given her withdrawal from the world, it amazed me that she had attracted a boyfriend.

I did not know what to do, but I reasoned that since I didn't have much information it was best not to say anything. I didn't want to be punished for keeping a secret from Mami. All I knew was that my sister had a boyfriend. I didn't know his full name, address, or telephone number. I remembered only that his first name was Joe and that he was *un negro*. In addition to Socorro's having disrespected our parents and disgraced herself, I knew our parents would be scandalized if they found out that her boyfriend was *un negro*.

My sister had violated my parents' authority as protectors. I went back to the living room and tried to comfort Mami, encouraging her to sip more cool water. She took a little and then rolled up in a ball on the sofa again. In a low whimper she said, "I am a good mother. How could this happen?" I went to her bedroom and took a blanket from the bed to cover her.

I felt so helpless, not knowing how to restore her sense of being *una buena madre,* the role that gave her life meaning. I sat at the end of the sofa feeling sad and guilty. Suddenly words had no meaning or importance.

I thought of asking Justa for help. Then I decided against it, since she was having her own problems with Jimmy, who had dropped out of school. What advice could she give Mami? My mind then turned to my grandmother. Abuela could help. Without disturbing Mami, I slipped out of our apartment and approached Abuela's. Before reaching her door, I stopped a minute to think. What would be the consequences of me revealing Chachita's secret? If my sister was with her boyfriend, Mami and Papi would crucify her for dishonoring them. Mami's immediate reaction to embarrassing situations was "What will the neighbors say?" The same friends who helped protect us were also vicious gossips who would ostracize a family with a holier-than-thou attitude. I hoped that Chachita was with a group of girlfriends, not this new man in her life, because the punishment would be less. But, remembering her elation over the gifts her boyfriend had given her, in my heart I knew she was with him.

I walked to Abuela's door, hoping she might find a solution. Abuela had a way of solving problems humbly, without ruffling too many feathers.

I knocked more rapidly and loudly than usual. I heard Abuela's slippers softly flapping against the floor as she walked to open the door.

"*Mi nieta,* what is wrong?" Abuela asked when she saw my face. "*Qué pasó?*"

"Mami's crying. Chachita has been gone seven weeks

and she is not in camp like Mami thought," I explained, bursting into tears again. Abuela's comforting arms embraced me, and she drew my head down and kissed its top. The scent of tobacco smoke permeated her clothes, soothing me with its familiarity. She rested my head on her shoulder and stroked my back to calm me. I felt clumsy, realizing that I had grown taller than Abuela and it was no longer possible for her to hold me fully in her arms. I was suddenly saddened by my inability to fit into the warm cushion of Abuela's bosom. She lifted my head and smiled as if she understood my feelings.

"Let's go look after your mother. Flora must be shattered, *la pobre*. We must be strong for her," Abuela said, solemnly pulling her door shut for emphasis.

We heard Mami's weeping through the front door as we approached. I opened the door cautiously, and we slipped into the apartment. Abuela walked to the sofa, where Mami was still lying in a fetal position. She gently stroked Mami's head and then placed her hands under Mami's chin. Lifting my mother's head slightly, Abuela told her, "I know you're disappointed. Chachita has acted irresponsibily and will pay the consequences. But you must be strong, ready to confront all that will come as a result of her misbehavior." Abuela's steady strength helped calm Mami. Slowly, she uncurled her legs and arms and lay next to Abuela, sobbing.

Abuela continued: "Children today want to test their parents. They don't understand that they only test themselves and their futures." Taking a bite out of her cigar, Abuela chewed without saying another word. We sat in silence for a long time as Mami slowly gained a frail composure. She raised herself to a seated position, her eyes swollen and bloodshot.

"You are not the first to face this situation, and you will not be the last," my grandmother told her. "There comes a time when children have their own thoughts and act upon them. There's no way of stopping that unless you lock them up, Flora."

"Luisa, you know how I've tried to be a good mother. I'm home all the time watching over my children," Mami cried, begging for understanding.

"My daughter, of course you are *una buena madre*," Abuela said reassuringly. "Now it's time for us to think, to decide on a solution."

Confused, Mami asked, "A solution to what? I don't even know where she is or who she's with. You know how defiant Chachita is, *una atrevida*. In her sneaky way, she tries to get what she wants. That's why I'm always watching her." Mami let out another wail. "I shouldn't have let her go to camp. But I thought it was a good opportunity." As if begging pardon for a grave sin, she added, "Luisa, she pleaded to go. She wanted to earn money for school clothes. You know that at her age girls like to dress up." Mami paused to think for a minute, and her hurt turned to desperation. "I'll kill her for disrespecting this house."

"Don't think or say those words," Abuela admonished sternly. "Words carry power to make happen even what you do not want to happen." Turning to me, Abuela looked intently into my eyes and asked, "Cotito, what do you know about this? Tell us. You won't be punished."

Standing in front of Abuela and Mami, I felt as if I would be punished if I told the truth, despite the assurance. My heart was beating so hard it throbbed in my ears. Tears gathered in my lids, and my lips trembled.

I looked from Abuela to Mami and then back to Abuela. "I really don't know much. Just that Chachita has a boyfriend and he gave her gifts."

Shocked, Mami jumped up from the sofa. "A boyfriend? How is it possible? It can't be." Pacing back and forth, her agitation growing, she asked, "What types of gifts did he give her? Tell us. Now!"

Looking toward the floor, I broke my promise to my sister. "She had lipstick, earrings, and a bra and panty set. Pretty silky ones with lace. Chachi was thrilled that she was going to spend time with him. I thought he was also a counselor at the camp," I blurted. Abuela sat on the sofa, watching Mami pace back and forth. I moved closer to Abuela, afraid of Mami's reaction.

She moved toward me, her hand raised and ready to strike. Her eyes filled with anger. I trembled, realizing as I spoke that I knew more than I'd thought.

Abuela said calmly, "Flora, I promised Cotito that she would not be punished. Honor my word."

Mami stopped herself, covering her forehead with her right hand and her mouth with the other. Tears streamed down her face as she realized that Chachita had probably spent seven weeks with a man. Slowly, the idea that her eldest daughter had committed the sin that she and the other mothers of El Barrio worked so vigorously to protect their virgin daughters from settled into her consciousness. "What a disgrace! She's a lowlife, no better than a street worker, *es una puta,*" Mami cried out.

Showing little reaction, Abuela simply said, "She is not the first."

The three of us sat in the living room without saying much. Mami moaned intermittently. The tears flowed freely from her swollen eyes. Abuela pulled out a cigar and asked me to get matches. I was glad to move, even if it was just for a quick walk to the kitchen and back to the living room. I gave Abuela the matches. The room soon became covered with clouds of smoke from her cigar. Sitting in the strong mist provided us a sense of isolation from one another. I trembled, knowing that Mami was angry with me. If it had not been for Abuela, I certainly would have been seriously punished. We waited for Papi and Chachito to arrive.

They got home late because the game had gone into overtime. Chachito's loud voice could be heard from the hallway, boasting about his winning hit. Laughing, Papi talked about the response of the other team's pitcher. "His mouth fell to the floor when he saw you hit that home run. He even threw his mitt on the ground." They burst through the door. "Where is everybody?" Papi shouted. "Flora, you should have seen your son today—he was magical."

Chachito shouted out, "Ma, every move I made was like a picture."

"We're in the living room," Mami called back to them in a crushed voice.

They walked in, filled with excitement. Chachito was holding a golden trophy.

Seeing the three of us, they immediately grasped that something was wrong. *"Qué te pasa, Flora?"* Papi inquired. When Mami shook her head, he shifted his glance to Abuela, seeking an answer. Chachito just stood there, looking from Abuela to me.

Mami was anxious. Having waited for Papi all afternoon, she attacked him with the news. "Your daughter is a *puta*!"

Although he remained outwardly calm, Papi's eyes registered his confusion. Abuela interjected, "Flora, relax." Looking at her son, she explained, "Chachita has not been to camp. We don't know where she is. However, we think that she is with a young man."

In his dusty clothes, Papi sat down on the cushioned living room chair. I waited for Mami to scold him for this. But if Mami noticed, she didn't care. Papi remained silent. "When is Socorro due back?"

"*Mañana*," Mami moaned.

"Who told you she has a boyfriend?" Papi asked sternly. When I heard Mami's answer, I felt myself shrink into the chair.

"She told Cotito," Mami responded without looking my way.

Chachito looked at me, wide-eyed. "Are you sure?" he said, surprised.

"Chachita showed me the presents her boyfriend gave her," I responded, avoiding Papi's eyes.

Abuela repeated, "She is not the first and will not be the last to act irresponsibly. Let's wait for tomorrow and see what happens." I appreciated my grandmother's calm way of diffusing situations and protecting me from my parents' wrath. She stood up and turned to Mami. "Whether it is good times or bad times, the stomach demands that we eat. Let's prepare dinner."

The following morning, Papi did not go to work. Chachito decided to take the day off as well. All day long, our parents whispered to each other somberly, ignoring Chachito and me. Abuela stayed in her own apartment.

When, in a low voice, I asked Chachito what was happening, he whispered back, "Chachita is in for it. I don't know what they're planning. Whatever it is, I know she'll live to regret what she did." Catching himself, he added, "You're too young to understand." But he was wrong. I did understand what was going on. And without question, I knew that whatever solution our parents devised, it would also impact me, but not him. If Chachita had sneaked around, my parents would assume I could do the same. And they might be right.

All day long Mami and Papi talked in private. The tension in the house was unbearable. Mami didn't prepare food. Chachito made sandwiches for us. Mami and Papi just drank espresso and had a bit of toast.

When Chachito tried to play one of his records, Papi scolded him. *"Estas loco?* How can you think about dancing at a time like this. Turn it off and keep it off."

The house was so silent that I could hear the ticking of the clock. We waited for Socorro's knock on the door. Finally, at five o'clock, we heard it.

Papi and Mami rushed out of their bedroom. Chachito, reading a sports magazine in the living room, quickly put it down. I was drawing in my sketch pad on the floor. At the sound of the knock, I immediately stopped.

Papi gave us a stern glance. "Do not say a word." He walked to the door alone. Chachito, Mami, and I stood a distance behind him. I held my breath and looked at Mami. She fidgeted nervously with her hair and the pockets of her pinafore. Next to us, with a worried look on his face, Chachito leaned against the wall.

"Who is it?" Papi called through the door.

"Me," my sister called back happily from the other side.

Papi calmly opened the door. There stood Chachita, a slight suntan on her chubby face, her new hairstyle contained in a hairnet. Still lost in the joy of her trip, my sister smiled as she greeted Papi. "Please, Papi, help me with the suitcase."

Papi helped pull her bag inside and then closed the door. "So, you're finally home, *hija*. How was camp?" His voice sounded forced and friendly.

"Wonderful," she responded, her voice bubbling with sincerity.

He turned the double lock to make certain the door could not be opened easily. *"Hija,* tell me, what did you do in camp these seven weeks?" he asked.

My sister glanced at the rest of us standing still as statues. She looked back at Papi and a cloud formed over her face. My father never asked us questions like these. It was always Mami who asked about our grades, friends, and school activities. In the evening as she served him dinner, Mami would inform Papi of all the happenings of the day, of his children's interests and our lives.

"Well?" my father probed, his voice strong and commanding. At a loss for words, Chachita remained quiet. Her body, fluid and relaxed when she had first come in, now stiffened visibly. With the door locked behind her and the large, muscular body of our father blocking the path to our bedroom, Chachita was trapped. Tension filled the air. No one dared break the silence.

Finally, unable to hold back her anger and dismay, Mami blurted out, "How could you do this? We did not raise you to be *una cualquiera,* just anyone!" Hysterical, she continued, "How dare you drag the name of this family through the mud?"

Each word Mami spoke shot a bolt of anger through my father. His back seemed to expand with his fury, and the muscles on his shoulders became more pronounced. Suddenly, Papi pushed Chachita against the door with uncontrolled force. Caught off guard, she bounced off it with a jolt. Before she could regain her balance, the powerful open hand of our father crashed against her face. Possessed by his own wrath, he cornered her against the door. He hit her. Again and again, he hit her.

I stood frozen and watched my father, his body coiled like a spring, attack his oldest daughter. It was as if, just in becoming a woman, she had wounded him with a knife. He slapped Socorro again and again until she collapsed against the front door. I screamed for him to stop. He continued to beat her as she slumped to the floor. Mami started crying too and pleaded for him to stop.

"That's enough, Pa, enough," Chachito shouted, pushing his body between our father and sister.

Chachita's face was blushed a deep pink, and her cheeks were swollen. A slight trickle of blood ran from her nose. Her eyes were wide, filled with fear and disbelief, overflowing with tears. But she didn't cry out, which infuriated Papi even more. "Your defiance will sink you," he said as his face twisted with disgust. Papi said to Mami, "Find out who he is. Arrange the wedding immediately." Mami stood crying, witnessing their daughter's punishment without attempting to stop it.

Chachito and I walked our sister to our bedroom. Chachita cried uncontrollably, then gradually calmed down. Surveying her injuries, Chachito asked, "Why didn't you cry out for him to stop? Why do you always have to be so stubborn? Look what it's gotten you."

Chachita didn't respond. She sat on the bed with the dazed stare of a mannequin. I looked at her face and tried not to cringe. Her cheeks, badly swollen, disfigured her features.

"Cotito, come here," Mami called out. She had prepared a basin of ice cubes and a washcloth. Wrapping the washcloth around several pieces of ice, she said solemnly, without looking at me, "Put this on your sister's face."

I took the basin into our room and placed it on the night table. Afraid to touch her, I handed my sister the washcloth. She applied the cold compress, remaining silent. I watched, yearning to express my apology for having divulged her secret, but terrified to speak. Chachita put down the compress and lay on her side of the bed without saying a word. I crawled onto my side of the bed, attempting not to disturb her further.

I was rendered speechless by guilt. If I hadn't said anything, would she have been hit? When confronted by our parents, it would have been her responsibility alone to tell them whatever she decided to say. Looking at the bruises on her face, I knew I should have held my tongue. But what would Abuela and Mami have said if they found out later that I'd known something and hadn't said so?

I broke the horrible silence. "Chachita, the counselor called and told Mami you weren't in camp. Mami was scared and crying. Then Abuela forced me to tell." I held my breath, waiting for her response.

Chachita remained silent for a long time. Then, in a whisper, as if to herself, she said, "It doesn't matter."

I searched her blank face, and she went on. "Sooner or

later, I would have had to confront the situation. I'm tired of being a prisoner in my own house because I'm not trusted. And what's so wrong with having a boyfriend?" I knew what she was thinking. Ever since he'd met Laura, Chachito still had tons of women. Had he ever been punished? Chachita was only one year younger. Why was her life so different from his?

"But Mami and Papi have already determined my future," she went on. "It doesn't matter what I think or want." Turning to the wall she said curtly, "Go to sleep."

But I couldn't sleep as, in the quiet of the night, Chachita tried to hide her crying. She turned on the radio, keeping the volume low, trying to muffle her sobs. In a tender lament, Tito Rodriguez serenaded us: *"Amor, perdóname, estoy pidiendo amor perdóname. Amor, ven bésame . . ."* Love, forgive me, I am asking that you forgive me. Love, come kiss me . . .

TEN

Toda Una Vida

Toda una vida, estaría contigo.

All my life, I would be with you.

— PEDRO VARGAS, "TODA UNA VIDA"

There is a point in every life when a confluence of forces sets your destiny in motion. For me, it happened in my fourteenth year, when everything came at me at once and I was changed, awakened to the harsh consequences of my sister's "mistake," to the power of my own budding sexuality, and to the possibility of a real education. My sister's fate would be sealed with a handshake between our father and a man with whom she had just hoped to find a little bit of freedom. In the pouring rain, a young man would declare his love for me and ask me, without asking, to wait for him. And I would begin my first year at a high school no one else from my neighborhood was attending, a place filled with strange faces and even stranger possibilities. For the first time ever, I would begin to think about my choices.

"Hurry up, Cotito, breakfast is ready. I don't want you to be late the first day," Mami called out to me.

I walked into the kitchen from my bedroom, and the aroma of freshly brewed Bustelo coffee lifted my energy. Mami handed me a glass of *ponche*—a vitamin concoction. *Pan caliente* with *queso del país* and *café con leche* were waiting for me at the kitchen table.

I had been accepted into Music and Art High School for my visual arts talent. Over the summer, Mrs. Segal, my junior high school art teacher, had gradually convinced Mami and Papi that they should encourage me to cultivate my drawing and painting talent. "Marta is bright and has artistic potential," she'd said. "After high school I'm sure she will be able to continue her studies." Mrs. Segal had visited our apartment several times, something unheard of in El Barrio. She'd pleaded with my mother. "Not everyone gets accepted to Music and Art High School. I've had only two students accepted. Marta is one."

Mami had had visions of me turning into a dirty panhandling artist on the streets of the Lower East Side if I went to Music and Art. My father's traditional thinking had been what finally allowed them to agree to my attending this prestigious, specialized public school. For Papi the issue was simple.

"Flora, what's the problem?" he'd told my mother when the teacher visited. "She's going to get married and her husband will take care of her. Let her attend. Cotito doesn't have to worry about working. Do you?" This remark had silenced and embarrassed Mami in front of Mrs. Segal, who represented the professional success Mami had wanted for herself and now desired for her children.

At every opportunity since Papi had told Mrs. Segal I would attend, Mami had tried to influence me to change my mind. "Your father doesn't know what he is talking about. Neither does Mrs. Segal. You need to have an education that leads to a real job. Be a secretary or a nurse, something that allows you to work if your husband cannot support you or he leaves you."

Mami spoke passionately, trying to make me understand the barriers that had held her back, which she felt were beyond her control. With Papi dressing in the bedroom, Mami made her last attempt this morning as I ate my breakfast. Standing by the kitchen sink washing the breakfast dishes, she said, "Look at me. Do you want to be me when you get to my age? Look at the cage your sister has gotten herself into. Do you want to be her? Is this what you want? Is it?"

Defiantly, she turned. Her eyes were filled with long-unspoken feelings. "I could have been a nurse. Look at me, old before my time with no future. Is this what you really want?"

I was speechless. It had never occurred to me to question Mami's existence or way of life, or if she was satisfied or happy with her choices. Actually, I'd never thought about it. Neither had I considered my sister's future. I remained silent, surprised by Mami's declarations.

I looked at my mother for the first time as a woman with unfulfilled and undeclared dreams, an individual with feelings and desires apart from Papi's and ours. Listening to her impassioned words, I had a sinking feeling in my stomach. Since Chachita could no longer do so, Mami wanted me to achieve her dream.

I felt uneasy. This was the first time I was going against my mother's wishes. Chachita's situation had caused Mami much pain and guilt. But to my shock, I realized with adult clarity that she was trying to persuade me to give up my dreams by making me feel guilty about and sorry for my sister and her. Not wanting to hurt Mami, but alarmed that she would impose her desires on me, I explained, "I can be an art teacher. I'm sure I can."

Shaking with emotion, she continued: "I love you, Chachita, and Chachito. I love your father. But that doesn't mean that I didn't want a career as a nurse. I came to New York to go into nurse's training. When I fell in love with your father, he insisted that I stop going to school so we could raise a family, so I did."

Placing more soiled dishes in the sink and rattling them as she worked, she said, "We'd be better off financially if I could work, but your father doesn't allow it. We have to count every penny and still we do not have enough money to make ends meet."

"Mami," I pleaded, "please try to understand that I plan to have a career. Just because I don't want to be a nurse or secretary doesn't mean that I won't."

She continued as if I had not spoken. "Now your sister's adding another financial burden. Her stupidity is leading her to an even worse future than mine, with a man she barely knows."

Mami was speaking as if Chachita had made the decision to marry instead of it being forced on her. "But Chachi doesn't want to get married," I blurted, as if someone else had spoken. Mami ignored me and kept on talking, a technique she used when she wanted to get her way.

"What future does your sister have? This man doesn't even have a job. *Mi hija,* consider your future. What future is there for you as *una negra* in the arts?"

I refused to let Mami confuse my future with my sister's. Mami was trying her best to help us succeed. Her idea of success, however, was based on very narrow views and beliefs. I looked at Mami and tried to figure out the words that would appease her.

I couldn't. "Mami, I'm going to Music and Art High School," I said simply. "Remember, it is also an academic high school. Mrs. Segal explained that if I do well I could go on to college and become an arts teacher just like her, or anything I want. Please don't worry."

Gathering my new loose-leaf book and an umbrella, I quickly left our apartment, terrified that if I stayed any longer Mami would somehow convince me to change my mind. I certainly had my own doubts. But my intuition kept assuring me that I was making the right choice.

As I stepped into the street, a downpour fell as if buckets of water had been overturned from above. My umbrella was no match for the torrential winds. I felt the spray of water against my face and clothes as I tried to keep the umbrella from blowing away. I struggled unsuccessfully to protect the school bag I clutched under my right arm.

As I passed by the neighborhood bodega, I saw Daniel, his usually friendly face partially covered by a floppy hat. Instead of his usual *buen día* he just grumbled under his breath as he struggled to open the lock to the shop.

Leocadia, wearing green plastic bags as a raincoat, dutifully cleaned the front of the storefront church, praising the Lord for His gift of rain. "The Lord knows what he does and why he does it." She repeated the phrase to no one in particular, then greeted me. "Praise the Lord today, tomorrow, and always, *darle gracias al Señor hoy mañana y siempre.*" The rain fogged her thick glasses. Nonetheless, she kept sweeping away the wind-blown trash that had accumulated in front of the church. I greeted her as always and kept walking.

On a day I should have been excited about my own future, I could think of little but my sister. I wondered what her future would be. Would her dream of working in the fashion industry ever happen? To help save for the wedding expenses, she had to work part-time and also attend school. Papi said that once she got married, it would be the responsibility of her husband to pay for her education, if *he* so desired.

Still taking classes, Chachita worked at a neighborhood dry cleaner's store. She spoke little and made herself scarcer than usual, hiding in our bedroom and pretending to do her homework. Caught in the trap of conservative Puerto Rican traditions that can nurture as well as suffocate, she didn't know how to escape.

In the evenings she would share her thoughts with me. "I want to run away," Chachita whispered, "but I have nowhere to go. I don't know anyone. Who would take care of me? This job is just temporary. I can't really support myself."

She wished Papi and Mami would just put the incident behind them and move on. "None of the neighbors know what I did," she lamented. "As far as everybody is concerned I am still a virgin. Why does it matter so much?"

"What about your boyfriend?" I asked.

"I like him. But I don't know if I love him. I just wanted to have a little bit of fun," she explained. "I didn't expect anyone to find out."

Our sister's dilemma and the uneasy tone in our apartment also changed Chachito. He barely spoke, trying to avoid being drawn into the constant bickering that Chachita's impending wedding was causing between our parents. Chachito's attention was directed to his friends and girlfriends. Now more than ever, when he was home he was constantly on the phone.

His sadness for Chachita registered in his eyes. They were no longer full of mischief. No longer did he tease Chachita and me. But Chachito was not so upset that he had stopped going to the Palladium, the Park Palace, and Hunts Point Palace. And his friends still came to the house to practice the magical steps that would distinguish them at the nightclubs.

Reynaldo came to our house on nightclub nights and, increasingly, would stop by to visit my brother at other times. He always found a way of briefly talking to me politely about school or the weather. But his eyes always said more.

When I arrived at the bus stop my thoughts were consumed with the rapid changes occurring to my family and to me. I didn't even notice Reynaldo waiting there. He was dressed in a hat with a brim and a beige trench coat, and his face was covered by a large black umbrella. "Young lady," he said, his deep baritone pulling me from my worries, "can I help you with your umbrella?" Startled, I looked up into his sparkling eyes and handsome face.

"What are you doing here?" I asked, flattered and pleasantly surprised.

"Can I ride with you to school?" he asked politely. "I want to talk to you."

"Why do you want to do that? Shouldn't you be at work?" I responded, suddenly worried. Reynaldo worked in his father's popular *cuchifrito* shop.

"I want you to be the first to know." He looked at me carefully, and for the first time since I had known him, he hesitated to speak. "I joined the navy," he said.

My heart churned, confused. Stunned, I looked at him. "Why?" The draft for Korea had recently begun, but no one we knew had yet been called. Was this how little he felt for me? Disappointment sunk in.

"I'd rather join the navy than be drafted by the army," he said. "I don't want to go, but there's no choice." He selected his words carefully. "I leave in two weeks."

He must have seen the shock on my face. Without his usual smile, he continued: "I want to create a better life for myself . . . and, I hope, for *you*, in the future. I need a trade, a skill. Frying pork fritters isn't going to make it. I don't want to get stuck in El Barrio."

The sound of honking cars, the splatter of rain, and the gasp of the oncoming bus disoriented me. People gathered closer, pushing to be the first on board. I looked at Reynaldo, hoping that he was kidding. His serious demeanor let me know otherwise.

When the bus doors opened, he looked at me questioningly.

I didn't want him to leave. I couldn't believe that in just two weeks he would be gone. "Will you ride with me to the school stop?" I asked, trying to hold on to him for a little bit longer.

Smiling for the first time, he teased, "I wouldn't want to scare off any potential boyfriends." Then, looking into my eyes for a reaction, he said, "Why do you think I waited for you in the rain? I wanted to be with you."

Taking my schoolbag, he led me to a seat near the back and sat down beside me. He nestled his nose in the nape of my neck and took a deep breath. "You smell like Maderas de Oriente. I love the fragrance of sandalwood, and so does my *indio,* my guardian spirit," he said in a smoky voice.

I wondered about his guardian spirit—I knew my Abuela had one, but I had not heard others speak of such things openly. As if reading my thoughts, Reynaldo explained. In a low murmur he said, "My aunt told me about my *indio.* She also told me to use Florida water on my handkerchiefs for protection." Then he added, "My mother and aunt also favor Maderas de Oriente." He smiled mischievously. "It seems like all the women I love wear this fragrance."

"This is my mother's perfume," I said.

"I'll get you a bottle of your own," he said softly, ignoring my comment. Resting his head on my shoulder, he inhaled deeply. My heart momentarily stopped as the familiar fragrance of Yardley pomade filled the air. The gentle scent of mint on his breath sent chills down my spine. His hair tickled my neck, and I started giggling softly, trying to push him away. No one had ever shown me this kind of attention.

"I love your laugh. It's natural, full of joy," he said, refusing to be moved. The sway of the bus pushed our bodies closer.

To calm my beating heart, I looked out the window, which was blurry with rain, and listened to the sound of the falling water. The people on the street looked like strokes of moving color. Stoplights became flashing Christmas lights as the rain's paintbrush created each passing scene. These fast-changing, unfocused scenes reflected my life. The clarity that I had known was increasingly blurred around the edges.

Smelling my neck again, Reynaldo repeated, "Yes, I will get you a bottle of your own." He caressed my hands.

"No," I told him, suddenly afraid. "My mother will want to know where I got it." I thought again of how much pain my sister's deception had caused our family.

"But I want to give you a gift before I leave," he said, putting his handsome face close to mine. "I want you to feel close to me while I am gone." He pouted slightly. "I don't want to leave you. But you know your mother and brother won't let me near you until you're older. Out of respect I must honor their wishes. And I would never hurt you. You know that, don't you?"

I knew he was right. But it didn't assuage the disappointment and hurt of his leaving.

"Besides," he continued, his voice filled with sadness, "things are changing here. El Barrio is getting overrun with drugs. None of us can stay here much longer."

I turned to Reynaldo, looking deep into his clear brown eyes with an unspoken question. I knew that *drogas* were becoming a problem for many of the young men in the neighborhood, and I feared for Chachito and him, too. He read my mind and reassured me.

"Your brother and I just dance and fool around. Drugs are not our thing. We both want the same things. To look good," he said with a flirty glance, "a good woman to marry, and, eventually, a family down the line."

I looked briefly out the bus window—watching people struggling in the rain. A young mother pushed a baby stroller filled with groceries and a young child. An old man hobbled along, walking with a cane in one hand and a broken umbrella in the other. An older woman struggled with a paper bag on her head to protect her from the rain. Young kids ran to school, bumping into anyone who got in their way.

Reynaldo rested comfortably at my side. I did not want to leave him or my home in El Barrio for anything new. I dreaded getting to my stop at 135th and Convent Avenue, wishing that the bus ride were even longer.

My life was changing too quickly. What would be the result? I turned to Reynaldo and nudged him lightly. "My stop is coming up."

"I'm awake," he said. "Just enjoying the softness of your body and tender hands."

We were sitting near the back of the bus. As we approached the stop, he stood up to let me slip out of my seat, then followed me off the bus. On the sidewalk, he handed me back my book bag and then playfully pulled it away and hid it behind his back. "Could I see you again before I go? Please," he begged, holding my book bag out of my reach as we walked down the hill toward the school.

How could I go see him when I knew Mami had her friends spying on Chachita, Chachito, and me? I hesitated.

"Okay, I'll come by your work."

"I'd like to walk you to the front door of the school. Can I?" He smiled, a glint in his dark brown eyes.

"No," I responded, a little too strongly. I had worked so hard and struggled with my parents to get into this school. Now I wanted to walk into the building on my own. "It's only a block. Please understand," I said.

Reynaldo smiled again. Placing his right hand on my cheek, he stroked me tenderly. I felt a warm current travel through my body. Then he lifted his left hand and caressed my other cheek. He bent down and kissed my forehead, then each cheek and, tenderly, my lips. I was thrilled and embarrassed by this public display. But I responded to his kisses, also kissing each side of his face and his full, soft lips. All too soon, he squeezed my hands and turned to leave.

I watched his easy, sensual gait as he walked up the hill to the bus stop, unable to tear myself away. When he reached the stop, he looked back. I saw the pleasure in his expression—he had not been expecting to see me watching him. He smiled and waved, touched his lips with his hand, and blew me a kiss. I did the same, pleased that I had waited. When he got on the bus, I walked toward the school, my heart beating so hard it felt as if it would blast out of my chest.

The morning had been filled with intense emotions that had shaken me like a rag doll. Walking up the steep hill toward the school, I felt overwhelmed by the new road I was about to travel. Without consciously thinking about it,

I started praying to the spirits for guidance. "Please help me do what I am supposed to do. Guide me to think clearly and to select the path I should take. Help me."

At the top of the hill, abundant trees with flamboyant green leaves stood out against the blue sky. The rain had stopped, and the sun's rays filtered through the clouds. The gray stone school stood like a castle before me. Rows of students walked quickly toward the doors, trying to arrive on time. I hesitated for a moment; then, without a glance back, I joined them.

ELEVEN

Hechos ... No Palabras

Hechos, no palabras, cosas que se graban.

Deeds, not words, things that are recorded.
— VICENTICO VALDÉS, "HECHOS ... NO PALABRAS"

Standing before the medieval bastion that was Music and Art High School, I felt a thrill travel my whole body. As I pushed open the massive wooden doors and stepped into the hushed lobby, my heart beat a little faster. Inside, dark wooden beams rose to a vaulted ceiling. Footsteps echoed off the marble floors with a deep-toned resonance. Awed by the building and what it represented, students spoke in muted voices as they walked down the wide corridors.

My first impression was that these students were

intense and interested in what they were doing. They moved with dignity and pride. I was immediately proud of my decision to enroll here.

Students came from all parts of the city to attend Music and Art High School. When I looked around the auditorium it was filled primarily with European faces. Occasionally, a brown or dark chocolate face provided a strong accent to the sea of white.

Walking down the aisle to the section designated for incoming freshmen, I felt as if everyone were looking at me. The unfamiliarity of the environment made me feel out of place. When I did make eye contact with another student, I was greeted with a curious glance or a spontaneous smile. I found a seat close to the front of the auditorium, wanting to make certain that I heard all the information being shared. Three teachers responsible for the introduction to student life at Music and Art stood on the stage.

They took turns talking to us. Like the student body, they were also white. This was the first time I was in a setting where I knew no one and was completely separated from my family, friends, and community.

Mrs. O'Sheredin, a robust older woman with curly bright red hair, identified herself as the lead counselor for the freshman class. Her amiable face was a rosy pink and her cheeks a light mauve. She was dressed in a light blue painter's smock, which she wore over a hunter-green dress. Her shoes were black and shapeless and looked comfortable. I had never seen anything like them, and maybe because of all the big changes that were happening to me, I focused on this detail. Her shoes resembled large cocoons covering her feet. I saw that both the female and the male teachers onstage and teachers in the auditorium favored these. In general, the teachers' casual attitudes and dress removed any apprehension I'd felt about wearing the right clothes. Looking around at the other students in the room, I noticed that the predominant style was casual, arty, and different from the styles we favored in El Barrio.

"You are now part of a family," Mrs. O'Sheredin began. "Today begins your four-year stay at Music and Art. You are partners in making your life at Music and Art a success." She spoke directly to different students in the audience as she paced back and forth.

"You're a team. Together you will learn, share information, support each other in your studies and at the end of the road—or I should say at the beginning of the road— you will move on to college and careers. Music and Art students have careers in all areas, not only the arts. But it is the arts that provide the inner creative eye to succeed." She waited, letting her words resonate. "Once a Music and Art student, always a Music and Art student. You will meet successful graduates wherever you go. Remember, they started here just like you. So welcome to Music and Art High School," she concluded proudly, registering our reaction to her words. Her speech removed doubts and opened doors in my mind that I hadn't even known existed. Mrs. O'Sheredin projected us successfully into the future, not doubting that we would complete college and have prosperous careers. I'd had doubts when I'd told Mami that the school would lead to a career. Mrs. O'Sheredin had no doubts. Now neither did I.

After a morning of low and high emotions, I felt it was safe to lower my guard here.

"Introduce yourself to the person seated next to you," another teacher prompted. "Share your names, where you are from, where you live, your likes and dislikes. Get to know each other."

The girl next to me had bright golden hair and blue eyes. She was chubby, and her wide smile reminded me of Howdy Doody. Her mouth was full of silver metal and rubber bands designed to straighten her teeth. The braces weighed down her mouth and squeaked when she spoke.

"Hi, my name is Lauren Carey. I live in Manhattan on the Upper West Side, at Seventy-ninth Street and Riverside Drive."

"Marta Moreno. I live in Manhattan, too, in El Barrio on 102nd Street."

With a confused frown, Lauren said, "I've never heard of 'El Barrio.' " Her pronunciation mangled the name of my neighborhood. "Are you sure it's in Manhattan?"

Immediately alarmed, I felt my attitude change from cautious calm to one of defiance.

"Yes, I live in El Barrio." I gave the *r*'s a distinct roll as I looked contentiously into her eyes. Mami's words immediately jumped into my head: *"Tú eres una negra*. What are you doing going to a white school? What will you do with an arts education?" What if Mami was right and Mrs. O'Sheredin wrong? "I'm sure it is in Manhattan," I added defensively, annoyed by the question. Does she think I'm stupid, I thought, that I don't know where I live *porque soy negra?*

Glancing quickly over the freshman class, I spotted only four dark-skinned students. Even though I didn't know them, I suddenly felt that I wasn't entirely alone. Accustomed to being surrounded by shades of the earth, I felt slightly more at ease to know that others who looked like me were also here.

We were divided into groups. Mr. Bloomstein, a visual arts teacher, guided mine. A short, middle-aged man, he was dressed in a white, open-collared shirt, a dark blue sweater vest, and baggy chinos. He had shocking white hair, and hanging from his mouth was an unlit brown pipe, which he caressed as he gave instructions. At each stop of our tour he had a joke to tell. Before a closed door in one wide hallway, he said, "This is the dungeon. Anyone who's unprepared is locked in this room." He opened the door and it was a closet full of brooms and garbage cans. We all laughed, releasing the tension we had been holding back. His silliness helped diminish my nervousness.

When I entered the painting studio, I was mesmerized. The room was filled with easels and students holding palettes and brushes, working on large canvases. The space buzzed with intensity as the students concentrated on their creations. Mature and self-confident, they provided a different image than the one I had of what being a good student demanded. They appeared to be self-directed, not followers.

Mr. Bloomstein explained that all visual arts students were required to take studio classes in drawing and painting. My heart jumped with joy as I imagined myself standing at an easel painting instead of sitting at a desk covered with the obscenities carved there by students past, as I had been forced to do in junior high school. The students here wore blue smocks like Mrs. O'Sheredin's. Most had individualized them with appliqués and trinkets and turned them into personal works of wearable art.

"Freshmen will start with introductory-level painting

and drawing classes. Make note of the supplies you'll need," Mr. Bloomstein said. I quickly pulled out a notepad and, filled with excitement, tried to write everything down. Mr. Bloomstein's crystal-blue eyes focused on each one of us as if he were preparing to draw us. He called out a long list of supplies, many of which I had never heard of: charcoal pencils, kneaded erasers, pastels, watercolors, and the appropriate paper for each of these mediums. "Any questions?" he asked.

A tall young man with unruly hair and paint-stained jeans asked, "What number pencils and brushes do you want us to use? What about the size and thickness of the paper? Will we be using oil paints this semester?" I was amazed by his questions. In middle school I had been told what to do and didn't dare ask questions. His list of questions was an education unto itself. I had used only the No. 2 pencils provided in school and an old bristle brush that looked more like the ones used to paint walls. At Junior High School 99 in El Barrio, we used typing and newsprint paper for our drawings and paintings. I had never even visited an arts supply store.

Lauren, standing next to me, asked, "Do we have to buy smocks and do they have to be blue?" Not wanting to appear stupid, I listened and did not speak. We were a group of twenty. Only two of us, another girl and I, were not white. I noticed that she didn't ask any questions either.

Toward the end of the session, Mr. Bloomstein turned his blue eyes on me. "Young lady, what is your name?" I answered, and he smiled. "Did you understand the list of all the materials you are to purchase for class?"

"I think so," I said, burning with embarrassment for his

having singled me out. Did I look confused? Did I look so ignorant?

"If you have any questions, don't be afraid to ask," he added, and I felt better. "Now I'll give you the rest of the day's schedule. Tomorrow you'll follow your full class schedule." Mr. Bloomstein began calling out our names and handing out our new programs.

"Go to your third period class now," he instructed. I looked for the room number of my English class, took the stairs to the fourth floor, and found the classroom.

Inside, when we were all seated, Miss Shaw, a tall, thin woman with light brown hair, gave out the class commandments. She insisted that students stand when speaking. Each word had to be enunciated clearly, and she stressed that our voices should boom outward as if we were actors on a stage. She passed out new English books, instructing us to immediately write our names on the inside front cover.

"I start teaching immediately," she said. "The first day of class is no different than the last." Her dramatic enunciation drove home her point. "When I call on you, stand erect and speak so that everyone in the room can hear you."

My seat was toward the back of the room. I slid down in my seat, trying to shelter myself from her icy gaze, trying to avoid having her call on me.

Sure enough, her eyes found mine. "Young lady." She echoed Mr. Bloomstein. "What is your name?"

"Marta Moreno," I responded nervously from my seat.

"Stand up, please," she commanded, already upset that I had not followed her instructions. I froze. "Your answer is not correct. You must say, 'My name is Marta Moreno.'

This is the proper way of responding to the question." She looked at me with a haughty glance.

"Marta, please start reading from the top of page one," she requested. Try as I might, I could not move my legs.

"Miss Moreno, did you hear me?" she called sharply. I nodded and, gripping my desk, tried to stand. To my horror, my notebook and English book fell to the floor with a crash. Embarrassed, I looked at the mess of papers spread around me and then up at Miss Shaw. She raised her penciled eyebrows, her green eyes wide as globes. "I'm waiting," she intoned.

Trembling, I bent down to pick up my books while everyone in class turned to look at me. No one offered to help. My limbs shook and my heart pumped hard against my chest. I focused on my hands and willed them to work.

Suddenly, a pair of warm brown hands appeared in my line of vision and began collecting my books. The girl was my height, with short, straightened hair. She quickly helped me gather the papers and book and put them on my desk. Then she winked and whispered, "Calm down. The old goat is crazy."

I smiled back in gratitude because I couldn't speak. Tears were already gathering in my lower lids. I tried to compose myself by taking a deep breath, but my knees kept shaking. I picked up my English text and found the first page. My hands wouldn't stop trembling. Perspiration trickled down my face. Hesitantly, fixing my eyes on the text, I started. "Da man said—"

"Miss Moreno," Miss Shaw interrupted, "please begin your reading again."

I glanced up at her amused face and repeated, hesitantly, "Da man said—"

"Stop, stop, stop, stop! Start again!" Miss Shaw shouted. Again and again, she forced me to read those three words. I started to cry in earnest.

"Miss Moreno, I want you to say *the* ten times in a loud voice," she instructed, oblivious to my tears, her voice tight. Holding up her hands and displaying her spread fingers, she kept count.

"Da, da, da, da—" I answered, counting.

"Miss Moreno," Miss Shaw said, anger bristling in her voice. "Place your tongue in between your teeth." Numbly, I pushed the useless lump out from my mouth and held it in my teeth as if it were a dead thing.

"Now say *th.*" She demonstrated, a triangle of flesh darting from her own lips.

The other students in the class had begun to laugh, and Miss Shaw didn't stop them. I was shaking, holding back sobs. My nose ran, and I looked down at my feet. I felt humiliated. Taught to behave and listen to my elders and teachers, I was momentarily paralyzed. The desire to flee the embarrassing situation won. I picked up my books and ran from the classroom, dropping some of the papers from my loose-leaf book.

Shocked, Miss Shaw called out, "Miss Moreno, where are you going?"

I kept running.

As I exited I heard Miss Shaw say to someone else, "Young lady, sit down immediately." When I turned, the girl who had helped me was running after me.

"Stop. It's okay," she called out.

At the far end of the vaulted hallway, we stood close together. She squeezed my arm. "Calm down. The old lady is nuts," she giggled.

Sobbing and scared, I just listened. She handed me a tissue from her purse, saying, "It's clean." After waiting for me to wipe my nose, she continued: "I'm Donna Stokes. I'm a music major. Are you?"

Shaking my head, I was finally able to raise my head and speak. "I'm an arts major." Donna was the color of dark maple with matching eyes, her skin shiny and smooth. Full-figured, her shoulders broad, she wore a white blouse and a dark blue, slim-fitting pencil skirt and flat black ballerina slippers.

"I like your Puerto Rican accent," she said soothingly.

I resisted the urge to ask, *What accent?*

"It's cute," she went on. "I'm going to learn to talk just like you."

Through my tears, I smiled at her, gratitude welling in my chest. This girl had heard me, truly heard me. It was as if a vessel inside me had filled with cool, clean water.

And though it would be hard, I saw that the path I had taken was the right one. With a new friend before me and all those who loved me behind, I would not be alone.

TWELVE

Conversación
en Tiempo de Bolero

Yo era muy joven para amar y no te sabía interpretar ...

I was too young to know how to love ...

— VICENTICO VALDÉS,
"CONVERSACIÓN EN TIEMPO DE BOLERO"

As soon as I walked into the building, I smelled Abuela's incense. I guessed that she was trying to clear the tense atmosphere that, with Chachita's impending wedding and my defiance of Mami, persisted in our family. Passing her door, I gave three rapid knocks to let her know it was me and called out, *"Bendición, Abuela."*

I heard her respond, *"Bendición."* When she opened the door, her tired eyes sparkled. *"Hija,* it has been a while since you visited. I'm happy to see you."

"Abuela, perdóname—forgive me, I have been so busy with schoolwork that I haven't had time," I answered. Following her inside, I noticed that Abuela walked more slowly than usual and with greater difficulty. She placed her hand against the wall for balance. "Abuela, what's wrong with your feet?" I asked, concerned.

"Hija, it's just old age. I'm an old hen," she responded, laughing. "These feet have worked hard. They have a right to be getting tired." Changing the subject, she said, "I'm cleaning the altars. Do you have time to help?"

I hadn't planned to stay long. But seeing the difficulty Abuela had in walking, I would have felt guilty leaving. I nodded and asked her to let me do the cleaning.

"Oh, oh, this is a surprise," Abuela said. "What do I do, then?"

"Just sit and relax and give me directions," I said as we walked into the altar room. I placed a chair next to the ancestral table—the *bóveda.* "What should I do first?" I asked, helping her sit.

Cupping my face in her hands, she kissed my forehead and said, "You fill my heart with joy. Remember when you were little how you sat on my lap? Now it's my turn to relax."

I hugged Abuela and promised, "I'll do some of my homework here to keep you company if you'd like. Is that okay?"

"Hija, you know you don't have to ask," she laughed. "Let's get started. I'll be a queen for the day."

I laughed too, answering, "You're my queen every day."

Pointing to the *bóveda,* she started giving instructions. "Empty the glasses and wash them. Be careful. They're narrow and break easy. I don't want you cutting yourself. I'll tell you how to arrange them when you bring them back. Meanwhile, in the large pitcher pour cool water." Squinting into my curious eyes—she had difficulty seeing but rarely wore the glasses Papi had bought her—Abuela smiled.

When I finished arranging the altar, she asked that I place the white flowers on the floor in front of the table. "Light the candle and place it next to the vase." Pointing to a wooden stool, she said, "Now bring it and sit next to me." Abuela pulled a cigar from the pocket in her apron. "*Hija,* there are matches right next to you. Light my cigar." I took hold of the end of the cigar and, with the wooden match, made a small hole at one end as I had seen her do many times before. I really didn't like the smell of smoke, and I even cringed as I put the cigar in my mouth and inhaled, feeling the heat of the smoke burn my mouth. The bitter taste of the tobacco made me cough. Abuela laughed and reached her hand out for it, saying, "*Dame el cigarro.*"

Abuela commented, "The spirits like the smell of cigars." We sat peacefully, admiring the arrangement on the altar. "A clean, well-cared-for altar also attracts their energy," she added. The small, windowless room came alive with the flicker of yellow light from the candle.

Abuela generally took her time in speaking. When she wanted someone's full attention, she paused for an even longer time before talking. She puffed on the cigar, and the haze of smoke spread out like a soft blanket around the room. I studied the image of Santa Marta la Dominadora and waited for Abuela to speak.

"Now tell me, what is the real reason for this visit?"

I smiled at how well she knew me, better even than I knew myself. Wanting immediate answers, I asked my questions all at once.

"Abuela, you always say that the spirits will help guide me. How will they help me? What must I do for them? How do I get to know them?" Pausing to catch my breath, I continued, "Do they really see more than we can see?"

"And where does all this sudden curiosity come from?" she inquired.

"I just want to know." I tried to be nonchalant, but Abuela quickly saw through my act. I didn't want to disclose that my interest was motivated in large part by Reynaldo's decision to enlist in the navy.

Lying to Abuela, I replied, "A friend at school says she has an *indio* spirit." Feeling my face flush, I mumbled, "I would also like to learn about my spirits."

"Why are you so nervous?" Abuela asked.

"No reason." I fidgeted in my seat.

"Have I ever lied to you?" I shook my head. "Then why do you lie to me?" Abuela asked without rancor.

"Why do you say that?" Caught off guard by her reply, I immediately wondered if someone had told her about Reynaldo.

"Because I know better. You don't have to lie to me, ever," Abuela said, looking toward the ancestral table.

Ashamed, I remained silent. "*Hija,* hand me the Florida water next to the cigar box," she said. I did so and watched Abuela as she reached out and poured drops of Florida water into the nine clean glasses. She turned to me and fixed her eyes on mine. "You are my granddaughter and this family is my life. My love is unconditional. It will never waver whether you do right or wrong. You don't have any reason to lie to me."

"I will never lie to you again, Abuela. I promise," I said fervently, embarrassed at having hurt her.

"Shall we start the conversation again?" She again inhaled deeply, letting the smoke pour out of her mouth slowly. The smoke filled the room as she puffed on her cigar. "Tell me what it is you want to know."

"Abuela, there's a young man who's interested in me. I like him, too. He just enlisted in the navy and is going away. Abuela, he asked that I wait for him. I don't know what to say. I want to. Should I?" I felt my heart pounding against my chest. Speaking about my feelings for Reynaldo was a new experience. This was the first time a man had ever expressed his love for me. It was also my first real attraction.

"You like this young man?" Abuela said, her gaze growing more intense.

"I think so, Abuela."

Amused, she gave me a piercing glance that made me quickly rethink my response.

"*Lo quiero*, I love him," I corrected. Saying the words was a relief. I sat more comfortably on the stool.

Abuela looked straight into my eyes as she kept smoking her cigar. At first I felt chills all over my body; then a warm, calming sensation embraced me. The intensity in Abuela's eyes took me back to Caridad's *botánica*. I remembered how Abuela had cared for Alma's spirit all those years ago. Though my mother had often reported the results of her visits to Abuela, I had never sat before Abuela's spirit. Although a bit uneasy, I wasn't frightened.

Abuela's body gently swayed back and forth and she closed her eyes, smoking the cigar, as her consciousness of herself drifted away. Suddenly, she opened her eyes wide and started laughing. She turned the lit tip of the cigar into her mouth and blew a stream of smoke over me.

"Buenos días si son de día, buenas noche si son de noche," said the spirit that possessed her. Good day if it is daytime, good evening if it is evening. Spreading her legs, she put her hands on her knees and hunched forward. The cigar hung from her lips. Abuela looked at me without blinking. Her eyes examined me all over, then focused on mine. The smoke-filled room lulled my senses.

Abuela reached out her hand, shook mine, and said, *"Shalam Malekum. Malekum Sala. Soy el negro Juango esclavo liberto. Vengo a la tierra a hacer caridad."* I am Juango, the African spirit, a liberated slave. I come to the earth to perform acts of charity.

I drew in a deep breath and nodded.

"Sayita, porque tú me llamas?" Little skirt, why do you call me?

Abuela's image was before me, but within her was the spirit that commanded her body. Abuela's movements were masculine. The spirit spoke with a strong, manly tone.

I hesitated, intrigued by the transformation, accepting it.

"I called you because I want to know my spirit guides," I responded, my voice sounding distant. The smoke was making me dizzy.

"Sayita, tu quieres hablar con este negro analfabeta?" Little skirt, you want to speak with this unschooled black man? *"Yo nunca fuí a la escuela, pero bruto no soy."* I never went to

school. But I am not stupid. Juango spoke in a creolized language, combining African and Spanish words, difficult to understand.

Perched in the chair, he started singing and moving to his own rhythm. *"Congo corama beti Congo cora. Congo corama beti Congo cora . . ."* He continued: "I've come from very far because you called me. There is much I want to say."

Removing the cigar from his mouth, the spirit grew agitated. He said, "I was not consulted on the situation of Chachita. The decision your parents made is wrong. But they're so blinded by their false pride that they won't change their minds. They will lament their decision in the future."

Defiantly placing both hands on his knees and looking directly at me, the spirit said, "Tell your parents everything I have said. I want them to remember my words. They will live to regret their decision."

"I will tell them," I promised, wondering why he was not addressing my questions.

Puffing on the cigar, the spirit continued singing and swaying to his song, *"Congo corama beti Congo cora. Congo corama beti Congo cora, wiri wiri mambo. Wiri wiri mambo."* Surprised to hear the word *mambo,* I paid closer attention to the song. He continued, entertaining himself: *"Wiri wiri mambo, wiri wiri mambo."*

Shifting his attention to me, Juango said, "Now let me talk with you." Again inhaling deeply and releasing the smoke, the spirit smiled mischievously. "I was in love many times when I walked on the earth. Love is good. It gives us a reason for living. It soothes the body and makes it come alive. It stimulates the mind. It makes what is between your legs throb with desire!"

At fourteen, I had never had an open discussion about sex with an adult. Trying to understand Juango was difficult enough, but talking about sex with a spirit possessing my grandmother's body was startling. I was embarrassed by the discussion. Looking at my folded hands, I remained quiet.

"Why are you ashamed of your feelings? Love and sex are part of the beauty of living. If you don't experience them, then you know you've become a spirit," said Juango, teasing me.

"*Sayita*, look at me." I looked up at Juango, who still had a mischievous glint in his eyes. "You came looking to know if this man is for you. Not about your own spirits." Juango laughed, again enjoying my shyness.

"*Mi sayita*, you thought you could fool El Negro Juango." Abuela's mystic eyes, controlled by the spirit, blazed with intensity. "I am Juango. I see more than you can see and understand more than you can understand. Remember, I am a spirit and I am everywhere. I have no boundaries."

After pausing to think, the spirit continued: "This young man that likes you is a good man. He truly has you in his heart. But, *hija*, there are too many obstacles in the way. Too many for you to spend your efforts trying to surmount them. In the end you will be chasing a dream, not reality. This path will take you away from your own path, from getting your education.

"Oh, he is a good man," the spirit said, nodding in agreement with his declaration. "But it will end before you know it. Still, enjoy the moment, enjoy the communication and letter writing while he is away. You will learn from him, but he is not for you now."

The room felt as if it were turning. I listened, trying to interpret and redefine the meaning of each word, refusing to agree with the spirit. How did Juango know that Reynaldo and I would be writing letters? I was still incredulous, not wanting to accept his message. I tried to clear the fog in my head that made it difficult for me to think.

"I want him to be for me," I heard my voice say, as if it belonged to someone else.

Juango responded, "He wants to wait for you. But he needs stability in his life now. He must anchor his life. You are still a child—you cannot be his anchor."

The gray smoke of the cigar was overwhelming. I could barely see Abuela although she was seated before me.

"Now let us talk about your spirits," Juango continued, without acknowledging my heartache. I was devastated and just wanted the discussion to end. I felt the tears swelling around my eyes.

"You have *una gitana* dressed in yellow and blue dancing around you. This gypsy is of two waters. She was a daughter of *las dos aguas*—of sweet and salt water. La Gitana makes you dance. This spirit loves to dance and is never still. She is a beautiful young mulatta, with dark hair and a strong body. *Pinta tu color,* she has your skin color and height. Her name is Rosario del Sol. This spirit solves problems through her movements. She cleanses you when you dance."

Puffing on what little was left of the cigar, Juango said, "Tell me, don't you feel much better after you dance? Aren't your problems soon resolved?" Never having thought about dancing in these terms I replied, "I think so."

Juango said, "You will see. This spirit stands to your left and works her enchantment early in the day. Play music in the mornings before you leave the house. You will see tremendous changes.

"*Sayita,* there is also a messenger from Obatalá, the force of creation. He comes in the form of an Arab dressed in white. On the turban that covers his head, there is a bright red stone in the middle of his forehead. He was a warrior in his time. This spirit controls your thoughts. *Este espíritu no te vende ni te traiciona*—this spirit will never betray you or give you away. He will help you surmount all your difficulties, whatever they may be. He is a spirit that seeks truth and justice. His name is Nacer. Lean on this spirit." I wondered how an Arab spirit could be ruling my thoughts. But I did not ask.

Juango, aware of my doubts, added, "You have been living with blinders over your eyes. Today those blinders have been removed. Wait and see."

He sat back on the chair and waited. Nothing was said for a long while. Then he spoke again. "There is a *conga* that stands to your right. She is a warrior, a *cimarrona,* a runaway slave. A young, beautiful woman with large brown eyes the color of chocolate, like her skin. Her black hair stands out like a sunflower. She has a very strong temper. That is where you get your stubborn streak. You must learn to control your temper. This spirit is a proud warrior and doesn't tolerate disrespect."

"Juango, what is her name?" I wanted to know.

"She carries the name of your great-great-grandmother, María de la O. Place a cup of fresh, cool water daily by your headboard for this spirit. *Ella parte por la primera*—she

confronts anyone that intends to do you harm. She is fear-
less.

"These are your main spirits. They walk with you. They
are always with you. The three are strong protectors and
will never leave you. There are others, but you will get to
know them in due time."

Silence filled the room. Juango fell into a pensive mood.
The stump of the cigar fell to the floor as the spirit shut the
eyes of Abuela. "I said all I want to say for now. I am leaving. Spray Florida water in the room after I have left. Tell
my *casilla*"—my medium—"to go to the doctor. She knows
she's getting weaker," the spirit scolded. "Take some of the
white flowers on the altar and cleanse my host, your
Abuela, when I am gone."

And just as suddenly as he had come, I felt Juango go.

Abuela sat listlessly in the chair. Afraid to touch her,
I waited, hoping that she would regain consciousness. As
if waking from a dream, she shook her head back and
forth. Abuela rubbed her eyes with her hands and then
looked at me and asked, *"Llego Juango?* Did Juango appear?"

"Si, he did," I responded, staring at Abuela. "He said to
spray Florida water around the room and cleanse you with
white flowers. Should I?"

"Yes, do it immediately," Abuela answered. She remained
seated while I completed my tasks. I sprayed the water, and
the floral scent immediately revitalized the room. "Abuela,"
I asked, "how do I cleanse you?"

"Hija, take the flowers from the altar. Spray them with
Florida water and sweep my body from head to foot. Break
the flowers at my feet. Then pour Maderas de Oriente into

your hands and cleanse me again. Do the same thing to yourself," she said.

"Abuela, why must we do this?" I asked.

"To remove the spirits' imprints." Abuela regained her full awareness as I performed the cleansing, first on her and then on myself.

"*Hija*, please clean up," she said weakly. "I'm very tired. The broom is in the kitchen."

I walked slowly, trying to gain control of my unsteady legs. I still felt light-headed and could not fully focus. Watching me clean the floor, Abuelita asked for an account of what the spirits had said. When I told her Juango had said she must go to the doctor, she said nothing.

I was saddened by the spirit's words. I worried about Abuela and, miserable, wanted my dreams of a relationship with Reynaldo to last. Silently, I questioned the spirit's knowledge. What if this visitor had just been my grandmother, telling me what she believed was best? As if reading my mind, Abuela said, "Remember, the spirits see more than we can see. They see the past, present, and future. They exist. It is through the confirmation of their predictions that we know they exist. You will have verification of Juango's words. Wait and see."

Returning to my apartment, I couldn't stop thinking of the messages that Juango had shared. I waited until after dinner, when Chachito and Papi were watching the fights on television. They would scream and holler every time their favorite boxer landed a punch. Chachita was buried in our bedroom, reading.

Washing the dinner dishes, Mami hummed along with the song playing on the radio: "*Yo sé lo que son los encantos de mí Borinquen, querida por eso la llaman preciosa isla del Caribe."* I know the enchantments of my beloved Borinquen (Puerto Rico), this is why they call her precious island of the Caribbean. She seemed relaxed and approachable.

"Mami, I need to talk to you," I said, trying to decide what to say first.

"Qué pasa—do you need money for art supplies again?" Twisting to face me, she kept her hands busy washing dishes.

"No, Ma." I hesitated. "Abuela said I must tell you what Juango said."

Mami, surprised, looked at me closely. "When was this?" she demanded.

"This afternoon," I responded, searching her face for her reaction. "The spirit came down while I was in her apartment." Getting closer so no one else could hear, I nearly whispered, "Juango said that you and Papi didn't consult him on Chachita and the wedding. He says you made the wrong decision."

Mami dropped the plate she was washing into the sink, and it shattered.

Papi called out, "Everything okay?"

"Todo bien," she called back, her voice sharp and bright. Turning to me, she said with a flash in her eyes, "That spirit doesn't know what he is talking about. We have made the right choice, and that's that. I do not want you to mention this again." She went back to cleaning the dishes, clattering them so noisily I thought they would break. Seeing her pain, I didn't have the heart to give her the rest of the message—that they would live to regret the decision.

The *misa* had not resolved my dilemma. My hope was that the spirits would provide a way for Reynaldo and me to overcome all impediments to the growth of our relationship. I was bursting, wanting to share my problem with someone. But Chachita was unavailable, mechanical. She was working nonstop, helping prepare for her wedding by sewing her own clothes and making reception gifts. Chachito, never one I'd share my feelings with, had narrowed his dating field. He was seeing more of Laura, who lived on the West Side, and Gladys, who lived on our block. Matriculated in college, he was one of the few in the neighborhood to avoid the draft. But with many of his friends gone, he was somber and distracted.

Reynaldo was convinced that our budding relationship could be maintained if we wrote to each other. In the short period before he left, I met him several times after school in the Conservatory Garden in Central Park, at 104th Street. I walked along Fifth Avenue to get there, the trees, filled with rich green leaves, were like protective umbrellas over our heads.

The circular garden and pathways formed a beautiful maze, with colorful flowers arranged like a stream of bride's bouquets. The filigreed stone arches were an idyllic location for newlyweds to take treasured photographs. It was the favored spot for Easter Sunday, when families from all over El Barrio took commemorative pictures dressed in their new clothes.

Reynaldo and I would sit under one of the arches, embracing each other and imagining our future wedding. In Reynaldo's arms I was convinced that Juango had made a mistake. I became persuaded that our bond would remain.

What did the spirits know?

I wanted to determine my own path. I didn't want it in the hands of anyone else. Whatever happened, I vowed not to let others determine my future. Not even in the name of love.

THIRTEEN

Que Pena, Here Comes the Bride

Dime lo que tú quieres para mí libertad.

Tell me what you want for my liberty.
— VICENTICO VALDÉS, "TE COMPRO MI LIBERTAD"

Six months after coming home from "camp," five months after my father accepted Joe's promise that he would marry Socorro, a date was set for my sister's wedding. In the weeks leading up to it, she could hardly raise herself from her bed. Each Saturday, to collect everything she would need, my mother headed out to the 116th Street community market with me in tow.

La marqueta consisted of a series of stores tucked underneath the elevated train from 110th Street to 116th Street along Park Avenue. Every time a train rolled by on its way upstate, the stores below shook violently. In the deafening noise, customers hollered out orders and vendors hawked wares that spilled out from the market onto the surrounding streets. From makeshift shops, people sold everything imaginable. Overflowing cardboard boxes lined the sidewalks, piled high with colorful shoes and clothing, jewelry, toys, tropical vegetables, meat, fish, game, and spices. As we walked along the strip, the sweet fragrance of flowers mingled with the stench of raw fish, shrimp, and oysters.

From one stall, Mami bought white satin cloth so my sister could design and sew her dress. "You cut a hard bargain, *señora, no estoy ganando nada con esta venta*—I'm losing money with this sale," the old vendor said, folding the shiny cloth into a bag for her. Mami ignored him, knowing that he was just doing his normal sales pitch. Mami had already rented tuxedos for Joe, who was not working, and for my brother, who was to be his best man.

"I don't want to be the best man," Chachito had argued. "I don't even know him."

"You know your sister—that's enough," Mami had responded.

Papi had bought a new blue suit, refusing to rent a tuxedo. "Why do I want to wear a tuxedo when this is not the wedding for my daughter I'd hoped for?" he declared.

Mami could not reason with him. He insisted that a blue suit would do the job. "Besides, I can wear it after the wedding for special occasions."

My maid of honor dress was a light blue, strapless taffeta borrowed from Teresa. In a pinch, it was easy for Mami and the other women in the neighborhood to forget that she sometimes worked as a prostitute. With her dark mass of hair, buxom chest, and thin hips, Teresa was always asked to be a bridesmaid or to lend a bridesmaid dress. She had a collection of birthday cake–colored gowns in her closet. Mami borrowed the dress for me, and my sister adjusted the strapless top to fit my smaller bust.

From another stall at the *marqueta,* Mami ordered Socorro's wedding bouquet and a single lily with a taffeta bow for me to carry. She watched every penny; her goal was to have enough money to rent a room at the Hunts Point Palace in the Bronx for a small reception. Papi was against it. "Why should we waste my hard-earned money celebrating your daughter's disgrace?" he argued.

"I don't want the neighbors to gossip, Clemente. You know if we don't have a reception they'll think that your daughter is pregnant," Mami argued back.

"Is she pregnant?" asked Papi.

"It doesn't matter. She'll soon be married." Mami refused to continue the conversation.

From a shop on 116th Street, she picked up cheap, predesigned wedding invitations. She planned to fill out the space left for the name of the bride and groom, date, and location. I told her that the invitations looked tacky.

"Do you know how much money we are saving by my writing out the details?" she shot back. "After all, people just quickly read the information and throw them out anyway."

"The invitations are ugly. Look at the paper. And the print is lopsided," I argued, trying to make Mami change her mind. She would not budge.

"I'll have them finished and in the mailbox by tomorrow. The savings will allow us to have a small reception for fifty people. This way the neighbors will think that the wedding was planned in advance and isn't some 'chippy-choppy' wedding."

"All the neighbors do is gossip. They don't care about anything except gossiping. You should be concerned with Chachita and what she thinks and wants," I said, tired of Mami making her decisions based on *lo que digan la gente*—what people would say. At age fourteen I was confident enough to let her know what I thought.

But she ignored me and bought the invitations anyway. That night, Mami sat at the kitchen table and quickly inserted the details. She wrote in Papi's and her name "proudly" announcing the wedding of their daughter. On the invitation she noted that the ceremony would be held at St. Lucy's Church, on 104th Street between First and Second Avenues. In her bold handwriting, she printed out the names of the bride and groom: Joseph Singleton and Socorro (Chachita) Moreno. The next morning, she had me take all the invitations to the post office. I looked at the hastily handwritten envelopes with sadness and promised myself that when I got married, my invitations would be professionally printed. I wanted gold or silver script printed to my own design on thick, ivory-colored paper.

The morning of the wedding, Chachita had no expression on her face. She walked through the apartment in a daze as the preparations went on around her.

Teresa insisted on doing my sister's makeup and fixing her hair. "What is wrong, Chachita? Are you nervous? Don't be. This is your special day, a day that you will remember and treasure for the rest of your life."

Having readied so many brides, Teresa felt herself an expert beautician. Armed with a basket filled with an assortment of eye shadows, eyebrow pencils, lipsticks, and other items, she sat Chachita in front of the vanity mirror in our bedroom.

Teresa's excitement was contagious. She bubbled as she spoke about the types of makeup she had collected. I rummaged through her collection with enthusiasm while my sister sat on the chair, looking at her image with disinterest.

With a hot comb, Teresa carefully curled Chachita's hair to complement the imitation-pearl tiara Mami had purchased. She put foundation and powder on Chachita's face and colored her lips with a soft pink lipstick. Teresa plucked her eyebrows and styled them down with a little Vaseline. Then she lined Chachita's eyes with a soft, dark brown pencil and dark brown mascara. Standing back to look at her work of art, she smiled. "Chachita, you're a beautiful bride. See how lovely you look."

Chachita ignored her, letting Teresa dress her without reacting. Finally Teresa began to realize that something was wrong. *"Qué pasa?"* she asked Chachita.

Walking into the bedroom at that moment, Mami responded, "Oh, she's just nervous. She'll change her tune once the wedding is over."

Looking suspiciously from Mami to Chachita, Teresa became aware that there was more going on than what was being said. She kissed Chachita lightly on her cheek, so as not to smudge her makeup, and said, "I'll see you at the church. Try not to move too much, so you don't sweat." With a quick smile, she left to get ready herself.

"Stop moping and change your attitude," Mami told Chachita. "You made your bed—now lie in it." I sat on the bed wishing that Teresa had volunteered to do my hair and makeup. "Cotito, start getting dressed. What are you waiting for?" Mami scolded. "I need to go and get your father's things ready so I can get dressed." With that, she turned and left the bedroom.

Chachita ignored our mother. She took a towel from the vanity and wiped the makeup from her face. She kept rubbing until her face took on a rosy tone and was wiped clean. Staring at herself, she took a different lipstick from the drawer and repainted her lips. With a tissue, she blotted her lips until they were a sheer red.

I removed the paper twists that I'd used to curl my hair and brushed it out. I dabbed some of my sister's lipstick on my cheeks as a substitute for rouge and slathered a generous amount on my lips. I stepped into the taffeta dress, with its many crinolines, and slipped on the shoes that matched. Unaccustomed to heels, I practiced walking around the room. Watching me wobble across the floor, trying to keep the shoes from slipping off, Chachita laughed for the first time that day.

Just as suddenly, she became morose. "We're ready. When do we leave?" she called out dully.

Mami shouted back, "Ten more minutes."

Finally we walked out the front door. In spite of all the problems connected to this event, there was a feeling of excitement. Rushing around trying to get the dress to fit right had made my spine tingle. I loved the outfit because it made me appear so much older. The heels made me two inches taller, even though I could barely walk. Chachita, in backless heels just like mine, demonstrated how I should hold my foot as, for the last time as a single woman, she left the apartment where she'd grown up. My silliness must have rubbed off on her because, crossing the threshold, we reached out to hug each other warmly and smiled.

Chachita walked to Abuela's apartment for her blessings. Abuela had refused to go to the wedding. Papi tried to convince Abuela again today, but she would not budge. Her faith in the spirits was absolute. She would not sanction any action that went against the desires of her spirit guides.

Justa also hadn't accepted the invitation to my sister's wedding. Her religion didn't allow her to attend churches of other faiths. Instead, she stood on the steps of our doorway and threw handfuls of rice in celebration of my sister's wedding. Her eyes filled with tears as she and her two sons sprayed us with rice while she exclaimed, "Chachita looks like a virgin dressed in white." Jimmy, tall and handsome, stood next to his mother, also spraying us with handfuls of rice while happily exclaiming, "My baby sisters are all grown up." Luis had a wide grin on his face, mimicking the smile of the others around him without understanding what was going on.

Abuela had scolded both Papi and Mami the previous week in our kitchen. Although she'd been too discreet to mention the wedding specifically, we'd all guessed what she was saying. In front of the three of us children, she had reminded them, "When you have had critical problems you have come before Juango to solve them. What was different with this situation?"

Nonetheless, eager to see her granddaughter on her special day, Abuela opened the door quickly. Dressed in a white cotton housedress, her hair wrapped in a white kerchief, Abuela looked Socorro over from head to toe. "I give you my blessings and those of all the spirits of our family. *Hija,* I am always here for you, *tú lo sabes,*" she said as she hugged Chachita. Abuela held a small amulet in the design of an African woman. Looking up at my sister, Abuela placed her hands under the open collar of the bridal dress and pinned the amulet to Chachita's bra strap. "*Hija,* carry this to remind you to turn to your spirits when you have a problem. They are more intelligent than humans." Abuela looked pointedly at my mother as she spoke.

Surprised by Abuela's comment, Mami opened her mouth to speak, but said nothing.

A fleeting smile moved across Chachita's red lips; then she turned to walk down the stairs.

Papi and Chachito were waiting for us at the car. They had shined it that morning and sprayed cologne inside for the occasion. Mami, Chachita, and I slipped into the back seat. Mami wore a lovely iridescent dark blue dress almost the color of Papi's suit. Her hair, rolled at the neck, was a sparkling white. Her high-heeled shoes made her appear taller and more sophisticated.

Chachito closed the back door after us. His tuxedo fit him perfectly. He slipped into the passenger seat without speaking. Papi also looked elegant in his blue suit. His hair was slicked back and freshly cut. They had both used Yardley pomade and Varón Dandy cologne. The car was a parade of scents.

Papi drove us to the church. No one dared talk. I kept sneaking glances at my sister's face. If she noticed, she didn't react. The car moved slowly from 102nd Street to 104th Street. When we stopped in front of St. Lucy's, no one moved. We sat there, wondering what to do next.

Mami was the first to speak. Refusing to say the name of Chachita's boyfriend, Mami said, "Chachito, go see if the groom is inside."

We sat in the car, waiting for my brother's return. It was a while before he reappeared.

"Chachita's guy is there. But the church is almost empty," he said. "The priest is waiting." Looking toward our sister, he winked and smiled, trying to ease the tension. Encouraging her to relax he added, "Come on, beautiful, you look wonderful." I caught a quick, loving glance exchanged between my brother and sister that spoke volumes. He understood her situation. He wished he could help her. Then, in a flash, they reassumed their previous cool dispositions.

Papi turned to Mami, Chachita, and me. "Go and wait in the outside lobby. I'm going to find parking. I'll be right back." When Papi was nervous he always tried hard not to let on, becoming more stern and commanding to hide his feelings. Rather than display tenderness toward his oldest daughter, he fought his emotions and turned distant.

Chachito helped us out of the car and we walked the few steps to the church. I couldn't help wondering at all the fuss about Chachita getting married in a Catholic church when we never even attended. We three children had been baptized at St. Lucy's, and our parents had had Chachito and Chachita make their first Holy Communion and get confirmed. As time wore on, their devotion had waned, and I had escaped these rituals. Yet if anyone had asked, we would all have declared that, yes, we were Catholic.

The air was heavy with expectation, all of us waiting for the others to say what we were feeling. But no one spoke.

When Papi arrived, the procession was complete. I turned to adjust my sister's veil and smooth out her dress. Chachita had designed a very simple princess A-line dress that fell below her knees. Her white satin heels made her taller than usual. In the miserable period of her "engagement," she had lost a considerable amount of weight and was now fashionably thin. Chachita had attached a short veil to the tiara, with tiny white lilies and rhinestones spread around the edges.

When I looked at her hands, they were empty. "Where are the flowers?" I asked.

Surprised, she glanced helplessly down at her gloved white hands. "I left them in the car."

Papi, annoyed, went back to get the flowers. Mami stared at us both and said nothing. A suspicious look crossed her face, and I knew she was wondering if this small obstacle might be an unlucky sign from the spirits to stop the wedding. Chachito and I glanced at each other nervously, hoping that all of these contained emotions would not erupt unexpectedly.

Papi handed the flowers to his oldest daughter without looking at her or any of us. He extended his bent arm so that Chachita could place her hand there.

"Cotito, walk down the aisle," Papi said sternly.

Trying to balance on the borrowed high-heeled mules, I started the wedding party, placing one foot forward and then bringing the other foot forward to join it; pausing; then placing the next foot forward, making a calculated, slow march down the aisle as I had seen other bridesmaids do at other weddings. A single calla lily shook in my hands. I tried to keep my eyes focused on the chapel and not look at the people standing in the pews.

St. Lucy's was almost empty. The unhappiness of our family found reflection in the mood and solitude of the church. Only three of Joe's relatives and a handful of friends from his neighborhood were present. His family did not approve of his marrying a Puerto Rican girl, just as our family disapproved of Chachi marrying out of her ethnic group. Lourdes, my sister's school friend, looked timidly at the sad little wedding party as we trudged slowly down the aisle.

There had been no money for an organist. Without music, the church seemed closed; the wedding party, intruders. Standing at the front of the church in their solemn black tuxedos, Joe and my brother looked as if they were participating in a funeral. Delivering his daughter to the altar, my father watched the ceremony stone-faced. My mother could not hide her sadness as Chachita repeated her vows in a whisper. Although my parents openly blamed my sister for this calamity, I knew they felt that, despite all their efforts, they had somehow failed her.

Joe reminded me of a frightened squirrel. He looked uneasy in the tuxedo, though it fit him rather well. His large eyes were constantly in motion, jumping from my sister to the pews to the priest. His voice trembled as he said his vows.

At the reception, the newly wedded couple were ill at ease. Inside the Hunts Point Palace, Joe led Socorro into the reception room as the guests chanted, "Here comes the bride, all dressed in white." People threw rice and confetti, and for the first time that day, the couple laughed a little. Chachita said, "Where are the beans?" The guests, accustomed to eating rice and beans as part of every meal, enjoyed her joke.

"Kiss the bride, kiss the bride!" the small gathering screamed out, rushing to greet the couple. Embarrassed, Joe turned awkwardly and gave my sister a clumsy kiss on the lips. Startled and unaccustomed to being the center of attention, Socorro turned her face away with an involuntary jerk. Finally, our aunt Moncha, my mother's younger sister, embraced Chachita and, pressing a small envelope into her hand, rescued her. "Put it in your purse," Moncha ordered, winking. "A little something to get you started."

The children who attended with their parents enjoyed Socorro's wedding reception more than anyone. They danced to the DJ's music and ran around the large room playing tag. Their laughter bounced off the walls of the dismal room, filling it momentarily with a welcomed distraction. Parents screamed out for their *hijitos* to be careful, to protect their Sunday clothes, to beware of getting hurt, but they paid no mind.

Sensing the discontent of the wedding party, the adults barely danced. They just sat in their chairs, talking among themselves and discreetly eavesdropping on the sparse conversations of our family and closest friends.

Thrown together less by love than restrictive mores, Chachita and Joe did not even know how to dance together. I watched them struggle to feel comfortable with each other, all of the scrutiny making them even more awkward. They didn't hug, laugh, or try to kiss. They occasionally talked in whispers, apparently oblivious to the inquiring faces turned their way.

The guests formed barriers. The Puerto Ricans congregated to one side, separating themselves from the African-

American guests. Joe's family members and friends sat at one large table, ignoring everyone else.

Finally, Joe's mother, an overweight women in her late sixties, decided to walk over to the bridal table. She wore a black dress with a rose pin at her collar. Her flat shoes were worn, and her large feet spilled over the edges like rising dough. Without acknowledging her new daughter-in-law or any of us, she said to her son, "Well, now, I'm leaving. Are you moving into the room tonight or tomorrow?" We all studied her face, shocked by her behavior. "It would be better tomorrow, because I haven't cleaned it yet." Joe's family lived on the Upper West Side.

Lowering his head, Joe spoke softly. "Mama, we'll be at a hotel for three days. We'll move in on Tuesday if that's okay."

"Where you get money for a hotel?" she asked harshly, without lowering her voice.

"It's a present from her parents," he responded, taking in Mami and Papi in a shy glance.

"Goddamn waste of money, if you ask me. You could have given me the money for food," she replied, not caring who heard.

Her hair disheveled and her words slurred, she looked from Chachita to Joe and said, "Son, you happy with your Puerta Rican gal? She looks like one of us, doesn't she? So what's the big deal?"

We all shifted uncomfortably in our seats, rendered speechless by her honesty.

Santiago, one of our neighbors, had agreed to take wedding photographs with our family's Kodak box camera. Enjoying his importance, he walked up to the table and insisted on taking a family picture, saying, "Let us get the mothers of the bride and groom together for a photograph." Mami and Joe's mother reluctantly moved to either side of the couple. "This is a happy occasion, not a burial," Santiago chided. "Give me a smile."

Mami was flushed and disoriented, trying to function in an obviously disjointed situation. Joe's mother was also scattered and lacking focus, and she clearly wanted to leave.

Like puppets, each took their place and smiled.

"Now the fathers," insisted Santiago, looking around. Papi stood up and walked toward the couple. Joe, sweating profusely, said, "I have no father."

"Good-for-nothing bastard. He should be burning in hell just about now," chuckled Joe's mother, to everyone's amazement.

Amused by Joe's mother's outburst, Santiago looked toward Papi. "Well, let's get Mr. Moreno to take a picture with the happy couple, since he has just gained a son."

Papi, unmoved by the comment, stood next to Socorro and Joe like a mannequin, without embracing them. I studied Papi's solemn face, wondering how he could be so detached and lacking in emotion. His daughter was going through a ceremony that no one wanted to happen, to live in a home where she wasn't welcome. Yet he and Mami stood by and let it all go on. Was this how much they loved her? Or was it that they, too, were prisoners of outdated traditions, prisoners of *lo que digan la gente?*

FOURTEEN

Tecata

Nadie al verme diría, es la droga que sin piedad me consume.

To see me no one would guess that it is drugs that without pity consume me.

— ARSENIO RODRIGUEZ Y SU CONJUNTO,
"MALDITA DROGA"

Sinking languidly against the concrete wall next to the bodega, his knees bent, Jimmy could barely hold himself upright. "Hey, sis, how was school?" he murmured. His sick yellow eyes stared vacantly, and his light brown hair was greasy from lack of care. He wore a stained beige shirt and gray pants covered with dirt from the streets. His shoes, coated with dried mud, were worn and untied. A gaunt face, drained of color, revealed little trace of the once-handsome features of my brother's childhood friend.

As teenagers, they'd gone to different high schools, and their friendship had faded. Chachito surrounded himself with slick-dressing mambo dancers, and Jimmy became a fixture on the block. He didn't dance or play sports. He constantly cut classes and fought in school. Justa didn't even know how many times he had been suspended from school. She often requested that Mami accompany her to Jimmy's school when she received letters complaining of his behavior.

Justa couldn't read or speak English. "Flora, please read this letter for me. I think Jimmy is in trouble again," she would ask humbly. When Mami translated the final letter, it said that Jimmy had been suspended from school indefinitely for hitting a teacher. After that, he dropped out permanently. Justa lost control over him. He lived in her house but came and went as he wished.

Mami tried to soothe her dearest friend, who, deeply religious, felt that God was punishing her. "You know that's not true," Mami said. "You are a religious woman and have devoted your life to the Almighty. He'll provide a solution."

At sixteen I began noticing a change in El Barrio. The popping sound of broomsticks striking rubber balls had ceased. Also gone were the innocent sounds of breaking windows from the force of stray balls and the clashing sound of players falling over the metal garbage cans used for makeshift bases. Now windows were smashed during break-ins and cans clanged when thieves ran from the scene of their crimes. Domino games were taken indoors as street violence became the norm.

WHEN THE SPIRITS DANCE MAMBO   215

Apartment doors were fitted with triple locks, and bats were positioned by those doors to bash in the heads of burglars intent on breaking in. Windows were barred with steel gates that could trap families inside during a fire. Absentee landlords cashed in their building's insurance checks for illegally set tenement fires. The shining rays of the sun dimmed on 102nd Street. In the shadow, the plague of drugs took hold. Jimmy was one of the casualties.

It was just as well that Reynaldo had escaped two years earlier. He had been right about the neighborhood soon being no place for any of us. I sighed, wondering for the hundredth time why, after the first letter he'd sent, he had not replied to the four I'd sent back. Perhaps the spirits had been right after all?

Arriving home from school, I walked in on a conversation between Justa and Mami. Justa sat daily at our kitchen table, crying and asking God for a solution.

"I spoke to *el pastor,* the pastor of the church, and he tells me to be patient. How can I be patient when my own son is stealing things from our home? He says that Jimmy has to give his life to the Lord for his salvation. *El pastor* says that Jimmy will change with God's help.

"But how will this happen?" Justa continued. "Jimmy refuses to go to church. He says that our church is a storefront with a charlatan for a pastor. He'll never give his life to the Lord as I have done."

Mami tried to explain that no one knew what was happening to the young men in El Barrio. "It is part of a mystery that must be solved," she told Justa. In helping Justa and other mothers, Mami was also attempting to appease her fear that Chachito might also fall victim to *tecata.*

Earlier that year, like so many other young men in El Barrio, these *tecatos* had been healthy, handsome, and filled with life. Pretty boys, they had spent their time chasing all the young women on the block. They cut classes, got into light mischief, and drew girls like bees to honey. Jimmy and his crew had projected a manly sexuality that was part of their slick, bad-boy attraction. Chachito, on the other hand, fashioned himself a man about town and surrounded himself with a crew of Machito look-alikes that followed the stellar mambo orchestras. Their reasoning was simple: the best orchestras drew the best dancers and the prettiest women.

Now Jimmy was constantly loitering on the corner of our block or sitting on one of the stoops with a group of friends. Sometimes they would unload merchandise for the bodega owner for a few dollars, then disappear for a few hours and return to the same spot. Over time, I noticed a transformation in their strong, muscular bodies. They became gaunt and looked haunted.

At first the boys using heroin attracted curiosity and attention with their cool, suave attitudes. With time, though, they began to seem odd, then pitiful. These young men had become the walking dead, cut off from the throbbing, healthy rhythm of the streets yet always present, like evil shadows.

In my junior year I witnessed Jimmy's decline daily as I returned home after school. One day in particular I noticed that he had sunk to an all-time low.

Disgust rose in my throat. I kept my mouth shut as I approached the dreadful shadow that Jimmy had become. No longer did he walk proudly down our street enticing young girls. He had become a parasite, trying to blend into the walls of a building until a body walked by. When someone did, he would beg for a cigarette, a light, a dollar, or coins.

"Can you spare some change? I want to get something to eat," he pleaded, dishonesty blanketing his face. He kept following the person until, exasperated, they finally relented.

The high-energy music that had previously set the block dancing now seemed forced, echoing a period that was quickly fading into the past. The block's mambo had been converted into a slow, sad bolero. El Barrio was becoming an abandoned lover.

In an instant, men who started using became strangers to their parents, friends, and neighbors, who, when passing the corner, would quickly walk by, clutching their bags closer, filled with fright, displeasure, and guilt. Quick glances and smiles were exchanged with the sons of friends who were feared now instead of cherished. Friendships disintegrated as parents refused to accept the suspicion of longtime friends or relatives that their sons were *tecatos*.

Walking by Leocadia's storefront church one day, I realized that even her conversation with God had changed. As she swept the sidewalk, she asked herself, "How is it possible that children we helped raise are now strung out on drugs?" Looking to the sky she pleaded, "God, what has happened? Don't forsake us."

Justa, too, was deeply devoted. She was like my mother's sister, our other mother. Without a husband to help her raise her two children, Justa went to church every evening and prayed for all the guidance of Jesus Christ and the Holy Spirit. Her faith glowed through her light skin, reflecting on all around her.

With great devotion, she cared for our family and her own. She brought us day-old bread distributed at the church. On Thursdays she shared her pound box of American cheese, also made available by the church.

Justa willingly prayed with neighbors and friends whenever they had a problem. Prayer was at the center of her being. That year she grew to accept that prayer would not change Jimmy, yet she hung on to her faith, remaining committed to the church.

Justa was at a loss to explain what had befallen Jimmy. "Flora, how can God do this to me? Luis *es un bobo,* he has Down's syndrome, and now Jimmy *esta en la droga*—he is into drugs. I have two lost sons. Why is God punishing me?"

Afraid to offend her God, she added appeasing comments. *"Dios sabe lo que hace*—God knows what he is doing," she sobbed, trying to convince my mother and herself as she sat at our kitchen table, her head in her hands. "God cannot be so cruel as to take my only able son."

Justa was only in her late fifties, yet she was afraid that she would die and her elder son would be left at the mercy of foster care. "If I die, who will take care of Luis? I had hoped that Jimmy would look after him." Every time she worried about Luis, Mami assured her that he was part of our family: *"Justa, tú sabes que es hijo de esta casa tambien."* He is also a son of this house.

Justa could not be convinced. Having dreamed her dreams, she could not let go of the notion that Jimmy should be responsible for Luis if she was called to join her Lord and Savior. Mami would hug Justa and say, "You are truly my sister, how can you offend me like this? If something was to happen to Clemente and me, you are the one that would care for our children, too."

Mami and Papi kept a watchful eye on my brother. When he fell asleep on the sofa, Mami carefully inspected his arms for traces that he had fallen prey to *tecata*. When my parents addressed the growing problem, my brother would ignore them or simply say, "Don't worry, I'm not stupid. You think I want to look like those idiots hanging out in the street? Look at Jimmy. Do you think I want to look like that?"

Chachito loved gazing into the mirror, inspecting every facet of his face and style. He even practiced the way he smiled. No, he was too narcissistic to use heroin.

At night, Papi and Mami whispered to each other in the kitchen. At the very table where other neighbors had come to open their anguished hearts, Mami would update Papi on the news of the day.

"Sonia was here today crying her eyes out. Her son Pepe stole her watch and rings. Last week, he took her radio. She doesn't know what to do. He has disappeared from the block.

"Sonia went to find him on One Hundredth Street, where they are selling that poison in the basements. One of the men there had her radio. So it's true." Mami lowered her voice even further. "Pepe is *un tecato*."

Papi's attentive silence was his only response. Finally, he spoke. "If Chachito gets close to *tecata*," he fumed, "I will kill him with my bare hands. How can a son violate the home of his parents?"

Confused by the sudden change on the block, Mami asked Papi, "How is it possible that we didn't know of this poison and suddenly it is everywhere, threatening our families, killing our children, our hope?" She spoke the words to Papi that she did not say to her friends. A source of comfort to Justa, Sonia, and others, she displayed endless strength, but in private with Papi she shared her fears.

Witnessing Jimmy's transition was frightening. At the same time, I felt a level of detachment as my interest in art and my school activities were drawing me away from the immediate concerns of my block. Although Mami insisted I be accompanied by my brother or sister when she couldn't get away, I was visiting the city's best museums, expanding my definition of the world. I was also struggling to keep up in my classes, having been unprepared for such rigorous academics by the public schools in El Barrio. Despite these struggles, attending a special school had created a false sense of superiority and arrogance in me.

Mami noticed it. *"Tú no eres mejor que nadie, deja esa actitud que estás desarrollando."* You are not better than anyone, so get rid of that little attitude you are developing. I ignored her, convinced that she was just trying to control my growth.

One day, on my way home, Jimmy called me and I didn't respond. "Cotito?" Jimmy repeated. Walking quickly, I ignored him. My back straightened, and I held my head high. Sweat broke out on my hands, one tightening around my patent-leather handbag and the other around the plastic handle of my unwieldy arts portfolio. The large portfolio flapped against my legs with a dull noise as I passed him by.

Slurring his words and unable to control his tongue, one of Jimmy's friends sneered, "You call that tender piece of ass your sister? She doesn't even know you."

"I'll kick your head in here and now," I heard Jimmy respond behind me, attempting to break through his stupor. "Don't you disrespect my sister."

Laughing, his friend jeered, "Shut up. You're fucked up."

As I walked more quickly toward home, their voices faded behind me with a sound like Abuela's Victrola running down. Shame and fear filled my heart. He had been part of our family. Jimmy had protected us as we protected Luis, making sure that he was sheltered from the neighborhood bullies, who teased him because he had Down's syndrome.

Mami would send Luis on simple errands to the bodega and give him coins, which he'd save to give to Justa for church. Luis loved Jimmy, his younger brother, with complete devotion. Sadly, Jimmy's addiction even drove him to steal the few coins that neighbors gave Luis for simple errands.

I had grown to detest Jimmy and his grimy friends, and now I'd begun crossing the street to avoid them.

Jimmy must have said something. The next day when I arrived home, Mami confronted me. "Why do you not respond to Jimmy when he greets you? He's like your brother," Mami scolded.

"He is dirt, trash, an addict! And you want me to talk to him?" I answered arrogantly. "He's scum and so are his friends," I continued, deriding him, oblivious to my mother's rising anger.

"Jimmy is family," she said, her eyes flashing. "And you never turn your back on family."

"No, he is not. Not anymore. He's filthy, a thief, a bum, a good-for-nothing, stealing to buy drugs," I shot back.

Mami's anger boiled over. She raised her hand and smacked me on the side of my face. Stunned, I didn't move as I felt the sting of the first slap, then a second, on my cheek.

"What was that for? I've done nothing wrong," I asked, bewildered, covering my cheeks with my hands.

"Again, I tell you, family is family. You don't turn your back on family. That could be Chachito, Chachita, or you on the corner. We don't know how or why this plague has hit El Barrio or who will succumb next. What I do know is that we have to stay together until a solution is found." Despite her anger, she hung her head sadly.

"Mami, this is a choice," I responded as tears spilled from my eyes. "He made a choice, don't you understand? This is not like catching a cold!" I heard myself screaming out of hurt, rage, and frustration. I realized that I was repeating word for word what my hygiene teacher had told my class about drugs.

Mami had never hit me on my face before. She was quick to scold or to pick up a cooking pan and tap us lightly on the head. But she had never slapped me in the face the way she had hit me now. Staring at me hard, she demanded that I sit at the kitchen table. She sat in the other chair and glared at me, nearly hyperventilating with anger. She looked away and stared at the floor. I, too, was infuriated. My body seethed as I held back my rage.

After a long silence Mami spoke. "Do you know who gave you the name Cotito?"

I stared back at her face, knowing the answer. She continued.

"It was Jimmy. He was so excited that I was having a

baby that he asked if he could name you. Chachito and Chachita wanted to as well, but they were so self-involved that they hadn't even chosen names by the time you were born. Jimmy had. He asked if we would name you Cotito."

I felt the anger in my heart beginning to turn to something else, but I hardened against this shift.

"When the church received shipments of cheese, powdered milk, and bread, Jimmy made certain that Justa set aside a special package for me so that you would be born healthy. He wanted a little sister. He asked if he could name you because you would be his special sister."

Mami's face was covered with tears as she shared her memories. But she didn't remove her eyes from mine. She used every word like a nail. Her stern expression was her hammer as she tried to pound kindness and compassion into my heart.

"When I went to the hospital with labor pains, Jimmy made sure that Clemente brought milk, even though it was unnecessary. Jimmy wanted to see you so badly that your father sneaked Chachito, Chachita, and him into the hospital room against regulations. Jimmy promised to protect you because he was also your older brother."

She paused.

"I am ashamed of you. Ashamed, do you hear me?"

Mami's eyes flared with anger. I recoiled, thinking she was about to hit me again. "How dare you not say hello or good day to the boy who named you."

Mami caught her breath, then went on. "If you treat a person like an animal, they will respond like one. Treat a person like a human being, they will respond as a human being. If they have lost their humanity, you must remind them of it."

Blinded by youthful arrogance, I kept my protective shield up and remained unable to comprehend the meaning of Mami's words. But not wanting to get scolded or slapped again, I promised to greet Jimmy.

The next day, coming home from school, I walked down my block as usual. Jimmy and his friends were at the same spot. Tempted to cross the street to avoid them, I resisted and walked by them instead. I held my breath, hoping that Jimmy would not speak.

"Good afternoon, Cotito, my little sister," he called after me, slurring his words.

His friend responded, "Stop wasting your time. You know she's a stuck-up little bitch."

"Nobody calls my sister a bitch," Jimmy said with clarity and strength in his voice, turning to his friend. The next thing I heard was his fist connecting with the jaw of the person who had spoken. I looked back as the young man crumpled to the floor.

Jimmy staggered, trying to bend to hit the guy again. I screamed out, "Stop! Stop it!" as I ran to Jimmy and tried to hold him up.

Jimmy's eyes were blurred, filled with tears. "I know I've fucked up," he told me. "You're ashamed and embarrassed to speak to me. I don't blame you. Promise me you won't mess up like me. Promise me."

I didn't know what to do. Jimmy was dirty, and his smell sickened me. Looking into his face, though, I could see the reflection of the old Jimmy there, reminding me of the family trips he had taken with us to Coney Island, the knee scrapes he had cleaned for me when I had fallen skating or running under the powerful spray of the fire hydrant.

"I won't, I promise," I said, trying not to cry. But I couldn't hold back my tears, mixed with pity for him and my shame at having been so contemptuous.

"Go home," he said. "Don't worry. I'm okay." He turned to inspect his friend.

"You sure?" I asked, watching his friend struggling to regain consciousness. I walked away as quickly as possible, wondering what weakness or evil resided in Jimmy and his friends that would make them destroy their lives.

Shaking, I entered the house without saying anything to Mami about what had happened. From that point forward, I always acknowledged Jimmy. He proudly boasted to his friends that I was his little sister and that I was going to a special school and would be successful because he and my family were watching out for me.

One week that summer, our apartment was broken into while we were at Coney Island amusement park. When we got home, our door was ajar. Papi went to Abuela's house and got a baseball bat.

He walked into our apartment cautiously, Chachito close behind him. The apartment was empty. Our television, radio, and watches, as well as Mami's Mexican coin bracelet and onyx stone ring, were missing. She started crying, less at these losses than because she was frightened by the first break-in we had ever had.

"Did we forget to close the door?" Mami asked Papi, bewildered.

Papi examined the lock and saw where it had been

forced open. "No, this was a break-in," he said, shaking his head. "Call the police so we can report what is missing."

My parents feared the police, never having forgotten an incident that had occurred soon after they were married. Before Chachito was born, Mami had rented an apartment in a tenement owned by an Italian couple in El Barrio. Because she was light skinned, they'd allowed her to sign a lease and had accepted the money for several months of rent. When Papi showed up to move in as well, the building's owner decided not to honor the lease and refused to return the money.

Papi refused to leave the apartment. He had a lease and a signed receipt for the money used as a deposit. The Italian couple called the police. Papi and Mami waited, knowing that they had all the proof needed to show that they were within their legal rights.

When both couples explained to the police what was going on, the men turned on Papi and threw him down the stairs of the tenement building. The police tore up the lease in Mami's face and told her to leave. When she asked for her deposit, the police took the owners' side, claiming that the Italian couple deserved the money as payment for the trouble my parents had caused.

In response to Papi's suggestion that she call the police now, Mami panicked. *"Estas loco*—are you crazy? Call the police? Don't you remember what they did?"

Angrily, Papi responded, "Well, we have to call them now." Turning to me, he ordered, "You call." As always, I obeyed.

While Mami, Chachito, and I sat in the kitchen waiting for the police, Papi went to the hardware store to buy a new lock. We waited four hours before the police showed up.

Finally, two white policemen came to our door. Taller and larger than Papi, they overwhelmed our small kitchen with their bodies and uniforms. They asked what had happened, and Papi began to explain.

Mami and I were still crying, frightened by the idea that someone had taken things from our home.

"What if they come back?" Mami asked.

"We could get killed in our sleep," I added.

The officers regarded us without sympathy.

Papi spoke again in his thick accent, causing the officers to look at him in confusion. Papi turned to me and asked that I explain.

"We came home and the door was open. Some of our things are missing," I said.

"What's missing?" One of the officers took out a pad and asked for details. In less than fifteen minutes, they were out the door. "We'll inform you if we find anything," one said, on leaving. "Make sure you change the lock."

Mami and Chachita called the precinct the next day to see if any of the items had been located. Upset by the police department's lack of interest, she gave up all hope of having her treasured onyx ring returned.

A cloud of vulnerability had entered our home with the thief. Papi placed a double lock on the door and demanded that we always keep it secured. On Saturdays when we spiritually cleansed the area in front of our door, we never kept the door open anymore. The custom of greeting and gossiping with neighbors also disappeared. The feeling of being imprisoned crept into our lives.

Mami sought out Jimmy.

She told him about the break-in, wondering if he knew anything about it. He told her he knew nothing. But he promised Mami he would find out who had broken in. It took him only a day.

That evening we heard a loud knock on the door. "Doña Flora, it's me, Jimmy."

Mami opened the door cautiously, as had now become her practice. She did this with everybody, including us. Papi had installed a lock with a chain that allowed us to look without fully opening the door.

When I heard it was Jimmy I left my bedroom and walked into the kitchen to hear what he had to say. He stood by the open door.

"I have some of the things that were taken. Others were already sold," he said apologetically.

"Where did you get them?" Mami asked. "Do you know who took them?"

After a long pause, he said, "I can't tell you that." He trembled as he stood there, his hands unsteady, holding Papi's watch and Mami's onyx ring. All the other items were gone.

Jimmy handed the things to Mami without looking at her face. "I'm sorry I wasn't able to find the other stuff." Shuffling his feet, he kept his eyes down. "If I see them, I will get them back, I promise."

Wiping his runny nose on his sleeve, jittery and impatient, he stood before my mother. Mami looked at him, her eyes watery and filled with sympathy.

"Clemente will be happy to have his watch. Thank you for also finding my ring," she said with tenderness.

Jimmy didn't move. He seemed to be waiting for something.

Mami suddenly realized what it was. "Do I owe you money for having retrieved our things?"

Without looking at Mami or me, Jimmy said, "Yes, I had to buy those items to return them to you. It was twenty dollars."

Mami looked at him and put her hand on his chin. She lifted his head so that he was looking directly into her eyes. "I don't have the money. I'll ask Clemente for it. Come this evening and he will give it to you."

Jimmy never came back.

A month later, Jimmy died in one of the basements on One Hundredth Street. Left abandoned, his body had swelled until he was almost unrecognizable. The slim, handsome features that had once enticed young girls on the block were puffy and distorted.

Justa did not have money to bury her son. The Pentecostal church members made donations, but the amount raised was insufficient to cover the burial expenses. Papi and Mami put in money, and Mami collected door-to-door to help with the burial. Carrying a tin can covered with Jimmy's photograph, Mami walked from building to building collecting money until the needed sum was gathered.

At the burial ceremony the pastor addressed us. "We have had to make many collections to bury our young. This year alone we have collected money to bury three of our sons. Jimmy is the fourth. We are a poor church with little savings. It embarrasses me that we couldn't raise all the money to help our *hermana* Justa."

Justa, dressed in black, sat in the front pew accompanied by our family. She rested in Mami's arms, crying uncontrollably. Mami tried to be strong, but she couldn't hold back her pain. None of us could. Not even Papi.

The simple coffin was almost too small to hold Jimmy's swollen body. Unlike the other mothers who had lost their sons to drugs, Justa had insisted on an open casket.

Most parents, scared and embarrassed, spoke secretly about the problem, behind closed doors. Others sent their children to Puerto Rico, hoping that removal from the neighborhood and being with their strong family members in the healing mountains of the island would cause their sons to kick the habit, just as young women were sent to Puerto Rico to hide their unwanted pregnancies. In this way, shameful secrets remained hidden from neighbors.

But Justa wanted everyone to bear witness to the devastation that *tecata* had waged on her son. With this casket, she made an open declaration, bringing to public light the destruction that drugs were causing to families and to El Barrio.

Mami bought the floral arrangement in honor of Jimmy that was placed on our tenement's front door, letting the community know that we had lost a family member.

Papi argued, "If Justa has no money, why should we waste ours on flowers? I'd rather give her more money for food."

Mami wanted Justa to see her son buried with all the traditional niceties. "Justa deserves this for her youngest son, and he does, too. She can eat from our kitchen, as will Luis."

A large arrangement of white carnations hung on the

entrance to our building until the flowers turned brown and the petals began falling on the steps. Justa wanted the flowers to remain as long as possible as a reminder to the young people on the block that *tecata* was a death sentence.

The ribbon read, "To Jimmy from your family. May you rest in peace."

FIFTEEN

De Qué Color Son Tus Bembas

"De qué color son tus bembas?" "Bembas colora!"

"What color are your lips?" "Red is the color of my lips!"
— CELIA CRUZ, "DE QUÉ COLOR SON TUS BEMBAS"

At the end of my junior year, Chachito surprised me by buying tickets for himself, Socorro, and me to a show of Palladium greats at the Apollo Theater at 125th Street in West Harlem. I was thrilled, and saw it as reward for having passed all my classes with decent grades. But Chachita, tied to her husband in an unhappy marriage, refused to go. To my astonishment, my mother allowed me to attend my first concert ever with Chachito as chaperone. Here was a small sign that Mami and Papi were loosening up and letting go of their outdated ways.

My brother, too, was changing. Laura, the belle of the Palladium, was pregnant. He was soon to be a father and a husband.

I was still not allowed to date. But with Reynaldo mysteriously disappeared from my life—I had begun to suspect that Mami had intercepted our letters—my in-school flirtations with two young Puerto Rican men, Rolando and Tommy, had begun to grow.

Rolando had *café con leche* skin and smooth hair combed so that one black lock slid down the center of his forehead. Unlike the other boys at school, who dressed in the standard artist uniform of white T-shirt and light beige chinos or jeans, Rolando wore aftershave lotion and silky suits and ties. His flashing smile spoke of mischief, and I knew he was the type of guy that mothers warned their daughters to stay away from.

One day, as we waited for Mr. Bloomstein to get to class, he approached me.

"Mami, your strong, muscular legs tell me that you know how to dance," he remarked.

"Whether I dance or not is none of your business," I shot back, arranging my painting supplies. I could feel Rolando's eyes clinging to me, examining the shape of my body. I had watched him eye other girls in the hallway. His heat radiated, sending warm, sympathetic vibrations up and down my body. The fragrance of his Brut cologne lingered around my work space.

"Why are you ignoring me, mami? I just want to get to know you," he murmured playfully. "After all, we're in the same class."

"The term is almost over. You should know by now that my name is not 'mami,' " I snapped.

Laughing, Rolando came closer and pulled up a seat next to me. Feigning annoyance, I turned around and asked, "What do you want?"

"The talent show is coming up, and I want to know," he crooned, his dark eyes locking on mine, *"bailas mambo?"* Do you mambo?

I looked at his face, searching for a joke. "Why?" I asked skeptically. "Do you?"

"I live at the Palladium," he responded, reaching out and gently stroking my arm.

"You're lying," I said, lifting his hand and placing it back in his lap. "They won't let you into the Palladium. You're too young."

He looked at me calmly, his eyes traveling up and down my body. "I'll show you right here and now that I'm not lying," he said, standing and pulling me out of the chair and into his arms. I was shocked and pulled back.

"Have you gone crazy?" I said, annoyed yet flattered.

Bowing, he extended his hand and asked, "Miss Moreno, may I have this dance?"

Enjoying the attention, I said, "Yes."

In a husky voice, his mouth close to my ear, Rolando sang, *"Changó ta venir, Changó ta veni, con el machete en la mano, tierra va temblar . . ."* Immediately, almost against my will, our bodies fell into rhythmic step. He kept the beat, imitating Machito's voice, and wrapped his arm around my waist, drawing me so close I could feel the ripples of his body. Then, comfortable with our rhythm, he swung me out and twirled me like a spinning top, dancing around me and bending at the waist, his shoulders grinding to the silent beat that pulsed between us. Completing my turns, I again fell into step with him as he swooped me into his arms. He guided us into a counterturn and then to a dramatic stop. Rolando dipped me low, his arm wrapped firmly around my waist. My heart leapt to my throat. Despite myself, I smiled.

"Marta, my sweet thing. We got it made," he whispered, smiling broadly as he raised my body from the dip. What he didn't know was that my mother would never consent to my dancing mambo in public.

Tommy, by contrast, looked like he had stepped out of a Hawaiian suntan advertisement: tall, with thick black hair and a deep golden tan. He was also an incredibly talented visual artist, his artwork winning the admiration of both the teachers and the other students. He was in most of my arts classes, and we'd quickly become good friends. The only problem was that he couldn't dance. He had two left feet.

Date or no date, I was thrilled to have the opportunity to see the artists I adored from their records and listened to on the telephone—it was almost a dream come true. If I couldn't dance to their music at the Palladium, then the Apollo would have to do.

It took me several hours to select an outfit. I readied myself as if I were really going to the Palladium. I turned my closet and drawers upside down looking for the perfect combination. Finally I settled on my new gray felt circle skirt with a poodle-and-chain design, a shiny pink blouse, and pewter ballerina slippers. I tightly buckled a wide, shiny plastic black belt around my thin waist. I combed by hair into a ponytail with an adornment that had two pink imitation-fur balls the size of Spaldings at its end. They bounced around when I moved my head.

"Cotito, what's taking you so long? The show's at seven," my brother shouted from the kitchen.

"Hold your horses. I'm ready," I hollered as I finished putting Vaseline around the front of my head and my ponytail so that my hair would glisten. I even put on a little lipstick my sister had given me. Fluffing out my bell-shaped skirt, I looked in the mirror approvingly, then made my entrance.

Papi, sitting at the kitchen table, looked up and smiled. *"Hija,* you look so grown up." Mami, collecting the dinner dishes from the table, turned around and opened her eyes wide, focusing on my lips. "And where did you get that lipstick?" she demanded.

"Chachita gave it to me."

Caught off guard at the mention of my sister, for whose unhappiness Mami felt responsible, she nodded. *"Esta bien.* A little lipstick is okay."

Anxious to leave, Chachito was already standing by the front door. He was immaculately dressed in one of his dark blue cardigan-style shantung suits. The suit jacket had no collar or lapels, and the baby-blue shirt he wore was accented with a pencil-thin, navy blue tie. He had on custom-made shoes, fabricated from the same material as his suit.

"Let's go now, or I'll leave you behind. I'm not missing the show because of your big lips." He opened the door and walked out in a huff. I ran after him.

We waited at the corner for the cross-town bus. Annoyed at the thought of missing the opening, my brother griped, "Didn't I say we had to leave by five-thirty?" Looking at his watch, he said, "It is almost six-fifteen. We're going to be late." I ignored him.

I turned my attention to Mirabel and her children, who were on the opposite corner.

Mirabel, a full-bodied woman with a rapidly expanding waistline, lived in the building next door. Just five years ago she had been the sexiest woman on the block, with a strut that made men melt with desire. Now she had three small children and a desperate expression on her face as she tried to cross the avenue carrying one child and a bag of groceries, pushing another child in a stroller filled with toys, and reaching out to grasp the hand of her oldest, who refused to be touched. She was panicking. The stoplight changed too quickly for her to cross the street safely with the children.

Still single, Mirabel was a source of gossip for Mami and her friends. "How many children does she intend to have, and from how many different men?" my mother commented each time she saw Mirabel trying to manage all her children alone.

Augustine, the block's self-appointed mayor, glanced her way. Ready to slap his winning domino onto a makeshift table, he was in a quandary over whether to help Mirabel first or wait his turn to play his last tile. Shooting Mirabel an enticing look, Augustine shouted, *"Preciosa,* give me a minute." Mirabel, with no other choice, tried to calm the children and waited. Triumphantly closing the game, Augustine stood up, knocking over the chair he was sitting in, and rushed toward Mirabel and the children.

With a flirtatious tinge in his voice, her savior said, *"Preciosa,* let me help you cross the avenue." Mirabel's four-year-old son started crying, refusing to take Augustine's hand. The more Augustine tried to appease the child, the more he cried. Confusion reigned, and the other men scurried to help. In the melee, Mirabel dropped her grocery bag, sending apples, mangoes, and oranges rolling in different directions. Her desperation turned to uncontainable laughter as she watched all the men dash to retrieve pieces of fruit shooting under parked cars.

When Augustine bent down to gather some oranges that had rolled under a car, the back of his pants split wide open. "Damn, what a frightening sight," Chachito chuckled. "Augustine needs to buy pants that fit an elephant."

"He looks like a hippopotamus," I remarked, enjoying the comical scene.

In the background, music from an old radio, a wire clothes hanger its only antenna, serenaded the street from underneath the domino table. *"Mira, mira, la ola marina, mira la vuelta que da."* Look, look at the huge ocean wave, look at how it turns.

The bus finally appeared. Traveling between East and West Harlem to get to my high school, I had witnessed the invisible line that changed El Barrio into West Harlem. Although El Barrio had a significant population of African-Americans and a fading number of Italians and Jews, the tone of East Harlem was overwhelming Afro-Latino and tropical. The beat of the *clave* encapsulated El Barrio. Once the bus crossed Madison Avenue, the sounds and tropical colors that hid our old tenement buildings changed.

As we crossed to the west of Madison Avenue, the population became predominately African-American. The melancholy blues of Billie Holiday and the raunchy rock-and-roll sounds of Fats Domino and Little Richard filled the air. The vegetable stands of East Harlem, hung with the flags of Puerto Rico, Cuba, and other Latin countries, were absent in West Harlem. Instead, the bright red, yellow, and green flags of the black liberation struggle of Marcus Garvey flew proudly from storefronts and buildings. Big posters of a young Martin Luther King Jr. covered lampposts and mailboxes in support of the nascent civil-rights movement. We saw street vendors packing up their crimson tomatoes, rich brown yams and potatoes, and leafy sprays of collard greens as the sun set. Last-minute shoppers hurried to make their final purchases.

I admired women with hats like parasols. Dashing young men with Al Capone caps tilted rakishly to the side wore oversized smooth camel-hair coats. Older women stood at the stands and felt the ripeness of the watermelons, examined the freshness of the greens, and looked over the assorted meats and fish.

Little girls played double Dutch and boys played "scullies," their bottle tops filled with pieces of orange peel. Stately older women walked down the street with their daughters and granddaughters, as we did with our mothers. East and West Harlem appeared to me as part of the same family, one tending to be lighter, like my mother and sister, and the other darker, like Papi, Chachito, and me. Yet it was evident that these two neighbors, although existing side by side, were different and set apart. My parents rarely ventured into West Harlem, but the younger generation was beginning to cross the boundaries. My brother and his friends often went to the Savoy, the Audubon Ballroom, and the Apollo Theater to catch their favorite artists, whether African-American, Puerto Rican, or Cuban. My brother and his friends' proficiency in

English and their clarity about also being black allowed them to function in both communities. I felt the same way.

The bus came to a stop right in front of the world-famous Apollo. The blinking lights surrounding the marquee highlighted the bold black letters spelling out the names of Tito Puente, Machito, Graciela, and others. I was awed by the splendor of the lights and the large crowd purchasing tickets. Chachito had ours already.

Stepping into the entranceway of the palatial Apollo, with its oversized photographs of the artists who had performed there, I felt I was visiting a grand museum.

Impatient, Chachito rushed us up the stairs. The band was already playing the introduction for Celia Cruz as, helped by the faint beam of the usher's flashlight, we found our seats.

Celia's tremendous voice preceded her appearance: *"De qué color son tus bembas?"* *"Bembas colora!"* *"De qué color son tus bembas?"* *"Bembas colora!"* The chant—What color are your lips? Red is the color of my lips—roared through the Apollo like rolling thunder. Celia sang and pranced across the stage, her red-and-white *rumbera* dress covered with layers upon layers of ruffles and lace, her glittering earrings moving like mobiles in the wind.

Resembling the figurine of the Spanish dancer that graced my Abuela's altar, Celia enthralled and possessed the audience with her grace and charisma. I imagined that my *gitana*, my gypsy spirit, looked and danced like Celia. Holding court, she commanded total attention. Her generous voice leapt from her fire-engine-red lips. Her voice, expanding like the wings of an eagle, rose to meet me in the upper balcony, where I sat paralyzed before the grandeur of the high priestess of song.

Celia danced rumba to the rhythms of the accompanying drums, then sashayed into a perky cha-cha-cha, smiling at the audience as she pulled her dress up to reveal a spectacular pair of sparkling high-heeled mules. The crowd's roar was deafening. Celia's wide smile registered her enjoyment and her approval of the crowd's response. Turning to Tito Puente, she said, *"Gracias, Maestro."* Tito Puente, dressed in a black tuxedo, raised his two drumsticks into the air like spears. They bowed to the audience, which screamed, *"Puente, Puente, el rey de los timbales."* Puente, Puente, the king of the timbales.

Chachito, overjoyed with the performance, whistled loudly, as did others. *"Uno más, uno más,"* he chanted along with the rest of the audience. I also jumped up and started screaming.

Then the band brought the tempo to a slow, reverent African rhythm, and the mood changed. The *conguero* beat slowly on the drum, replicating the sound of my heart. Celia's voice sang, *"Eleguá y Ogun de la región Africana, guerreros valiente."* Eleguá and Ogun, gods of Africa, valiant warriors.

This mention of the divinities that lived in my Abuela's house startled me. The repertoire honored those warrior spirits that had traveled from Africa to Harlem. I couldn't wait to tell Abuela that the gods that she worshipped were also at the Apollo. With a soft, lingering tone, Celia ended the song by saying, *"Moforibale."* In honor of the gods.

"What does that mean?" I asked my brother.

"I don't know," he responded without looking my way.

His attention was focused on Celia. "Ask Abuela—it's probably some African word."

Then, with a coquettish glance at the audience, Celia screamed out, *"Azúcar!"*—Sugar!—and started singing, *"Azúcar pa ti, mi negro, azúcar, azúcar pa mi, azúcar, mi negro, es de Mayari."* Sugar for you, my *negro,* sugar, sugar for me, sugar, my *negro,* is from Mayari." The crowd soared, singing along with Celia. Turning to Tito Puente, who was posing like a matador, his drumsticks ready to stab an imaginary bull, she said, *"Bueno, Maestro, y qué?"* Maestro, what's happening? He responded with a drum roll, causing the crowd to let out a thunderous roar of approval.

Puente's hands moved across the timbales like a flash of lightning, sending waves of rhythm into the audience that brought us to our feet. The audience screamed, *"El rey, el rey!"* Fueled by the heat generated by the audience, Puente's energy rose even higher as he attacked the timbales with greater rhythmic fury. The audience fell silent watching the "king" perform as Celia pranced across the stage, the long train of her dress whipping at her command. Holding court, she moved majestically across the stage, gazing out at her adoring public. When Puente finished, we all stood up again, screaming, *"Toca, Tito, toca, toca, toca."* The roar of the crowd, the entrancing Celia, and the hypnotic live music infused and took over my body in ways that my brother's calls from the Palladium had not begun to.

Celia again raised the front of her dress to her knees, revealing her shapely brown legs, which moved in syncopation to the rhythm of Puente's timbales. Her shoes flashed silver in the darkened auditorium. Celia had her black hair pulled back in a large chignon, accented by a tiara made of pleated red cloth that resembled an open fan. Her head danced to the movement of her feet. Her hips jutted from side to side, absorbing the rhythm into her body. The crowd was uncontainable as Celia taunted them, *"De qué color son tus bembas?"* What are the color of your lips? The crowd responded, *"Colora!"* Red! She retorted, *"Colora, colora, de que color?"* Red, red, what color? The audience, now in a frenzy, responded, *"Bembas, colora,"* red lips. Chachito and I stood up, caught up in the commotion, dancing in place and screaming out, *"Colora, colora!"*

Chachito couldn't help sharing bits of information with me throughout the concert. "See the man with the gray hair conducting the band? That is Pedro Knight, Celia's husband. He played with the orchestra La Sonora Matancera when Celia sang with them.

"Tito Puente is a master. Watch his hands."

The audience, a mixture of Latinos, African-Americans, and European-Americans, had been drawn to the Apollo to witness the greats of the Palladium. Their response was one glorious expression, as they danced in their seats and in the aisles, to the amazement of the ushers. Communities that often were distant in their everyday lives were one as the spirit of mambo took over their hearts. We all clapped to the sound of the *clave—ta-ta-ta, ta-ta, ta-ta-ta, ta-ta*—and the thunderous sound made the walls of the Apollo shake.

After Celia, the blazing, robust sound of Machito's band's trumpets called out his sister Graciela. Graciela took center stage, her body soft, inviting, and generous. Flamboyantly sensual, she responded to the shouts of the men in the crowd with a coquettish smile. Laughing, she let her hands roam her ample hips. The audience roared their appreciation. Her auburn hair sparkled, and she acknowledged the warm reception with a slight bow and a cheeky smile. Her generous, deep red lips were very expressive, and with each movement of her eyes, Graciela sent a message to the audience without saying a word. She played the audience, and they loved it. *"Graciela, así, así es, así es*—Graciela, like that, it's like that, like that," they teased in return, heightening the sexual innuendo.

Her hands caressed the microphone suggestively. Although short, she stood tall, showcasing her large chest while projecting an elegant sensuality. Her insinuating movements drove both males and females in the audience wild. Deep moans could be heard intermittently as the men jokingly responded to her teasing. "Ay, José," they shouted out, requesting her sexiest song. "No, not yet," she laughed raunchily, her accented English sweet on her lips. She turned to her brother-in-law, musical director Mario Bauza, and waited for his signal. Her suave brother, Machito, looked out at the crowd, greeting people who called out his name. "How you doin', men?" he shouted out, acknowledging the praise and love the audience so willingly shared.

In his crisp black tuxedo, Bauza stood before the band at military attention. He raised his right hand, and the theater went absolutely silent. The anticipation grew. He lowered his arm, and a burst of heralding trumpets and trombones beckoned the audience. The voices of Machito and Graciela joined in, moving in sync to the rhythms of their signature song, "Tanga," pushing the crowd to a state of sublime ecstasy. Pulled by an invisible force, the audience became part of the show, dancing in the aisles, screaming with glee, and clapping to the *clave*. Machito, a mocha-colored, husky man, possessed a warm, flirty, yet innocent quality. His precise, smooth movements were captivating. Watching him, I understood where my brother and his friends had acquired some of their fashion sense, their cool, and their dance moves.

My brother was in a trance, watching the musicians he loved serenade the packed theater and giving me a running commentary. "Look at Mario Bauza—he is a genius, yet he stays in the background quietly conducting the band.

"Watch how Machito moves—he dances without much effort. His body is one with the music.

"Graciela is unbelievable. Look at that woman."

Finally, the band slowed down for the sensual bolero "Ay, José." Graciela's deep, sensual voice soared above the music, taunting and inciting the audience: *"Ay, José, así no es. Ay, José, hazlo otra vez. Así, así, ayeeee."* Ay, José, don't do it like that. *Ay, José,* do it again. Like that, like that, *ayeeee*.

With its overtly sexual, teasing lyrics, the song had the audience laughing and singing along. *"José, así,"* Graciela ended with a slow, erotic moan. The crowd erupted. *"Así,* Graciela, *así,* like that, Graciela, like that," they cheered. Laughing, Graciela thanked the audience coquettishly, scolding them tenderly to settle down. Then, in a voiced filled with honey, she said, *"Mucho aché para todos*—blessings to all."

Rising from my seat, I shouted out my admiration with the crowd, reveling in the force of my own voice and the vibrations resonating throughout my body. The beat of the *clave* had woven itself into my heart, and the melodies flowed through my veins, breathed new life into my body. The music called out to me in a language that tantalized and invigorated all my senses.

Dressed in the clothing and singing with the voices of angels, the musicians had graced the stage with unparalleled elegance, the shades of their skin and their generous features reflecting their audience. These images, sounds, and rhythms blended, conjuring in me the beginnings of inner strength. Screaming the names of these gods and goddesses at the top of my lungs—"Celia, Graciela, Tito, Machito, Mario!"—I felt all timidity flee from me. Here, before men and women whose music tugged the audience's deepest core and exalted all of us higher, I began to feel how much the power of creativity mattered. If I were a creative person, I might matter in the world. I understood the love my brother and Abuela had for this music, how essential it was to the soul, how it made my soul come alive.

I, too, would be an artist.

On Monday I described the concert to Donna as we walked to our music-appreciation class. I became a performer, imitating Celia and Graciela and trying to replicate the fury of Tito on the timbales.

"Celia is your color," I told Donna, "and has a butt that sticks out just like yours." I tried to sway hips I didn't have as I walked.

With her well-endowed breasts and hips, Donna pushed me aside and demonstrated the undulating walk that only women with hips can do. "You mean she walks like this?" The other students in the hallway stopped and watched as Donna imitated Celia Cruz, whom she had never seen.

"Shake it, baby, shake it," shouted Rolando, on his way to class. Donna relished the attention.

"Chocolate is sweeter and tastier than milk," she shouted back as she strutted down the hall, her hips rising and falling like a slow-moving wave.

I danced in place, shaking my shoulders and playing imaginary maracas. I tried for the sensuality of Graciela, imitating her sassy look and caressing my body as she had done.

Donna burst out laughing. "Girl, you don't have boobs or butt! Be still," she teased me.

We laughed all the way to class.

"Lend me a record so I can play that Latin stuff at home?" she asked. "My parents will probably holler, 'What is that mambo jumbo stuff?' I'm almost as Puerto Rican as you now!"

I laughed. The other students in the small classroom had turned around almost in unison. Donna stuck her tongue out at them. The students turned back again, indignant. I couldn't stop laughing.

"Quiet!" Miss Jackson, our music teacher, reprimanded.

I placed my hands over my mouth, trying to muffle my laughter. But I laughed louder as Donna began to make up Spanish words.

"What's the problem, Miss Moreno?" the teacher asked.

I couldn't respond because I was giggling so hard.

Imitating my accent, Donna asked Miss Jackson, "Do you have Spanishee recordos? I want Spanishee recordos,

I am tired of those." She pointed to the stack of records in the corner of the room.

"No, I do not," Miss Jackson said, with a tinge of real anger. "If you bring one in, we might play it."

I joined in, asking, "Why don't you have records of Spanish singers?" I meant Puerto Rican and Cuban artists. For better or worse, Donna's boldness had helped me out of my shell.

We had become the center of attention, and the other students turned to look at us, some annoyed and some amused. Some students began talking among themselves. Miss Jackson shouted, "I want quiet."

Emboldened, Donna went on: "We are tired of hearing the same music over and over again. Who cares about Beethoven and Mozart anyway? Their music is boring."

Miss Jackson's rosy complexion turned a deep red. Her thin lips quivered as she tried to control her anger. "It is unfortunate, Donna, that you find the works of the greatest composer-musicians of the world boring." Her terse words cut like a sharp blade.

Her piercing brown eyes looked directly at Donna, ignoring me. We had been kidding, but the situation had taken a serious turn. I stopped laughing and watched Miss Jackson.

"I don't understand why, if we are students of all different backgrounds, we are not taught music celebrating *all* of us," Donna pressed.

"The objective of this class is music appreciation," replied Miss Jackson, saying each word as if she were grinding it into Donna's head. "The classics."

"I'm not stupid, Miss Jackson," Donna said with the

same cutting tone. "Music appreciation can include jazz, rhythm and blues, and the classics you play." At a loss for more examples, Donna said, "It can even include Spanish music, right, Marta? People like Ma-chito, Sela, Bazooka, and others," she said, confidently mispronouncing the names of my beloved heroes. The names of other artists were totally mangled as she continued to argue with Miss Jackson.

"Marta, do you agree?" Miss Jackson asked me.

I took a deep breath. "I agree with Donna," I said, trembling inside, hoping my voice didn't convey my fear. "The class should include music from different parts of the world."

I looked at my friend, who was all of a sudden aware that she had been getting herself into trouble. Not knowing how to back out, she remained quiet, her eyes wide open.

Miss Jackson asked, "And what type of music would you include?"

I blinked, then opened my mouth. "Tito Puente, Machito, Celia Cruz, Graciela, Cortijo y Su Combo, Ramito, Bobby Capo, Mirta Silva, Daniel Santos, Tito Rodriguez . . ." I rattled out so many names in a short time that I surprised myself. The concert, my mother's love of *jíbaro* music, and my brother's mambo records all popped into my mind, giving me a sense of pride and power.

"Well, they must not be famous or very important. I've never heard of them," the teacher responded flippantly.

"Celia, Puente, Machito, and Graciela filled the Apollo Theater for Sunday's performance," I replied, offended at her dismissive tone.

Regaining her nerve, Donna asked, "Have you heard of Fats Domino, Eartha Kitt, Little Richard, Miles Davis, Aretha Franklin, Pearl Bailey? Have you heard of Frankie Lymon and the Teenagers?"

Angered by our insistence, Miss Jackson sarcastically responded, "Music appreciation is about classical music, music that will live forever. Your examples are of music that is contemporary and not classical. Music that will fade away, that people will not remember in a few years."

Donna and I fell silent, trying to contain our anger and our feelings of ignorance at not being informed enough to defend our own music. We knew it was important, lasting music, but we could not explain why in her terms.

Our music had a beat that penetrated our hearts, calling spirits down and elevating our souls. Our *clave* rippled through our blood, creating kings and queens that soared beyond the limited borders of our neighborhoods.

Our tempo allowed us to dream. Tito Rodriguez reminded us of the meaning of love. Celia Cruz called on our African gods and goddesses. Graciela spoke to our beauty and sensuality. Machito celebrated the elegance of our men. Puente reminded us that we were the children of warriors, and Mario shone with our endless creativity. Vicentico and Mirta Silva acknowledged that we were also human, vulnerable, sexual, and enchanting. How could we make Miss Jackson understand?

I knew that our classmates listened to "black music," but they wouldn't defend it. What hypocrites they are, I thought. Many of the students came around when we were playing music and dancing, wanting to join in. Yet they remained quiet now.

Raising her hand, Donna asked Miss Jackson, "Do you know black gospel music? That is our classical music."

"Gospel is religious music. It is more like popular music; it is not at the caliber of classical music," the teacher argued.

"Shit, I am outta here," hissed Donna, her anger now full blown. Miss Jackson, ignoring her, proceeded with the class. She put on a Beethoven symphony.

"I can't stand this class, and I am not wasting my time listening to the same boring music over and over again," Donna told me. On the verge of tears, she started clapping her hands.

Miss Jackson, startled, looked up immediately. The other students turned to stare. The teacher said, "Donna, stop this silliness immediately."

Then my friend began to sing at the top of her voice, "Oh, when the Saints, come marching in/Oh, when the saints come marching in/Lord, I want to be in that number/When the saints come marching in." I was amazed by Donna's courage. Swaying to the song, she reminded me of Celia Cruz controlling the stage at the Apollo. Donna's movements declared that she was in charge. She was the *conga* spirit that Abuela had said stood beside me, strong and resolute. I felt compelled to act. In supporting Donna, I was also acknowledging my strength.

Repeating the phrases, I joined in, singing and clapping my hands. Donna smiled, her eyes shining with tears that were anything but silly.

Donna stood up now and sang. Her melodious voice chimed like church bells on Sunday morning. As she sang, more energy filled her voice, and she started stomping in place.

I stood up too, singing and imitating her stomping movements. Our classmates were stunned. They didn't know how to react. Some laughed, some giggled, and others just stared with their mouths opened. No one joined us.

Nervous energy pumped through my body.

Then Donna started marching out of the classroom, and I followed. Our hands in the air, we sang, "Oh, when the saints, come marching in/Oh, when the saints come marching in/I love to be in that number/When the saints come marching in."

From the hallway, the noise we heard was faint at first, but it, too, grew in strength. It was the sound of our classmates clapping for us.

SIXTEEN

Joining the Spirits

Congo corama balancongo cora, wiri wiri mambo.
Congo corama balan congo cora, wiri wiri mambo.
— RITUAL SONG TO THE CONGO SPIRITS

A light knock sounded on the front door. When I opened it, Abuela stood before me. *"Hija,* you don't visit me anymore. I miss you," she remarked. It was a Saturday. She had brought me a dish of her special fried chicken, but instead of coming in, she handed it to me across the threshold, her hands shaking slightly. These thin, wrinkled hands were fragile, and she could barely lift the plate.

Although it must have been happening gradually, I had been caught up in my own tribulations, trying to determine which colleges to apply to in time for the fall 1959 semester and preparing for my high school final exams.

The times had changed. My parents were now support-ive about my continuing my education and having a ca-reer. Perhaps they had begun to regret their behavior with my sister, who was stuck in a miserable marriage, her dreams of being a fashion designer jettisoned.

Involved in my own world, I had not been attending to Abuela as I had in the past. Her brown face was covered with deep wrinkles, and her eyes possessed a mystified distance. I realized that Abuela was growing weaker and was not invincible. She seemed thinner and shorter. Or was it that I had grown taller?

"Sorry, Abuela. I have so much homework I can barely keep up," I told her with a pang of guilt. "I promise I'll visit you more." My love for Abuela was profound. How could I have taken her presence for granted?

Abuela smiled and passed her small, thin hands over my head. She turned to go back to her own apartment. As she walked down the hall, I noticed that her gait was more un-steady than ever. When Abuela didn't respond, I knew that my absence had caused her pain. I felt even worse.

She dragged her feet at a weary pace. Her narrow shoul-ders hunched, causing her to look even more frail. I stood watching her white kerchief drift down the dim hallway, her terry-cloth slippers softly flip-flopping against the tiles. Her body was devoid of energy, and her image left a trace of sadness that frightened me. "Abuela, make sure you lock the door," I shouted, and I waited to hear the bolt click.

It was true that high school was a tremendous amount of work for me. I'd had to take remedial classes every year to catch up with the other students, and I had been overwhelmed with new academic courses and art homework. In the little free time I had, I wanted to enjoy the new teenage dancing shows on television or listen to the new records coming out of Motown. But after this encounter at the threshold, I realized how delicate Abuela was and made a point of being with her more.

Every day after school I would stop at Abuela's and sit quietly in her sacred room, drawing and painting canvases filled with the colorful flowers and figurines that adorned her altar. Abuela watched me work, smiling her approval as the images dear to her heart began to appear on my sketch pad.

"Hija, what happens to these drawings of yours? Who sees them?" she asked me one day as she admired my sketches. I described my classrooms. I told her about my classmates and my teachers and the critiques that were a part of each art class.

"What do they say?" Abuela wanted to know. "Do they understand what your drawings represent?"

"No," I told her, "they don't know or understand about the spirits."

"Then what do they see?" Abuela asked with curiosity, not comprehending why I painted objects my viewers didn't know the meanings of.

"Abuela, they see the colors, the forms, and how they interact," I responded, parroting my teacher. "People react to how the painting makes them feel," I said, trying to make my explanation sound important.

Abuela asked, "But how can they understand their feelings when they don't know the meaning of what motivates them?" Swaying in her chair, Abuela watched my face register confusion. She was amused by my inability to answer her questions to her satisfaction. "Cotito, what's the point of not understanding the meaning of what you see, hear, touch, and feel? *Hija*, spirit makes you dig deep inside yourself to understand the purpose of your existence. We are here for a reason. "

"Abuela, looking at paintings is a personal enjoyment. It makes you feel good." I tried to simplify my teacher's explanation.

"Spirit makes you see, feel, taste, and understand more," she countered. "That is the beauty of spirit. It's not in the image or the symbol. It is the intangible, what you don't see, that is spirit. But you know it is there. How can you paint that?" Abuela asked me, trying to get me to dig deeper than my present understanding.

"Abuela, now you sound like my teacher. He says that we should look behind the image," I explained, attempting to unite the different perspectives of my teacher at school and the woman who had been, in so many ways, my first teacher. Abuela giggled, but I noticed how tired she was and the difficulty she had in sitting too long. I asked if she wanted to listen to music.

"*Hija*, play something soft so we can continue talking," she responded. I walked to the old Victorola and put on one of her favorite songs, "Boriquen, la Tierra del Eden." The sounds of Bobby Capo singing about Puerto Rico, the land of Eden, flowed through the apartment. She closed her tired eyes and listened. Her clothes fell loosely about her fragile body as she sat enjoying the music.

Then, smiling, she said, "I never thought about it, but

I'm sure that I could have been a professor on the subject of spirits."

As I spent even more time with Abuela, her altar room became the subject of more of my paintings. Instead of looking at the old photographs of the family, I played her vintage records and concentrated on creating images I thought reflected the spirits.

Abuela consistently reminded me that I was missing the point, that instead of painting the literal images, I should try to capture their meaning in my drawings and paintings. I essentially dismissed her in my mind, feeling that since my Abuela had never been to school, her good intentions could not replace the knowledge of my teachers and the information I was acquiring. I was a young woman now. I imagined she knew less.

In the winter of my senior year Abuela fell ill. Her thin body shriveled before my eyes. Having smoked and chewed tobacco most of her life, Abuela developed terminal lung cancer. Refusing treatment, she insisted she wanted to stay in her apartment, surrounded by her spirits and her loved ones. When Papi insisted she go to the hospital, her response was resounding. *"Que no.* I know what is best for me. I haven't lived all these years for nothing." Her refusal made her illness advance quickly.

None of us could convince her to go to the hospital. The doctors provided medication to help deaden the pain. When my father tried to reason with her, she told him gently, "My life is not in the hands of the doctors. It's not in your hands, son. It is in the hands of the spirits." I felt that Abuelita was not only ill but heartbroken, disappointed by the deterioration that was beginning to surround us.

Abuela was saddened by the loss of what she called *el espíritu de la humanidad*—the human spirit—in El Barrio. She often said, "What do we have on earth but the spirit of humanity?" All her life she had enjoyed walking to the nearby bodega. Sometimes she would sit in front of our stoop talking with neighbors. Now she was a prisoner in her own home because of street fights and the drug epidemic. Abuela had also been badly hurt by the death of so many young men in the neighborhood. Asked by some families who respected her spiritual knowledge to perform the nine-day ritual for lifting the spirits of the deceased, she'd been directly involved with the pain these families experienced. Although Abuela had not performed the ceremony for Jimmy, since Justa was Pentecostal and did not believe in spirits, she kept his photograph on her altar. For families that believed in *espiritismo,* or spiritism, Abuela was asked to supervise the home ceremonies. Abuela also gave the family spiritual guidance and support. At her advanced age, and in our troubled neighborhood, these were draining responsibilities.

I noticed that she had begun talking about having lived too long.

"*Hija,* I think it is time that I join the ancestors. I am too old to keep witnessing the destruction of our human spirit, our humanity." When Abuela spoke about death, I got very upset and asked her to stop, threatening to leave the apartment. She responded, "*Hija,* what happened to Jimmy and the others is not natural. But at my age death is nothing to be feared. It is natural. I welcome it.

"Those younger spirits do not know that they are no longer with us. They do not want to leave because they have just begun to experience life. How painful it is to el-evate spirits that should have been present to send off their elders."

Abuela had photographs of the young people who had joined the spirits on her ancestral table. *"Hija,* look at those beautiful faces. It hurts me deeply to realize they are no longer with us. Look at them. Carlos Colón, Armando Soto, Vicente Cruz, Orlando Gómez, and Jimmy. What a pity."

When I mentioned that all of this was too much for her, she responded simply, *"Es mi obligación y deber."* It is my ob-ligation and duty.

Papi and Mami insisted that we all spend more time with Abuela. The source of our family's spiritual strength, she grew more and more pensive and withdrawn as her ill-ness consumed her body. Papi placed a hospital bed in Abuela's altar room so the images of her spirits would sur-round her.

Mami was Abuela's main caretaker. Chachita, who had moved back to the neighborhood with Joe, also took care of Abuela. My sister was a great help, and the relationship between Mami and her became very loving. When she wasn't working at the dry cleaner's, she was always in our house helping out or in Abuela's apartment.

She listened, now, to Mami's advice. "Chachita, mar-riage is not like the movies. It requires work, time, and pa-tience. Don't be so impatient." Papi and Chachito would pass by Abuela's daily and run whatever errands were nec-essary. Chachito and Laura had set their date for the up-coming month.

But it was Mami who sat all day with Abuela, preparing

broth for her that she rarely drank. When I came home from school, I relieved my mother at Abuela's bedside. Daily, I watched her wither, becoming weaker and more distant. Her eyes were almost always closed.

When she found the strength to open them, an opaque gray film prevented her from recognizing visitors. I sat next to her bed and gently caressed her forehead. Her skin was like tissue paper, lifeless and lacking the warmth that I had basked in as a little girl. Tenderly I stroked her forehead and her wiry gray hair. "Abuela, please get better. The family needs you," I whispered into her ear, hoping that she would respond. Sometimes a slight smile or a subtle movement of her thin fingers signaled to me that she had heard.

Sometimes she would utter a word I could understand. *Hija* would slip out occasionally when she became conscious. Other times she spoke with her spirit guide Juango.

I remained obsessed with planning my future.

I had been accepted to an upstate college specializing in the arts, but my parents decided I couldn't go. They felt that at seventeen I was too young to be away from home. Mrs. O'Sheredin immediately gave me an application for New York University, which was still taking late registrations. She also helped me apply for student loans and get a partial scholarship. If I got in, I told myself, I would at least be at the other end of the city. Tommy, the studious artist for whom my feelings had begun to deepen, also decided to apply to New York University. I was elated.

When I cared for Abuela, I talked to her, hoping she was listening. One night, I sat next to her and filled out the application for NYU. Mami had left to fix dinner, thinking that Abuela was asleep.

"Abuelita, I am filling out a new application for college. I can't go upstate. Mami and Papi won't let me."

She murmured, *"Oh? Esta bien."* Happy to hear her voice, I stood up and held her hand, wanting her to touch me.

Abuela started talking, but she wasn't talking to me.

"Juango, porqué tú estás aquí?" Juango, why are you here? I began to feel the presence of Juango as Abuela spoke. "I didn't call you. Are you calling me?" Abuela's eyes were closed, and tears were streaming down her face. The skin on her slender face fell softly around her cheeks like thin gauze. The white sheet outlined her small, frail body. The halo of white hair that surrounded her head gave her an ethereal quality that was stunning. I felt she was being called, but I didn't want her to leave me.

I tried to keep Abuela in the realm of reality. But every day, she talked more and more to her spirit.

"Abuela, he is just here to help you get better," I said, growing more fearful as she embraced Juango and stopped asking for any of us.

"Juango, where is my dress? Why didn't you bring it?" Abuela asked. "I can't dance without my dress," she whispered.

I quickly looked at the figurines on her altar, which had seemed larger than life to me when I was a little girl. I noticed that they now appeared small. Yet they shone like precious jewels, awakening deep memories of sitting with Abuela before our family albums and listening to our music. The statue of Marta la Dominadora that I loved stood as a symbol of the strength I hoped to one day embrace. La Madama, a strong, motherly black figure, spoke to me of the importance of family. La Gitana reminded me of the joys that life can bring us. El Viejo Congo, of the grand-fathers I had never met and wished I had.

I felt these figures' acceptance and welcome of my being in the room with Abuela. I felt them although I could not see them. The spirit of the room inspired strength and helped me care for Abuela.

It appeared as if she had fallen asleep again.

I took the opportunity to clean the ancestor figures on her altar, changing the water of the *bóveda* and replacing the flowers. As a little girl, I'd done this task just to be with Abuela. Replacing the glasses of water now, I felt a sensation of chills through my body. When I positioned the cool, water-filled glasses on the table, they quickly filled with bubbles. Abuela had explained to me that the bubbles were caused by the spirits letting us know that they had come to visit.

My stomach fluttered to see such a thing, but I was pleased that the spirits were present. As Abuela had re-minded me, it was not an image that spoke of spirit, but small signs like these.

I made certain to dust the lace tablecloths and the many colorful decorations on the altar. I burned Abuela's fa-vorite sandalwood incense in hopes that she could still smell the fragrance she loved.

I realized that the room was a mosaic reflecting the spir-ituality and history of Abuela's journey to El Barrio. The old wooden statues of Catholic saints mourned her illness. The framed sepia photographs of my uncles and their mother recorded special Easter and Christmas gatherings she'd loved. The dark brown, frayed dress she'd worn when she left Puerto Rico was neatly folded and stored in a small wooden box filled with camphor balls.

On her *bóveda,* pieces of brown paper with the names María de la O, Chachito, and Tomasa were pinned under a large glass cup. Too inexperienced to fully understand the spiritual value of the altar's contents, I nonetheless believed that cleaning it would help my beloved grandmother make a peaceful transition into the realm of the spirit world. I knew by now that this journey could not be stopped.

I went to Abuela's record player and turned the crank that rotated the antique turntable. Looking through the pile of old records, I selected the one with the fewest scratches. The voice of Celina filled the room. *"Santa Bárbara, bendita da me tu bendición . . ."*

I felt the energy of La Gitana dance in the room, twirling around Abuela's bed. The vibrant gypsy moved majestically, creating her own music with the clapping of her hands. I could see her feet moving to a hidden rhythm, dramatically circling around Abuela's bed. The gypsy's image slowly faded away as the record came to a stop.

I held Abuela's hand and spoke to her. "Please don't go yet. I want you to see me graduate next month. Chachito's getting married a week after that. We need you there."

There was no sign she had heard me.

I tried again: "Abuelita, I plan to go on to college to study art education. This course will prepare me to become a public school teacher." I thought, but did not say, "It will take me out of El Barrio."

From 102nd Street, the rhythms of mambo tumbled from a passing car, startling me. I looked at Abuela. The soft hum of her breath let me know she was sleeping and her pain had subsided.

The younger kids on the block shouted out, "Ring-a-levio," and their voices, mingling with the staccato commentary of the neighborhood ladies presiding from their stoops, rose up to remind me of the continuous energy that motivated all of our existence. At first, my heart sank as the protective, familiar noises of my neighborhood captured me and held me prisoner. I wanted to escape. Then, suddenly, as if the spirits had opened my ears, I heard. I understood.

The music sounded out all around me. It was all one composition, and always had been. Celia, Graciela, Machito, Tito, Vicentico—these elegant, beloved musicians held up my own image in their capable hands and reflected it back to me, offering a shimmering vision of who I was and who I might become. Their music reverberated through the streets of El Barrio, elevating all of us on its wings, and rooting us, too, to the spirits of our ancestors. In our streets and tenements and crowded kitchens it called out, reminding us of our journey. *You are beautiful! You are strong! You are spirit! Celebrate! Dance!*

The energy of La Gitana, the warrior spirit of Changó, and el mambo were all aspects of the same sacred energy that had traveled with us from Africa to the Caribbean to El Barrio. Abuela had been right when she'd taught me that *los espíritus bailan mambo*—the spirits dance mambo.

Spirit comes in many forms, and one of the most beautiful is the spirit that lives in the music. That lives in dance. That lives within. Spirit calls—*espíritus llaman;* the music calls—*la música llama.* We must respond.

My hand in hers, I felt my Abuela move.

She moaned. Her face cringed from the pain she was

feeling. I held her hand tightly and tried to calm her. "Abuela, here. Take your medicine."

She wouldn't open her mouth. I tried to gently open it for her. She wouldn't let me. I felt her squeeze and grip my hand. I held hers tightly as well and waited.

And then Abuela released my hand. Slowly, slowly, the spirits claimed her and she let me go.

She let me go.

Epilogue

My love for my family and El Barrio are my foundation. As a young girl trying to comprehend how I "fit in" or not, I always knew that I was loved by my family and friends. When we're growing up, varied strands of thought guide all of our lives in ways that are unique to each of us. My caring family members, teachers, and counselors were profound influences in helping me see beyond the borders of my community while remaining rooted in my cultural experience.

My mother joined the ancestors in an ambulance on the way to Metropolitan Hospital in 1968, when she suffered a heart attack. I am happy that she lived to see me become a public school teacher. This filled her with endless joy. My father lost his memory after a heart attack and joined Mami in 1990, having witnessed my work in building cultural institutions that celebrated our creative traditions. He was most proud of my role as the second director of El Museo del Barrio, making this institution independent from the New York Board of Education and internationally known. Papi was filled with pride that the Museo was located in his beloved El Barrio.

Sadly, my sister, Socorro, whose deep unhappiness eventually led to drinking and an addiction to pills, died somewhere in Florida. I heard of her death from one of her twin daughters, who did not know the date or the precise location. My brother's womanizing led him to Venezuela, where he died in 2000, abandoned by a money-hungry young lover in a penthouse in Caracas. While my mother passed before her heart could be broken by her children's fates, my father lived to witness the unraveling of both of their lives.

I am the only remaining member of my nuclear family. Chachita's twins, DeAlma and Florinda, and Alberto's children, Melody and Edgardo, also remain as branches of the same tree. Laura, my brother's elegant first wife, is my best friend—the elder and the keeper of our family's memories. There are no accidents, and recently I was on a beach in Puerto Rico with my granddaughter when I met again my childhood friend Myrta, who now lives in San Juan. What a joy to relive childhood experiences and share our journeys to adulthood. In researching this story, I've also had the opportunity to speak on the phone with some of my brother's old Palladium friends and learn about the depth of his passion for dancing and how much Chachito's friends treasured his friendship and leadership. Talking with Reynaldo rekindled teenage emotions long hidden and cherished.

I realize that my growth also helped my parents grow, allowing them to see the realization of dreams that were not possible in their time. My growth has allowed my two sons' nurturing and that of my granddaughter, nephew, nieces, and friends. It is like tossing a rock into water: Through the generations, our cultural traditions spiral out in new ways, allowing possibilities that were not available to my abuela, parents, or siblings in their time or to me.

I honor them. It is they who have allowed me to be.

I clean my *bóveda*, washing the glasses and placing them carefully in parallel rows. I listen to the voice of Celina praising Changó, letting the music lead me to the many memories and experiences I have shared with my loved ones.

I place white flowers and light a candle to honor the loving spirit guides, family members, and friends who have joined the spirit world and who protect my family and me. This simple ceremony makes them come alive and takes me back, allowing me to trace the contributions they have made to my formation. This action helps me recall the good they did and the difficulties that they successfully surmounted so I could achieve dreams they could not because of the barriers they faced in their time and place.

Abuela's story has since taken me to the town of Loíza Aldea, where I walked the roads that she did with her grandmother, María de la O. With my sons, Sergio and Omar, and my granddaughter, Kiya, and daughter-in-law, Jenna, I've walked the streets of Loíza, Puerta de Tierra, and Old San Juan, looking for the buildings where my father and uncles grew up so my descendents can have memories that connect them to their ancestoral lineage. My visits to Caguas, my mother's birthplace, have helped me understand the traditions that informed her views and how she translated and applied them to my siblings and me. These were rules that both strengthened and hurt us.

Spirit lives in each of us and through us. It is in the beat of our hearts, in the movement of our bodies, and in the creativity of our thoughts. As I dream of a more enlightened future for all of us, I realize this: It is in sharing the many stories and experiences that contribute to our lives that we will jointly form a reality that allows us to dream and to achieve what is best for us as family and community members. We need to help one another dream dreams that our ancestors had to defer. A dream deferred hurts us all. A dream realized helps us all.

When music flows through our bodies and enlivens our spirits and awakens our soul and humanity, we can all dance mambo. When the spirits dance mambo, I know that our memories live.

Acknowledgments

IBAYE, BAYE TONU— I PRAISE THE SPIRITS OF MY FAMILY THAT CONTINUE TO GUIDE ME

So many members of my family are now part of the spirit world. I praise their strength and vision in surmounting many barriers so that their stories could be shared: María de la O, Tomasa Osorio, Luisa Palacio Correa, Maximo Dueno, Donato Moreno, Flora Cruz Marcano, Clemente Moreno, Socorro Moreno, Alberto Moreno, Justa, Jimmy, and Luis.

KINCHAMACHE— I HONOR THE NETWORK THAT CONTINUES TO ENCOURAGE AND SUPPORT MY DREAMS

I honor Laura Moreno, who joined our family when I was fourteen and has been a sister and pillar of strength throughout most of my growth. To my sons, Sergio and Omar, who have taught me the depth of a mother's love.

To my nieces and nephews Melody, Heriberto, Chino, and Norma, who have birthed with my soul daughter Jenna and my son Sergio the next generation. To my granddaughter, Kiya, and my grandnieces and grand-nephew Erica, Elyssa, Kailani, and Jovan, who are now coming of age and have opportunities that were unavail-able to the generations before them. I hope that they will learn from the past and conquer and eliminate any obsta-cles in positive ways so that the future generation, now embodied by my grandnephew Matthew Naseem, can benefit from their achievements and with his warrior spirit open the road for the next generation.

This book is dedicated to our young. It is my hope that the stories of the past will help you negotiate the wonders within our cultures and those of the broader community. The challenges are many. We still combat racism, discrim-ination, sexism, lack of quality education for all, and social and economic stratification and intolerance. Our genera-tion battled against racism, cultural myopia, and crime in the hopes that our children would be protected. We fought for equal opportunity and parity to ensure that you would receive opportunities that would improve the lives of us all. There were many victories, and defeats as well. The dream is that your efforts will secure many more successes ensuring that our cultural communities remain strong and healthy.

To my spiritual family that is an endless network of sup-port: Yari, Cindy, Danetta, Monifa, Assada, Naima, Nyoka, Kim, Brenda, Donna, Djinji, Bobby, and Khadijah. To my godparents, who are now spirit, Zenaida and Elpidio, who further open my spiritual vision. To the ultimate padrino, J. Michael, muchas gracias.

My gratitude and deep appreciation to my soul sisters: Kyra Ryan, my personal editor, who made me delve deeply into my memories. To Mari Brown, my agent, and Rachel Kahan, senior editor, for having embraced my memoir and seen it to completion. All three have become part of my extended family circle. Muchas gracias.

MODUPE—THANK YOU

About the Author

MARTA MORENO VEGA, PH.D., is founder and president of
the Caribbean Cultural Center/African Diaspora Institute,
cofounder of the Global Afro Latino and Caribbean
Initiative/Latin American and Caribbean Studies Program
at Hunter College and the Caribbean Cultural Center.
Dr. Vega teaches African Diaspora Studies at Hunter
College/LACS and El Centro de Estudios Avanzados de
Puerto Rico y El Caribe, among other locations.

WHEN THE SPIRITS DANCE MAMBO

MARTA MORENO VEGA

A Reader's Group Guide

1. Abuela tells Cotito the heartbreaking story of being rejected by her own mother because of her skin color. How has this tragedy, and the experience of being raised by her grandmother, Maria de la O, affected Abuela's life and attitudes as an adult?

2. Cotito is fascinated by the photograph of her grandmother as a young woman, sailing alone to New York. In the photo, Abuela wears a borrowed dress, carries a borrowed suitcase, and watches her gorgeous country slide away from the hold of a ship built "like an enormous metal coffin." She describes this young Abuela as "the woman at the crossroads." In what ways is Cotito herself a young "woman at the crossroads"? What borrowed burdens does she carry, and which ones does she shed in the course of the memoir? What is her "coffin"?

3. What does the drama with Alma in the *botanica* teach Cotito about male/female relationships? How do the neighbors' attitudes toward Alma contrast with Abuela's approach? Why doesn't Cotito question the strange events she witnesses that day?

4. When Papi decides to take the family to Rockaway Beach instead of their usual destination, Orchard Beach—nicknamed

"the Puerto Rican Riviera"—Cotito suffers her first bout of self-hatred and embarrassment about her family's ethnic ways. She is acutely aware of the spectacle they create by cooking on the beach while other families quietly enjoy "sandwiches neatly packed in plastic bags and picnic baskets with fruit." What defining moment does her meltdown lead to back at the apartment? How does it polarize the family?

5. What conflicting advice do Mami and Chachita give Cotito when she gets her first period? Do you agree with Chachita's assessment that by keeping information at a minimum, Mami "just wants us to stay her babies. She's trying to stop us from growing up"? Is it that simple?

6. Cotito receives mixed messages about love from her neighbors in *El Barrio*. When one man stalks his wife in a jealous rage, paranoid that she is cheating on him, Cotito concludes, "this, I supposed, was love." When Mami enrages Papi by taking driving lessons against his wishes, Cotito overhears her mother's nervous telephone conversation with a friend: "'He just loves me too much. That's why he doesn't want me to work or go out.' The thrill in her voice suggested that somehow my father's anger was an expression of his love." How does Cotito interpret these jarring lessons as she moves into young adulthood?

7. Cotito is repeatedly warned not to talk to Teresa, the neighborhood prostitute. Yet Teresa is summoned by all the neighborhood women when they require help with gowns, makeup, hairdressing, or anything uniquely feminine and presentational. How does this paradox reflect the conflicted way in which the women of *El Barrio* deal with their sexuality? Why does Teresa's power over her own body frighten them? Why does Papi allow a prostitute to prepare his daughter for her wedding day?

8. How does the influx of drugs into *El Barrio* contribute to Abuela's decline?

9. While Chachita struggles desperately against her parents' attempts to determine her future for her, and ultimately caves in to their pressure, Cotito strikes out on her own with little resistance other than mild verbal sparring. Why are their experiences so different?

10. Chapter ten opens with: "There is a point in every life when a confluence of forces sets your destiny in motion." What are these events? How does Cotito's acceptance to the Music and Art High School open her eyes to her mother's repressed dreams? What gives her the strength to defy her mother's wishes?

11. As Cotito approaches school for the very first time as a child, she is eager for everyone in *El Barrio* "to bear witness to how special I looked on my first day of school." How is her sense of pride challenged immediately upon arriving? How does this episode foreshadow her experience at the Music and Art High School years later?

12. Cotito is repeatedly struck by the contrasting ways in which her siblings' budding sexuality is greeted by their parents. Mami and Papi "encouraged Chachito's philandering," in part because it banishes any fear of homosexuality and in part because his robust manhood is a continual source of pride. Chachita, on the other hand, is violently castigated for her interest in the opposite sex: "It was as if, just in becoming a woman, she had wounded [Papi] with a knife." Do these conflicting attitudes toward young men and women still exist in the Puerto Rican community today?

13. Immersed in the power of music, Cotito experiences an epiphany about her future while attending a concert of

Palladium greats at the Apollo along with her brother. What is this revelation? How does her experience of music differ from her brother's? From Abuela's? Are their three distinct experiences equally spiritual?

14. As a girl, Cotito's ideal of womanhood is a composite of the seductive sensuality of Saint Marta la Dominadora, the powerful legs of Katherine Dunham, the enticing smile of Dorothy Dandridge, the piercing eyes of Abuela, and the sexy hauteur of her brother's many girlfriends. What features of her own do you imagine the adult Marta Moreno Vega has added to this intoxicating mix?